Thinking about God

Dorothee Sölle

Thinking about God

An Introduction to Theology

WIPF & STOCK · Eugene, Oregon

Wipf and Stock Publishers
199 W 8th Ave, Suite 3
Eugene, OR 97401

Thinking about God
An Introduction to Theology
By Soelle, Dorothee
Copyright©1990 SCM
ISBN 13: 978-1-4982-9576-5
Publication date 8/5/2016
Previously published by SCM, 1990

Contents

Preface

Some years ago I taught a class on 'Liberation Theology for North Americans' along with a dear friend and colleage of mine. The list of 'instructors' for this class read: 'Robert McAfee Brown, Dorothee Sölle and 31 Others'. I recall most gratefully those 31, and the many others to follow.

This book developed out of several classes I taught at Union Theological Seminary in New York City. I am most indebted to my colleagues from the theological field, especially James Cone, Tom Driver, Beverley Harrison, Christopher Morse and Donald Shriver, because they continually questioned my positions and nourished my enthusiasm for theology.

Back home I reworked the material and gave a series of public lectures in Kassel, sponsored by the Interdisciplinary Task Force in Feminist Research, along with the Faculty of Education and Humanities of the Gesamthochschule Kassel.

In revising the text I have largely kept the lecture form and also incorporated questions and contributions from the audience and those many fellow teachers to whom I express my gratitude. Martina Gnadt has been a special help in transcribing the manuscript and revising the text. Marilyn Legge of St Andrew's College, Saskatoon, Canada, was the most helpful and effective tutor in my introductory class in New York, and has now shaped up the section 'For Further Reading' for the English-speaking world. I am grateful to her for additional references and bibliographical details. Last but not least, my *compagnero* Fulbert Steffensky has read the text critically and helped to improve it. It is good not to write a book all by oneself.

Hamburg, July 1989

1   What is Systematic Theology?

In this series of lectures I shall attempt to give an introduction to the basic questions of contemporary Christian theology. However, I find the word 'introduction' on the one hand too pale and on the other hand too authoritarian. I would like to offer an invitation to theological thinking because I want to communicate something of the joy in doing theology, of the enthusiasm which can come over one and also turn to anger in the face of a botched theology which belittles human beings and reduces God to a potentate. The sheer enthusiasm and the attacks of theological fury which I sometimes get – what used to be called the *rabies theologorum* – go together. But above all, I would like to communicate something of the beauty and the power of religious and theological language, because I feel encouraged and supported by this tradition. Hence my invitation to think about God.

And that brings me to the first difficulty. There is such a thing as mineralogy, because minerals exist and scientists can become knowledgeable and expert about them. Theology, too, is an -ology, derived from the words *theos* (God) and *logos* (teaching). But can there be any Logos, any systematic and rational clarification, of God? If theology were simply a 'theory about God', analogous to ossology (the theory of bones), then it would be an insult to God, blasphemy. The object of theology can only be the relationship between God and human beings: in other words, reflection on the experiences that have compelled human beings to talk about something like 'God'.

Karl Rahner defines theology as 'the conscious effort of the Christian to hearken to the actual verbal revelation which God has promulgated in history'.[1] Rahner expresses the element of the relationship between God and human beings by beginning on the one hand from God's 'revelation of the word' in history and on the other from the 'believing person', who alone can do theology. In this definition the Logos lies in the 'explicit concern' which comes about scientifically and methodologically and leads to a 'reflective unfolding of the object of knowledge'.

Many years ago, when I was teaching religion, I once visited Martin Buber in Jerusalem. I had thought of myself as a theologian, as a teacher. He looked at me for a long time and eventually said: 'Theology – how do you do that?' At that point I understood for the first time the depth of the difference between Hebrew and Greek thought: how can one grasp the experience with God of which the people in the Bible tell – that God encounters them, challenges them, requires something of them, gives something to them, refuses them? How can one grasp this living but many-sided experience in a system with the help of technical terms and logic? Certainly the Hebrew Bible contains an implicit understanding of the existence of human beings before God. But this understanding is seldom the object of systematic theological reflection. Only when Christianity spread into the ancient world did 'its best thinkers seek to make their doctrines comprehensible to this world; and it was inevitable that for this they should utilize the language and conceptuality of Greek philosophy'.[2]

The wish to communicate and to reflect on particular experiences thus stood at the beginning of the remarkable synthesis of Greek and Hebrew thought which is represented by Western theology. There remains a tension between the thought which masters its object and orders it, as represented for example by Aristotle, the father of the mediaeval scholasticism developed by Thomas Aquinas, and a thought which listens and responds, of the kind attempted by Luther and Calvin, which stands closer to the Hebrew Bible; it also runs through this series of lectures, with a stress on Hebrew thought (cf. 173f. below). Perhaps we must concede that there are two kinds of knowledge: one is cognitive and makes use of the Logos; the other follows the significance that the word 'know' has in Hebrew, when for example we read, 'And Adam knew his wife Eve and she became pregnant' (Genesis 4.1) – it comes about through union with that which is to be known. In this light I now want to correct my remark about inviting you to attempt to think about God and say, 'I invite you to love God.'

But do we need theology and its concerns about method to do that? Do we not rather need another language, of narrative and prayer? I

think that faith does not come from theology, from reflective acceptance, but conversely, that faith, the experience of God, comes first,
and reflective acceptance is a second stage. However, this second step
is necessary – for several reasons. The experience of faith must
continue to be subject to criticism inwardly, among believers, to
prevent each and everything from emerging as an experience of the
divine. Let me give an extreme example.

A Contra captured in Nicaragua, who had bestially murdered a
number of people, was asked in an interrogation whether it was true
that those who were killed – as practising Catholics – wanted to pray
first. His reply was: 'Everyone has his own faith. Everyone does what
his faith tells him. I am a Christian, a Catholic...'[3] That is an example
of a kind of faith which is completely beyond rational communication.
The dialogue is broken off. Subjectivism and anti-intellectualism here
go hand in hand. While faith is certainly more than theology, it
necessarily also calls for critical reflection, self-understanding, if it is
not to come to nothing in the subjectivism of 'Everyone has his own
faith.'

The consensus among those who share in the experience of faith
must constantly be brought out. Protestants think that this does not
come about through a teaching office from above, but through
the community. 'A Christian community is competent to judge all
doctrine,' says Luther. Another reason for the necessity of theology
is the relationship between believers and the outside world with which
they communicate. It is necessary to bear witness to one's experience
with God. That happens in the confession of people who emerge as
witnesses to God, like Martin Niemöller and Oscar Romero; it also
happens in reflective, responsible theological discourse. Dietrich
Bonhoeffer's *Letters and Papers from Prison* are an apt example of the
coincidence of the two forms of testimony and theological thought.

Three elements which govern systematic theology can be recognized
in these preliminary reflections. The task of systematic theology is to
identify these three elements and at the same time to relate them to
one another. The elements are:

Scripture and tradition, or: the *text*;
the historical situation of the text and its interpreters, or: the *context*;
the community of believers, or: the *people of God*.

Text, context and people of God are fundamental concepts in any systematic theology. It has to take account of all three elements and may not play one off against another. A theology which only repeats scripture and tradition in as it were an ossified way and does not articulate what this text has to say in the present context fails in its task for the people of God. A dialogue must develop between text and context which is related to the people of God as the subject of faith. Here is an example.

At the beginning of the 1980s a public discussion arose in West Germany involving the Sermon on the Mount, which was often reprinted in the newspapers at that time, and the peace movement. Such a dialogue has an audience; it is not just disembodied scholarship. In it there is an explanation, development and criticism of the faith of the church. Tradition, situation and the 'agency' of those who feel committed in their actions belong together. To this degree systematic theology presupposes links in two directions: with the Word of God and with the church. It provides information 'about the praxis from which it emerges and about the experiences which are had in this praxis'.[4] If we do not understand the praxis of the experiences of God as these are related in the 'text', in other words if we do not connect them with our own experiences in our own context, then there is no necessity to confess God as reality.

But does that not bring theology very close to faith? Yes, it does! It *is* an act of faith! How does it differ from faith? The classic answer to this question is given in the scholastic formula *fides quaerens intellectum*. Faith struggles for the clarity of its cause. This definition of theology contains three elements: a presupposition (*fides*), a reflective action (*quaerens*), and a result (*intellectum*). The presupposition of theology is that it is practised by faith. Theology is not the same as religious studies. The formula *fides quaerens* takes into account the fact that there are also quite different forms of the self-expression of faith, for example a *fides cantans*. Faith also comes about as a singing, dancing, silent, fighting faith. But one of its forms is the quest for intellectual clarity, for comprehensibility.

The scholastic formula speaks of seeking, questioning faith. It is not a faith free of doubt which deceives itself in naive optimism over its own difficulties with God. *Quaerens* (in search of) also means that faith cannot exist without its shadow, doubt. Faith without doubt is not stronger, but merely more ideological. The search into which living faith throws us cannot be content with cheap grace, naive trust that all will go well, superficial charity which does not get to the root of things. A faith which seeks practical understanding of itself as participation in the reality of God cannot spare itself the trouble of rational grappling with the conditions for a worthwhile human life. The best scientific methods at our disposal for developing greater justice are good enough. It is not a sign of strong faith but of weak faith if our quest ends quickly and if faith shuns the light of reason.

By comparison, love too is constantly in search of its own understanding: *amor quaerens intellectum*. A love which does not want to know the 'you' in 'I love you', which is afraid of perceiving strange other things in the other, is a weak love, which puts illusions above truth. Real faith always bears within it the wish to convince, to convey itself, to communicate with others. The remark which I sometimes hear from young people, 'You can't understand that, it's how I feel', is a breaking off of communication, giving up the effort to make oneself understandable, self-isolation. It expresses not only great loneliness but also an ideology of solitude. It says: we cannot share all the important things with one another; no one understands anyone else; there is no agreement about our central feelings and experiences; they escape language. This ideology is widespread: faith contradicts it.

That is still true in another sense. Faith is certainly my personal affair, but it is always also more than just my private affair. The faith of Christianity was there before I was born, and it will be there after my lifetime. It lives in and through a society. It is the faith of the church – even if we often cannot see it because the church has been distorted to the point of being unrecognizable. But despite this the church represents a continuity; it lives by remembrance and promise. It listens to the witnesses of faith and recalls them, and it hands on the promises of the community.

I must add something about *fides*, the faith that does theology, which does not become clear enough in the traditional notions of faith as holding to be true and faith as trust. Faith as what I hope for, that towards which my life is directed, my 'project', as the Latin Americans say, is not just an internal or meditative matter. Faith is a form of praxis. My active life, my wishes, my hopes, my anxieties – all these are part of my praxis. Just to think of the mere sequence of actions in our life would be to misunderstand praxis. What we do not do, what we go along with, what we are silent about, is also praxis. And just as faith needs theology in its search for self-understanding, so the praxis of our life constantly needs interruption, interiorization, theory, intellectual assurance, clarification, self-criticism, which then lead to more conscious praxis. There is a circular movement from praxis to theoretical reflection (1) and back again to changed praxis (2). This circle of human learning is also a circle of human life: faith needs theology to understand itself and to communicate, but the significance of this theological theory is to lead to a deeper faith. Theology is not there for its own sake but to help us to grow into faith. The thought-model of theology begins and ends with praxis, lived-out faith.

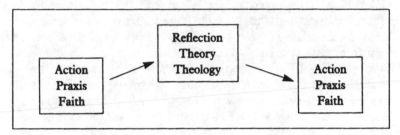

2 Orthodox, Liberal, Radical – Three Basic Theological Frameworks

Theology has the task of interpreting scripture and tradition in a particular historical situation for the community of believers. That is a formal definition, the content of which can lead to very different consequences. There is no one theology, but extremely different theologies, even in one and the same historical situation. During the Vietnam War, for example, in the United States Cardinal Spellman could be blessing soldiers and weapons while at the same time Quakers and Mennonites blocked the trains carrying their deadly freight by lying on the tracks. What conceptions of God, Christ, sin, being human, stand behind these different positions?

I would like to distinguish in a paradigmatic way three different forms of theology which seem to me to be relevant today. This division has its problems, because there are always overlaps, connections, cross-fertilizations everywhere, and established 'schools' in no way determine the field; nevertheless it seems to me to be useful. I know the three present basic frameworks of orthodox, liberal and radical theology, and understand them as three houses built in different periods of faith. I would like to invite you to enter them and look around. How are the basic concepts of Christian faith interpreted within these different paradigms? By paradigm I mean, as does Thomas Kuhn, that 'general constellation of convictions, values and modes of experience which are shared by a particular community'.[1] How are creation, sin, grace, resurrection, church interpreted in these theological paradigms?

When I was studying theology in Göttingen in the 1950s, apart from

the fundamentalists, whom nobody took seriously, there were two
relevant positions, which were identified with Karl Barth and Rudolf
Bultmann respectively. At the beginning of the 1960s, and above all
with the student movement, these positions and the controversies
associated with them faded away. A long period of mistiness over the
theological landscape followed: no mountains towered high; there
were no works which created particular schools; no controversies
going to the roots of things – or at least that is how it seemed. Instead
of that there were rediscoveries, cautious assimilation to empirical
reality, catching up with the humane sciences like psychology, soci-
ology and psychoanalysis.

This diffuse situation changed at the beginning of the 1980s
with the strengthening of fundamentalism on the one hand and
the liberation movement on the other. Nowadays there are three
recognizable theological tendencies which I want to call orthodox or
conservative theology, liberal and radical theology, or liberation
theology. In all these 'pigeonholes' it is important to keep in mind
the links between the 'theological' and the 'political'. These three
theologies are basic theological and political models, each of which
relates to both theology and politics. There are no basic theological
convictions which then can, but need not, also find a political application. Nor are there, as conservatives like to suggest, political options
in theological guise. Rather, basic theological distinctions underlie
the political conflicts: tell me how you think and act politically and I
will tell you in which God you believe.

This is the place for a story about a pastor working in industry, who
in a television interview in front of the factory gate said, 'There ought
to be a notice here saying "Here you are leaving the democratic
sector".' The next day he was called in by his superintendent. A
complaint had been made by the highest authority. 'The highest
authority? Do you mean God? Or the bishop?' 'No, the board of
directors.'

The dissent between positions is in fact theological and political.
Any serious theological statement has a political focus, related to the
way the world is shaped. In the death of Jesus, no matter how much
it may be interpreted in a theologized and spiritualized way, Pontius
Pilate and with him the power of the state are present, as is attested
by the second article of faith. Statements without such a focus may be
'correct', but they are irrelevant; they answer questions like how many

angels can stand on a pinhead. The statement 'The earth is the Lord's' (Psalm 24.1) challenges the domination of the multi-national corporations.

I did wonder whether I should speak of two contemporary theologies which I would then have to call 'theology of liberation' and 'theology of the bourgeoisie'; or whether I should be more subtle and put the two very different expressions of bourgeois theology in a conservative and a liberal camp. I imagine that many people who work in the church need this more sophisticated analysis, because in practice they are confronted in their everyday life with the two species of bourgeois theology and are often torn apart by the conflict between them, although they really dream of a transcending of bourgeois theology into liberation theology.

Orthodoxy is understood to be 'right believing' (here I leave aside the use of the term as a proper name for the Eastern churches, which are in communion with Constantinople). Orthodoxy means 'right faith' in contrast to error and heresy as conscious and deliberate rejection of a doctrine. In Protestantism, orthodox theology came into being after the Reformation and was nourished by it; it flourished from the end of the sixteenth century to the eighteenth, when in the wake of the European Enlightenment a new way of thinking slowly became established, without the traditional theology, sometimes called 'classical' theology, ever completely disappearing. Rather, orthodox theology was given new impetus more through the revival movements of the nineteenth century and later fundamentalism. In the twentieth century, as a result of Karl Barth's 'dialectical theology', which is called 'neo-orthodox' in the United States, it achieved a new significance of quite a different depth, which in some ways points forward to radical liberation theology.

So what is 'orthodox theology'? Its starting point is the Bible and the dogmatic tradition. Belief means the acceptance in faith of the truth revealed in the tradition. This 'revelation', which is inaccessible to reason, has taken place only and exclusively in Jesus Christ. Old and new Protestant orthodoxy are agreed in the fact that – in contrast to the scholastic theology of Catholicism – there can be no harmonious scheme of nature and supernature, in which human beings and God, nature and grace, reason and faith, philosophy and theology, belong together like a natural basis and a supernatural superstucture. In

schematic form we might follow Hans Küng in describing scholastic
theology as operating on two levels of knowledge:[2]

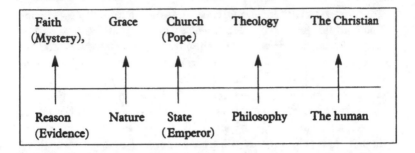

This Thomistic synthesis of reason and faith within a unitary culture
which is regarded as good and necessary, if not adequate, understands
Christ as standing 'above culture'. Here I follow the interesting
investigation by Richard Niebuhr (1894-1962) on *Christ and Culture*,[3]
in which a typology of the different relationships between culture and
Christianity is presented:

Christ above culture
Christ of culture
Christ transforming culture
Christ and culture in paradox
Christ against culture.

The Christ above culture presents the attitude of synthesis between
nature and supernature which is characteristic of Catholic orthodoxy.
Here there is no deep, unresolvable conflict between culture and
Christ. The two entities have to be understood as complementing each
other and can form a synthesis. The danger of this theological position
is that the stabilized synthesis may become a smooth identification, a
kind of culture-Christianity, which Niebuhr calls the 'Christ of
culture'. The two are no longer distinguished, and phenomena develop
like culture Protestantism or milieu Catholicism, in which the Christian element no longer represents a challenge.

In its understanding of itself the Reformation tradition breaks with
the synthesis in which tradition plays an excessive role and leads to
this identification. It replaces it with a dualism which sees Christ and
culture in a tension which remains paradoxical, and is indissoluble

within history. Fidelity to, belonging to and loyalty to a particular culture is always in conflict with fidelity to Christ. Diastasis, separation, critical distance, is part of Protestantism from the beginning; in the minority churches of the Reformation the principle of Christ against culture penetrates deeply, to the point of shaping the lives of radical pacifists. Diastasis plays a great role among all Protestants.

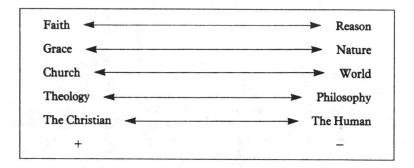

A critical minus appears under reason, nature, the human, and above all governs the thought of orthodoxy. Luther called Aristotle 'Narristotle' (a word-play which is impossible to reproduce in English – in German Narr means fool), and reason a 'whore'; that does not seem too absurd to me, given that fifty per cent of all scientists and technologists are now working in industries and places of research related to military purposes!

The productivity of the diastasis is the 'Protestant principle'[4] of the criticism of 'this world' and all its idols: it must have a place outside, a vision of the wholly other. The maintaining of this place outside, which makes it possible to say no to the idols of 'this' world, is perhaps the greatest strength of the orthodox Protestant paradigm. That proved itself in Germany in the church struggle against National Socialism.[5] The Barmen 'Theological Declaration' of 1934 is an expression of the diastasis. Its theses are an example of the productivity of orthodox theology and also of its limitations. The first thesis runs: 'Jesus Christ, as he is attested to us in Holy Scripture, is the one word of God which we have to hear, which we have to trust and obey in life and death.'

So speaks a theology anchored in conservatism and shaped by the neo-orthodoxy of Karl Barth. Men and women are subject to the Word of God; they are to 'hear', 'trust' and obey. All other 'events and powers, forms and truths', cannot, as the explanatory repudiation attached to this thesis runs, be recognized as revelation. In the context of the controversy with National Socialism and its German Christians it was clear what 'truths' (for example the superiority of the Arian race), what 'other powers' (for example blood and soil), and what 'figures' (the Führer Adolf Hitler), were meant.

But outside its historical situation this thesis, like much within the orthodox paradigm, is theologically ambivalent. What does it mean to hear Christ as the one Word of God, if some Christians assert that only heterosexual love counts as obedience to Christ; that it is sin to love another person of the same sex?!

Orthodoxy has a specific blindness to its own cultural provisos: its understanding of marriage, the bringing up of children, the morality of work is uncritical in an Enlightenment way; orthodoxy lacks any suspicion that it might be an ideology. Its reflections are far too detached from any context. Therefore it is possible for the Barmen theses directed against the German Christians nowadays to be interpreted in the following way, in a mixture of neo-orthodoxy and conservatism.

Any political involvement on the part of the church is to be condemned. Jesus Christ stands above all worldly systems; to join his party means not to become involved in the struggles of this world: being a Christian creates a certain detachment from any practical involvement in a political question. As Christ is the one Word of God, no systems, whether they be socialist or capitalist in their economic theory, emancipated in respect of the role of women or obsessed with the preservation of the *status quo* in their policy on the family, can ever be identified with him. Jesus Christ stands above all. The church must distance itself from the world and preserve the so-called 'eschatological proviso'. If the second thesis of Barmen proclaims the 'joyful liberation from the godless ties of this world', the conservative exegesis of this confession assumes that all ties of this world are in themselves godless, and not just some, as the historical context of Barmen suggests. The lack of context is elevated to become a principle of theology. Other conservatives have used the christocentrism of neo-orthodoxy to oppose the hermeneutical approach of the ecumenical moveement and its assertion that 'the world sets the agenda for the church'. They have even depicted representatives of liberation theology as kinds of

German Christians. For them, Christ is beyond culture and history, an unchangeable, autonomous, divine being, beyond all our hopes and visions, which are then consistently regarded as a purely ideological assertion and are all equally remote from the one Word of God.

With the European Enlightenment the paradigm of theological orthodoxy gave way as being untenable. The new liberal theology which arose, supported by the bourgeoisie, was stamped with the critical spirit of the Enlightenment. The priority was established of reason over faith; of philosophy with its approach to human beings over theology; and of the new interest in the natural sciences, going along with with natural philosophy and natural religion. Kant defined the Enlightenment as the 'courage to make use of one's own under-standing'. From the clash of old orthodoxy and the new, secularized, spirit a new model came into being, that of liberal theology. It developed new forms of criticism of the Bible, the church and the state. It attempted to reconcile the modern scientific consciousness, which understood itself primarily to be anti-religious, with Christian faith. It did away with many incomprehensible authoritarian principles and opinions which had become offensive. It rejected the paradoxical strangeness of Christian existence and the Christian God. It tended towards an understandable interpretation of Christianity, in which its alien character in the modern world increasingly disappeared.

I want to mention three premises of liberal theology here:

the validity of science
the historicity of religion
the unity of culture and religion.

One foundation of liberal thought is the validity of science: the whole space-time continuum is an object of scientific research. There are no exceptions in which one says, 'Science must stop asking questions here.' The result of this universal validity is that the hypotheses of the sciences are regarded as authoritative in the sphere of natural and historical facts. For example, the origin of nature and the origin of the different species and forms of life are the subject of a scientific explanation. This of course causes difficulties with any dogmatic method. Religion loses the function which it had in earlier times, that of explaining the world.

Where does everything come from? How is it that there are butterflies and stones and people? If science claims to be able to explain the origin of the world and individual phenomena in it, then one cannot resort to a mythological explanation and say, 'But in the Bible it's different!'

There is a fundamentalist trend in the USA whose followers call themselves 'creationists'. They take the Bible literally and are opposed to the teaching in public schools of a biology in which the origin of human beings is described from a scientific perspective. They explain that this corrupts their children and goes against their faith. Here – in a small island in society – we have a remnant of the dogmatic method of thought.

The second presupposition of liberal theology which I mentioned is the historicity of religion, indeed all religions. That means that all writings, all confessions of faith, dogmas, all church constitutions, expressions of piety, Christian customs, prayers, came into being in history. In biblical scholarship this basic insight leads to the questions: 'From what period does this psalm come? Did it come into being before or after the exile? What experiences are expressed in this creed? How did this institution, this arrangement, this religious custom, this church teaching, come into being?' When, for example, was the doctrine of the omnipotence of God fixed? When was it no longer adequate for theologians to speak of the power of God, and when did they put a special stress on omnipotence? A central historical question for feminist theology is when women came to be described as the bearers of sin, as vessels of sin. In what theologies? Why in Tertullian and not in Jesus? To discover these differences we need historicity as a methodological principle, permission to ask questions. Since when has that been so? It was not always like that. There is something liberating about knowing that particular thought-forms, convictions and customs do not hold from eternity to eternity but are historical forms of expression which must necessarily be subjected to examination and understood in terms of their origin. That applies to all religions which make similar claims to absoluteness. Indeed there are also Islamic and Jewish fundamentalisms, though in the view of liberal theology all these fundamentalist standpoints must also accept the historicity of religion: they came into being at a particular time, in particular circumstances of a social, economic and historical kind. Liberal theology is not to be criticized because it thinks historically, but because it does not do so consistently enough, and often gets stuck in a reduction of reality to a mere history of ideas.

The recognition of the historicity of religions has led to one of the most important moral and political postulates of the liberal era, that of tolerance. Tolerance is grounded in the assumption that we have no right to make a religion or an expression of religion absolute and give it sole and absolute validity as opposed to others, which are then declared heretical.

The third liberal premise is the unity of culture and religion. It is an Enlightenment principle that a religion which completely repudiates a culture (for example, creationism), destroys itself. Religion must stand in a living relationship to the culture around it and cannot in the long run encapsulate itself in a group which has quite different rules of life and customs and, for example, in our day still persists in wearing clothes in the style of hundreds of years ago or travelling in horse-drawn vehicles. After the shift at the time of Constantine this position of 'Christ against culture' historically became that of very small churches and sects. I have a deep sympathy for the 'no' that these churches say, for example, to a culture which unquestioningly adapts itself to militarism. But this 'no' risks becoming a pure encapsulation, a mere 'count me out'. At all events, the liberal paradigm is furthest removed from this counter-cultural Christ. It mixes up culture and religion to the point that they often become indistinguishable, and Christianity consists only in obedience to certain bourgeois customs and rules of life, like getting married in church. That is the 'Christ of culture' or, to use a sociological expression, 'civil religion'. Cultural achievements are then so linked with Christianity that a false unity is suggested, as in the cliché 'Christian West', which was a cultural definition of the restoration period of the Adenauer epoch. But at any time of official fusion the theological question needs to be asked whether the church of Jesus Christ does not also have to oppose the normative culture.

I suppose that most of us owe our best experiences of faith to liberal theology. Its humanity, its comprehension and its intellectual honesty, which forbade it to leave its own understanding at the church door and offer a sacrifice of the intellect, are values which cannot be surrendered. But it is now impossible to overlook the shadow side of this theology. Here I want to mention two main points of a criticism of liberal theology: one relates to the consequences of its assumption of the need for the separation of church and state, and the other is its consistent individualism, which has perhaps most changed the Christian message.

Liberal theology affirms the separation of church and state as a liberating basic principle. In fact it is absolutely necessary for an economic and socio-political system which functions according to the principle of the free market economy to distance itself from the moral, religious and transcendent dimensions of human existence. At the early stage of liberalism the rising class of the bourgeoisie handed on an enlightened vision of an autonomous society which was no longer dominated by the church or the strange alliance of nobility and clergy. The liberal state had an interest in protecting itself from a church which was regarded as being hungry for power. Nowadays things are the other way round: the church as a middle-class institution often has a great interest in keeping out of the political and economic decisions of the modern state. Official Protestantism, which we have to see as a form of bourgeois religion, has withdrawn into the moral and transcendent aspects of Christian faith. It has silenced its social and economic demands for the whole of human life and its society. The church in its bourgeois Protestant form adapted itself to the demands of modernity, the Enlightenment and science. But in this process of adaptation it lost its critical and prophetic voice because it recognized a division into two worlds – a realm of economics and politics, and a private realm – with religious matters falling into the latter. Both realms had a specific, autonomous identity; together they represented the historical reality of the bourgeois era.

But this prestabilized harmony was deceptive. It did not do anything for the human rights of racial minorities like the Jews in Europe or the Blacks in the USA. The promised equality was only the equality of white men. The basic view of liberal theology has done nothing for the poor; the separation of church and state has not functioned either in a positive way, for the landless peasants or for the industrial proletariat, bringing emancipation, or even in a conservative way, simply by protecting them – and that completely ignores the marginalized masses which now live in the Third World.

Bourgeois liberal ideology asserts that the modern world has created a historical situation in which the state sees to economics and politics while the church protects and saves the soul of the private individual. But this liberal myth has never really functioned for the oppressed. When state oppression took on new forms in the twentieth century, for example concentration camps, and when torture became the rule in many countries, the myth of the separation of church and state collapsed, and at least some parts of Christianity rediscovered their own visionary claim to change not only the private individual but also society. The collapse of liberalism, which brought Fascism into being in the twentieth century, posed a challenge to the church and polarized it – in Nazi Germany, in Franco's Spain, and now in South Africa and Latin America. The harmony of the separation of church and state could not stand up in the light of increasingly totalitarian states. And the church under Hitler, Franco, Pinochet, Somoza and increasingly the CIA saw itself challenged by the violation of human rights. An apparatus of state which calls for absolute obedience and total surrender to its ideology now compels the church to rethink its own history of liberalism. Can a theology maintain its integrity within the laissez-faire separation of church and state? That was not possible in 1933: liberalism more or less failed in this situation, just as liberal theology already failed in 1914 at the outbreak of the First World War (to the despair of Karl Barth!). Nowadays – in the face of the technological megamachine – it is called on not just to leave the destiny of creation to industry and the state.

In view of the catastrophes of our century, the division of competence made by liberal theology, which understood the state, economy and technology as autonomous spheres free of religion, and banished faith into private inwardness, is untenable. In Western Germany and Britain, theology is under massive pressure from society and industry to limit itself to the soul of the individual; the church is to make clear the meaning of life to the unemployed and in no way to raise questions about the causes of unemployment.

The second starting point for a criticism of liberal theology is its individualism; that is its chief distinguishing mark. Liberalism regards human beings as individuals who find comfort and peace of mind in faith. Modern life deals harshly enough with all of us, and the stress, the competition and the solitude of men and women are tremendously great – it is precisely in this field that Christian religion is to bring consolation and healing as redemption for all evil. From this perspective the kingdom of God is completely suppressed in favour of the redemption of the individual. 'Deliver us from evil' is more important than 'Thy kingdom come', although both petitions in fact belong together. This bourgeois theology is the work of the white middle class, relatively well-to-do, dominated by males and with an androcentric thought. It takes no account of the impoverished masses of this earth; the starving appear at most as objects of charity. Otherwise problems of sexual ethics or the ethics of dying are far more important in this theology than social, political or ecological questions.

Alongside this, for about twenty years there has been a theology which is not done by people who are white, relatively well-to-do and almost exclusively male: the theology of liberation. In it the relationship of faith to the world is not understood along the lines of the liberal division of work; rather, the task of theology itself is redefined. It consists in collaboration with God's work of liberation. Faith is not primarily a comfort in an ordinary and often lousy life, but another way of living, hoping, acting. It means a revolution in the human heart which corresponds to the word which Jesus said many years ago to a crippled man: 'Arise, take up your bed and walk!' (Mark 2.9). Christ does not just comfort us but changes our lives. As with the first disciples of Jesus, who were poor and ignorant people, the majority of them women, so today in the communities of faith growing at the basis, a new way of living together, sharing, organizing, celebrating and fighting is coming into being. Faith and action, theology and politics – in the broad sense, not the professional sense of the word – here belong together. In a great many cases this form of a new life means that Christians are despised and avoided, and no longer tolerated in many professions: in the Third World, persecution, torture and death for the sake of the faith are becoming increasingly more frequent.

The theology of liberation represents a change of perspective. It comes into being among the poor in the South African townships, in the refugee camps of El Salvador, among the textile workers of Sri Lanka. It comes into being among those who are oppressed on account of their race, their sex and/or their class situation. But that does not mean that they are not important for us here. We are not uninvolved in the wretchedness in which people suffer today in two-thirds of the world; we are part of its problem. At international conferences, for example UNCTAD, the representatives of the United States, Britain and West Germany are usually united against all proposals made by the poor countries on the economic situation. We are not onlookers, we are not victims; we are agents who have a share in causing the misery. Therefore liberation theology is not just some theological fashion which we can follow or ignore, but the expression of faith offered to us today by God, including those in the First World who live for liberation: liberation from the frightful role of causing misery to the innocent, condemning children to death by our financial policy, and suppressing the hopes of the poor by police regimes, military dictatorships and open war.

Liberation theology, too, is orientated on the one Word of God, on Jesus Christ. But it does not leave this Word without a context, standing above time or related to individual souls in their depths. For liberation theology, the one Word of God is the messianic praxis of Jesus and his followers. Christ is not the one Word of God because he is formally superior to all ideological or religious challenges, because in contrast to all others he speaks of God. The appeal to God is ambiguous, and the weakness of conservative theology is that it points to God only assertively ('But our God is the right one'), only theoretically. The basis of faith is not that it was Christ who spoke with divine authority; the basis of faith is the praxis of the poor man from Nazareth who shared his bread with the hungry, made the blind see, and lived and died for justice. Obedience to authority does not get us any further; praxis does.

In liberation theology the principle is that the poor are the teachers, and so we learn most today from the poor and through the poor: not technology, not knowledge, but faith and hope. By 'poor' we understand the victims of history, those who are damaged in a concrete situation. In theological discussion we sometimes speak of the 'epistemological privilege of the poor', namely that it is easier for them to understand the gospel, God's word for the world. Here the concept of poverty occupies a remarkable position between absoluteness and relativity. In itself it is relative: in a social situation something can be regarded as poverty which in another context would be extreme luxury. We need think only of how our poor look from the perspective of the 'Third World'. But this sociological relativity is relativized yet again in liberation theology, because God's preference for the poor, this 'preferential option for the poor', again introduces an element of absoluteness. In *any* situation, God is with the poor and for the poor, with and for the tormented and oppressed in the most varied circumstances. Their fights for liberation and their attempts to rebuild a new and more just society have become *loci theologici*, theological contexts, from which the Word of God is interpreted and the presence of God is experienced. That is in no way relative, and one cannot say, 'Yes, but we must also consider what becomes of the rich.' No, we are also to learn to think from the perspective of the poor – in each new Trident submarine that we give ourselves! For God has opted for the poor.

In a conversation about the situation of the peoples oppressed by Western countries, a young Swiss teacher recently asked me from where I could derive any hope. At first I wanted to reply to him, 'From my faith in God, who once rescued an oppressed people from slavery under a great military power.' But then it struck me that it is not really 'my' faith which bears me up. It is really the faith and the hope of the poor who do not give up. As long as they do not despair and give up, as long as they go on, we do not have the least right, whining and resigned in an analysis which counts money and weapons but does not see the pride and the combativeness of the violated, to say, 'There's nothing one can do.'

Radical theology goes to the roots of our anguish at our helplessness and assures us that 'all things are possible', as one of the liberation stories of the New Testament says (Mark 9.14-29).

Reformation	Enlightenment	Left Wing Of The Reformation
Orthodox	**Liberal**	**Radical**
Dogmas	Validity of science	Collaboration in God's work of liberation
Revelation Timeless faith	Historicity of religions Unity of culture and religion, separation of church and state	Perspective of the poor of women of victims of oppression
	Textual criticism Criticism of institutions Criticism of rule	Contextuality
Christ and culture in paradox (Protestant model) Christ above culture (Catholic model)	Christ transforming culture Christ of culture	Christ against culture Christ and culture in paradox
	Trends in contemporary Protestantism	
Fundamentalism Evangelicals New Religious Right	Mainstream within the church	Liberation–theological minorities in the Women's movement Peace movement Ecological movement Solidarity movement

3   The Use of the Bible: From the Orthodox to the Liberal Paradigm

I have described the different basic theological approaches and now want to develop them following the major themes of theology. These great themes, forms, myths, statements and the expressions of faith associated with them like prayers, sacraments and religious rituals, represent a shared religious culture: all Christians refer to creation and redemption, all believe that the Bible is a 'holy' scripture. The Bible is the 'Word of God', and I would add the Latin theological expression *norma normans*; it is the normative norm, i.e. the norm that sets rules: the binding, limiting norm which according to common Christian conviction makes it Holy Scripture.

In what sense is the Bible the 'Word of God'? What does such a statement mean within the three theological paradigms? I shall begin with the Protestant-Orthodox position which developed in Europe out of the Reformation and was expressed, for example, in the 1577 Formula of Concord.

The great period of Protestant orthodoxy extended from the Reformation to the Enlightenment, around two hundred years. Offshoots of it have survived down to our time. This orthodoxy is a kind of scholastic system which was developed on the foundations of the Reformation. One of its most important characteristics is the doctrine of the Holy Spirit, defined authoritatively: this belief in scripture was not so basic to Christian faith either earlier or later. To quote the Formula of Concord: 'We believe, teach and confess that the prophetic and apostolic writings of Old and New Testaments are the rule and norm according to which all teachings and all teachers must be evaluated and judged.' In other words, 'We believe, teach and confess scripture as the basis for all teaching and all teachers.'

Such an effective basis, which even extended to church law, explains many conflicts between orthodox officials and deviant pastors. Time and again pastors and even more, of course, laity, were regulated, disciplined or oppressed on the basis of this interpretation of scripture, which was understood to be authoritative. Scripture was held to be literally true, and literalism (belief in the letter), as this attitude is also called, was expressed in two doctrines about the origin of the Bible. One claimed verbal inspiration and the other personal inspiration. The former notion was that God dictated the text word by word to the authors of the Bible and the latter that God gave inspiration to the authors of the Bible so that what they wrote is directly the word of God. These doctrines had to be developed because Protestantism had done away with the pope and so had abolished a particular form of church authority. The opportunity thus given for discussion free of domination was soon lost: at most it remained alive on the left wing of the Reformation (in its understanding of the Holy Spirit).

For the mainstream of the Reformation an answer had to be found to the question who really decided on disputed questions. Appeal was made to the Bible, leading to excessive stress on the letter of the text. This principle was never taken so far in Catholicism, because the combination of scripture with a tradition understood in broad terms prevented it from becoming biblicistic. In the early church and during the Middle Ages the authority of scripture was guaranteed by the authority of the church. That could no longer be the case within Protestantism, and as a result scripture acquired excessive authority: not only scripture itself but consequently also those who represented and interpreted scripture, i.e. the pastors and church officials.

Orthodoxy developed a dogmatic method of thinking. It began from a revelation which was utterly remote from the relativity of history and lived in an absolute sphere: God – revelation – Holy Scripture. From the conservative perspective there is some comfort in the elevation of the Bible above time: the eternity of God speaks from the Bible. 'As it was in the beginning, is now and ever shall be, world without end, Amen,' says the liturgy. That is a strong statement. We change; there are ups and downs in the life of the individual and in history; but above them stands this unassailed world of God. If one says to such people, 'The Bible too belongs in the historical sphere;

the Bible too speaks from historical people to historical people,' they
are terrified. What is left? Is not everything shaking? Is there no
timeless truth which is valid for ever?

There is a deep longing in human beings to have something which
is unchangeable and not hurt by the confusions of history. The
relativity of history destroys the quest for the absolute – or perhaps it
would be better to say that it destroys rest in the absolute.

Eternity is quiet,
the passing world is loud.
God's will goes silently
above the earthly struggle   (*Wilhelm Raabe*).

That is how religion was and is felt to be.

The piety which goes with orthodox theology rests on a religious
feeling which is attached to an already existing salvation history. It
accepts God's saving acts in humility, waits for God's intervention
from heaven in patience, and also lives in a present full of suffering
with innermost certainty of the goodness of God, the forgiveness of
sins and eternal bliss. Trust, humility, patience, certainty, are the
pillars of this piety, which, as is often said, 'holds fast to God's word
and sacrament'. To understand orthodoxy productively, one must
also take into account its cultural expression. Its best representatives
live by a deep piety bound to the Bible and dogma. In this sense Paul
Gerhardt and Johann Sebastian Bach were formed by orthodox
Lutheranism, and can only be understood in that context. We can
learn better what orthodoxy was really about from them than from its
fixed formulation in dogmas.

If we take the Reformation as the time of a religious revival, a living
movement, the orthodoxy which followed it is a time of consolidation
in which static elements like authority, tradition and institution have
become dominant, first of all in the sphere of doctrine and dogma. The
Augsburg Confession (1530) was canonized, and any new theological
view which emerged was measured by it, and any deviation condemned. Martin Luther, the thinker of deep contradictions, who
wrote very much for his own time when he took up a particular
position, became a dogmatic authority. But Protestant orthodoxy was
never 'pure doctrine'. Rather, it also regulated state and cultural life.
In the interest of maintaining 'law and order' in the state, and by
means of state power, it safeguarded the rule of the authorities, which

at that time had a confessional stamp. Theological, political and social rule became culturally established in the medium of orthodox theology. Indeed it has to be said that with increasing secularization the original theological content of this conservative orthodox theology and its living piety faded away more and more, while the form of life shaped by the authorities and the states and an authoritarian fixing of thought continued to be regarded as 'Christian'.

We still encounter caricatures of orthodoxy, distortions of its former life, in many places. Let me give an instance which I have experienced repeatedly in recent years. I have met older people who from the beginning of the 1980s for the first time have gone 'on to the streets' and seen a form of life which is not governed by state authorities as an expression of their faith. Because they read the Sermon on the Mount and began to believe in the non-violent Christ, they had to break with the paradigm under which they had grown up. They knew Christianity only in its socially conservative form. It was new to them that it had quite different consequences from those of unassuming bourgeois prosperity. Although they were virtually no longer aware of the content of the faith of Protestant orthodoxy, for example its understanding of the Bible, christology, the doctrine of the last things, they had been unconsciously stamped by the orthodox model. For them, to be churchmen and churchwomen was to accept the authority of the father: the physical father, the heavenly Father and the state father. They lived by the tradition of what is regarded as normal, usual, taken for granted, and an awareness of what the church stands for as an institution had been firmly stamped on them.

Precisely those people who are remote from the church think that they know very clearly what the church may be and what it may not be, what it stands for and what it does not touch on or is not concerned with. The living heart of the orthodox exposition of Christian faith has long disappeared from their horizon, but the elements of 'neutralized religion are everywhere present in the way in which the mentality of bourgeois society has been stamped... one is poisoned in them as by parts of corpses'.[1] In fact I think that most of what Tilman Moser calls the 'poisonings of God' in the present derive from an encounter with a dead, lifeless, rigid form of religion, as though all that were left of Christianity were this unholy Trinity:

The authority of the father, the state and of order

The tradition of subjection, lack of intellectual freedom, anti-intellectualism, resignation to fate and a wrong understanding of obedience

The institution of the church as a factor of power, which leads to adaptation and rest, often 'contentment'.

This belief in authority, tradition and institution was not the faith of Jesus. The new Enlightenment, liberal paradigm begins with three norms of criticism. Criticism of the text of Holy Scripture, institutional criticism of the church and its representatives, and criticism of the rule of authorities and powers which legitimate themselves as being 'appointed by God' or belonging to 'the order of creation' belong at the foundations of liberal theology. Gotthold Ephraim Lessing (1729-1781) always kept in mind the connection between obedience to the Bible and the obedience of subjects when he raged against 'bibliolatry', the idolization of scripture. 'Away with the head first – with the consequent improvement it will already turn out as God wills' (*Anti-Goeze*).

The paradigm shift represents the replacement of a method of explaining the world: the scientific method takes the place of the dogmatic method.

Dogmatic method	Scientific method
Revelation	Possibility of proof
Supernatural truth	Historicity
Timelessness	Relativity
Absoluteness	

But what does that mean for the use of the Bible? What significance does the Bible 'still' have, as people often ask? In orthodox thinking the Bible was the 'word of God' without any ifs and buts; in the liberal understanding (in terms of method) it is regarded as a book like any other. This change was disquieting for many people. The hermeneutical break experienced by Christians who have grown up in the closed world of religious fundamentalism and are confronted with historical-critical scholarship is still shattering today. It is painful, and is therefore often rejected in favour of an authoritarian fixation on an understanding of scripture which seems to me to be very dangerous within a tradition like that of German Protestantism, because it has allied itself so closely with tendencies in the authority exercised by the state. The choice of scripture which is made here – and any dealing with scripture is selective – speaks volumes, when one thinks, for example, of the excessive stress on Romans 13.1 ('Let everyone be subject to the powers that be') in comparison to Peter's confession in Acts: 'We must obey God rather than men' (5.29).

The paradigm shift has changed two things in the relationship of believers to the Bible. It has relativized the Bible and it has historicized it. 'Relativism' is to be understood as a critical revision of the Reformation scriptural principle *sola scriptura*, by scripture alone, which means that we gain comfort and certainty of faith only from scripture, and not from the tradition, which the Reformers criticized as Roman. However, the questioning of the eighteenth century is no longer about this contrast, but about the significance of Holy Scripture generally in a comparison of the different religions and confessions. Why should the Qur'an or the Bhagavadgita be less 'holy scripture' than the Bible? Why should God speak exclusively in the Bible?

Lessing gave an answer with the parable of the ring in *Nathan the Wise* (III.7), which is among the best of liberal theology. Nathan tells the story of three brothers who appear before the judge, each claiming personally to have received from their father the ancestral ring which makes him 'prince of the house'. The rings which they present are so similar that the authentic one cannot be recognized, and the statements of the three brothers are equally credible:

The father,
so each claimed, could not to him
have falsehood shown; and ere to him
so dear a father could a suspect be,
he must suspect his brothers,
while of them prepared to think the best,
must hold them guilty of the falsehood done
and seek to find the traitor, vengeance take.

Here Lessing is criticizing zealous, self-certain orthodoxy, the 'gross possessors of the truth' who believed that they had the true, the absolute, religion.

What was at stake in this controversy can be understood only if we know how orthodox church rule kept men and women in spiritual tutelage for centuries. Here I am thinking particularly of Galileo Galilei, who was forced to recant scientific knowledge by being shown the rack and instruments of torture. We cannot suppress such historical events from the history of the church, and it is to the credit of liberal theology in particular that it took them seriously in its self-criticism and its own revision of Christianity.

In Lessing, the judge reminds the disputing brothers that the authentic ring, the true religion, the Bible that is appropriated, must have the power to 'make beloved, acceptable before God and man'. As the brothers are disputing, none of them can have the authentic ring.

> And so you are all three
> deceived deceivers. For your rings are fakes.
> None is authentic. That ring, we suppose,
> must have been lost.

Here attention is shifted from the ring itself to its power, to what it really brings about. Religion is there to make us more human; if it does not do that, we can drop it. The judge admonishes the three brothers:

> Let each be zealous freely to show love,
> without alloy, and free from prejudice.
> Let each one strive with each to bring to light
> the power of the stone set in his ring.
> May help come to this power with gentleness,
> with honest friendship and beneficence,
> and innermost submissiveness towards God.

Lessing makes a double move characteristic of liberal theology: he relativizes the foundations of religion but strenghtens its practical reference. What is the practical significance of this relativization of the foundation for the relationship of liberal theology to the Bible? Liberalism represents a new attempt to understand what it means that the Bible is the word of God. Liberalism says: it *is* the word of God, but it is spoken by human beings. That means that it comes from historically-conditioned human beings who are capable of error, who perhaps did not know particular facts of science and were not aware of particular historical facts.

There are mistakes in the Bible. For example, Joshua says: 'Sun, stand still over Gibeon!' (Joshua 10.12) The basic notion here is that the sun travels round the earth, and because 'Sun, stand still' is in the Bible, Galileo Galilei was condemned. The modern scientific knowledge that we are not the centre of the world was felt to be a revolt, something that destroys all order.

Liberal theology with its criticism of the Bible waged a similar struggle: the experience of scientific and historical truth stands over against the revealed truth of scripture. Historicity confronts revelation. An understanding developed that there are contradictions in the Bible, that different things were told in different ways in different versions, that now 4000 (Matthew 15.32-39) and now 5000 (Matthew 14.13-21) people are fed miraculously, that on one occasion women and children are not included, and on another occasion they are not mentioned (Mark 8.1-9). It is undeniable that there are different traditions and different writers in the Bible who told the stories each in a particular way, especially as they were often based on oral tradition.

The anxiety of the orthodoxy of the time and of many pietists from the fundamentalist camp today has been a motive force in the centuries-long struggle over the Bible. The transition from the orthodox to the liberal paradigm lasted for a long time; it was more a paradigm shift than a paradigm change. But the power of such a paradigm recognized by a community can be measured today by the fact that in our churches and far beyond them, the liberal paradigm is for most people as naturally and unbrokenly true as the orthodox paradigm once was. It just seems to be superior to orthodoxy, which is regarded as retrogressive.

Its weaknesses are hardly noted within the male-directed white middle-class church of the First World. The historical transition towards a theology of liberation in which we find ourselves worldwide – from an ecumenical perspective – is denied or even fought against by many people. Paradigms are only valid for a time, and today we are facing a change which does not derive from the guilds which have done theology hitherto, but which is being brought about by others. Elisabeth Schüssler Fiorenza, who in my view is the most significant feminist theologian of the present day, speaks of the deep 'cleft between the interests of the community of faith and those of historical biblical scholarship'.[2] This gulf rests on the shift of theological paradigms which I shall be investigating in the next chapter. Here, first, I had to describe the liberating role of liberal theology. But what had a liberating effect in the eighteenth century, the historical-critical method of biblical scholarship, can no longer satisfy a living community today. What was bread has become a stone.

The Bible as the Word of God

Orthodox	Liberal	Liberation theology
Word of God	Word of God spoken by humans	Word of God spoken by/ to the poor
Literal Literalistic	Relativization of the Bible Historicization	speaking in the historical context from/to the oppressed
Verbal inspiration		
Personal inspiration	Shell and kernel (Harnack et al.)	binding on the community
	Symbolic truth (Tillich)	
	Existential truth (Bultmann)	

4   The Use of the Bible: From the Liberal Paradigm to the Paradigm of Liberation Theology

I have already pointed out that living Christian community today finds itself in some tension with dominant biblical criticism whenever it has deliberately entered into a commitment.

'Commitment' (Spanish *compromiso*) means taking on an obligation, devoting one's life, an attitude without which faith remains merely a world view, an intellectual opinion. A group of Christians committed in this sense will be ready to hear the voices of our brothers and sisters from the exploited two-thirds of the world; it will establish links with Christians from South Africa; it will hear the cry of fellow creatures, pay attention to the trees or the seals. It begins to get involved, but then often feels left in the lurch by the theologians. It receives only stones from them, not bread; an explanation of the Bible, not how to use the Bible in the current battles.

It seems as though the liberal paradigm has lost the power to communicate the confidence of faith and the hope of faith; it still affords consolation in difficulties in personal life, but that too remains in the superficial realm of individualistic psychology. A combative hope (and there is no other kind) for the preservation of creation, an end to militarism and the vision of a justice other than the murderous economic 'order' under which we now live – none of these things seem to grow within the liberal paradigm. Is not this spiritual weakness connected with liberal theology's relationship to the Bible? It emphasized very strongly that the Bible is not an unassailable authority, as orthodoxy thought. But does that mean it is only a collection of universal principles and timeless norms? What intrinsic authority does the Bible actually have? Do we really need it?

My own theological development was determined by the offshoots of liberal theology (Friedrich Gogarten and Rudolf Bultmann). I owe a great deal to this theology; without it I would have turned away with a shrug from an orthodoxy that was fossilized and a neo-orthodoxy that was intolerably authoritarian.

But as I became increasingly conscious of the history first of my people and later of the rich world, and even later of my femininity, I was driven beyond this paradigm. In 1971 I wrote a 'political theology' as a critical response to Rudolf Bultmann. That was a still tentative first step towards the new paradigm of liberation theology, which at that time in Europe we called only 'political theology'.[1] In attempting to say in retrospect what liberal theology has given me, I want to be careful in the way in which I formulate its understanding of the Bible: it attempted to rescue the authority of scripture in a non-European way. It saved the inner truth of scripture precisely by putting its external truth – its God-givenness, its unity, its consistency – radically in question. It failed to see the problem of this separation between 'inner' and 'outer' because the problem was deeply rooted in its own framework of liberalism. Negatively, two points of liberal biblical exegesis seem to me to be questionable or at least in need of supplementation. One is the limitation of the historical-critical method to the question of the 'authenticity' of a particular text. Did things really happen like that? Did Jesus in fact walk on the water? Anyone who puts the question in this way only has a choice between fundamentalism and historical criticism; the symbolic, existential perception of the text, which points to a new experience in one's own life, is lacking. The fixation on this problem of 'authenticity' has helped to blind people to questions of the social, political and economic context.

Connected with that is a second, methodological point of criticism, and that is the hermeneutical approach, which is largely in terms of the history of ideas. Liberal theology finds timeless norms and statements in the Bible. Despite its insistence on the historicity of scripture it does not go far enough in historical-critical terms, because it leaves out issues of social history. Only to another perspective of involvement, to a perspective 'from below', which knows suffering and oppression in its own context and does not exchange them for neutrality and objectivity, does the Bible open itself up and its continuum of text-context appear as truth. For the hungry the Bible then becomes bread.

Here I want to present three thought models of liberal theology in which an attempt is made to affirm the inner authority of the Bible and in fact to understand it as God's word.

I have identified one model with the expression 'kernel and shell'; here I am going back to Adolf von Harnack's book *What is Christianity?* which appeared in 1900. In this book, a bestseller from the beginning of the century, Harnack attempts to explain Christianity to his educated audience in Berlin and in so doing to separate kernel and shell. The unpalatable shell of the fruit is its time-conditioned covering which comes from a past world-view. Real faith relates to the fruit, the kernel. Using another image for this, Lessing had already asked ironically: 'Then do only those who swallow the packet along with the medicine become healthy?'

What is the heart of the gospel for Harnack? It is the love of God for the individual. Each individual man or woman has an infinite worth. God has 'so ennobled the human soul that it can and does unite with him'. That is the conception which stands at the heart of the gospel: 'Jesus Christ calls to every poor soul; he calls to everyone who bears a human face: You are children of the living God, and not only better than many sparrows but of more value than the whole world.' That is a liberal humanistic theology which also addresses non-believers. Being a child of God has this significance: 'Someone may know it or not, but a real reverence for humanity follows from the practical recognition of God as the Father of us all.'[2]

Thus the gaping abyss between the New Testament and ourselves is bridged; then as now, human beings can 'acknowledge' God as Father. It does not become clear how far they need God and whether this Father is the God whom the women workers on the conveyor belt need. The dialogue partner of this theology is the bourgeois, educated, enlightened male.

Another important attempt to hear the Word of God in, with and under the words is that of Rudolf Bultmann. As a New Testament scholar all his life (1884-1976), he was occupied in radical, historical biblical criticism which separates out sources, uncovers what is inauthentic, discovers contradictions and asks questions like: Which words really come from Jesus? Which stories come from the earliest community? However, for Bultmann this academic work of New

Testament exegesis with the aid of the historical-critical method is accompanied by an interpretation of the Bible in terms of human existence which he regards as an absolute necessity. He calls it 'existentialist interpretation'. For him, what is decisive is more than a rationalistic biblical criticism in which really nothing is left and one asks afterwards, 'What shall we do with all these pieces?' It is an attempt to understand the Bible in such a way that it says something to us *now* and challenges us *today*. It is important that the Bible is not just about the fact that two thousand years ago Jesus fed five thousand people with bread and fish but is also about where this miracle of feeding happens today. This story, which has been handed down several times in the New Testament, was interpreted in orthodoxy as proof of the divine power of Jesus. He can do what no one else can. He alone can do it and he alone accomplishes it. The meaning of the miracle is not that the hungry people are filled but that the divine power of Jesus, which is superior to the world, is demonstrated.

In liberal theology, instead of this there is stress on the togetherness of human beings, their community, their capacity to share, which is called forth by Jesus. One commentator thinks that, faced with the hungry crowd, Jesus said to the disciples something like this: '"We must show a good example to the rich, so that they share their provisions," and he began to give his food and that of his disciples to those sitting nearest to them. This action worked, and immediately there was an abundance of food. Without him the people would never have shared the bread; they would have gone on fighting endlessly over this bread, would have torn one another apart, as they have done as long as the world has existed and will do so until it comes to an end... When they looked up at him, the Son of Man, they reflected that they were all brothers, children of one father... They understood that "mine" and "yours" mean death, but "mine is yours" means life.'

Bultmann also stands in this tradition, with a special stress on the life-creating word of God. Bultmann's theology has often been called a Word of God theology, and in fact the living, transforming word plays a major role in it. As he says in a sermon: 'That is in fact the one real miracle, that the word of the redeeming grace of God encountering us in Jesus creates us anew; that it frees us from ourselves, that is, from our old sinful nature, and makes us a "new creation".'[3] It is remarkable to note how a theology which deals so extremely critically and analytically with the words of the Bible, its literal text, remains almost orthodox about the 'Word'.

However, the concept of the 'Word of God' is also demythologized in Bultmann. It happens as an ordinary oral communication from one person to another. There is no formal criterion with the help of which one could identify it as divine. Whether God's word comes from the pulpit or from the radio or from the kitchen chair, whether it is introduced by 'Thus says the Lord', with 'Good grief', or 'In the name of the mothers' doesn't matter. Luther says, 'As often as God's word is preached, it makes the conscience happy, broad-minded and sure towards God... But as often as the word of man is proclaimed, it makes the conscience in itself sad, narrow and fearful.'

So the criterion of the Word of God is the future which it opens up. The word is God's word if it makes people human – happy, broad-minded and sure. Those who are freed for their humanity will also no longer fail to give other people the true Word which opens up the future. However, in applying the term 'ordinary' to the Word of God I did not do so meaning that it is often or indeed normally what happens between men and women. What is normal is that people fail over the word which makes the way clear.

It is evident that this kind of theology of the Word of God which I learned as a student seeks to get beyond mere truthfulness. Here the claim and the limitations of liberal theology become recognizable. It is open to what liberation theology will later go on to call 'praxis'. It is not yet capable of identifying this praxis of faith more precisely. It remains – and this I have learned this from my teacher Friedrich Gogarten – in the sphere of personal relationships. Today, in place of 'Word of God' I would prefer to say 'the praxis of Jesus'. At any rate, here the connecting links between the liberal approach and that of the theology of liberation become evident.

Another important attempt to hear the Word of God in the human word, which similarly points forward to liberation theology, is the concept of the symbol, which Paul Tillich has developed. Tillich has made it clear that religious language is essentially symbolic and not representative.[4] I would like to explain that briefly via the use of the word 'God', which is one of the most ambivalent words in the world. You can understand almost anything you can think of by it. 'In God we trust' appears on every dollar bill! Is that the Father of Jesus Christ, or is it another God? That is a question we have to raise whenever the word 'God' appears. Tillich says that the word of God has a different structure from the words 'desk' or 'table'. The word table is a definite and unambiguous designation, even if I say the equivalent in other languages. So named, the table can be made of wood or metal, be white or green. These are accidents; but the essence of the table, that which makes it the piece of furniture that it is, is given in the word. And correctly so. So we rely on words. But the word 'God' does not belong in the same category. When we say 'God', that is only a symbolic approximation to something that we cannot grasp with our words. Tillich calls it 'ultimate concern'.

God is always greater than any talk of God. I think that it is immediately evident that God must be more than all our words, that God always means something more behind them, something that we perhaps have not formulated at all, that God 'is' essentially, ontologically, something 'other' than a table, if one is going to use the verb to 'be' here at all. 'There is' the table, 'there are' the Himalayas, but you cannot say 'there is' God; when confronting God the objectifying approach of a detached observer is meaningless and impossible.

Symbolic language is language which must remain aware of its own limitations. Dogma is then symbolic God-talk from a paradigm which is now finished and has become largely incomprehensible. The notion of symbolic language plays an important role in contemporary discussion about feminist theology. Patriarchy easily confuses its concept of God with God and does not understand that even the statement 'God is the Father of all human beings' is a symbolic statement and not a real description. The moment I make that a non-symbolic, i.e. a reified, dogmatic statement, which rules out other statements like 'God is the Mother of all men and women', my thought of God is too small. I have reduced God to the spiritual horizon and shut God up there.

Nowadays, in many places theological thinking pushes beyond the liberal paradigm but gets caught up in its own horizon through a distinctive characteristic of European, post-Enlightenment theology to which Gustavo Gutiérrez, one of the fathers of liberation theology, has drawn attention.[5] Gutiérrez asks who is the dialogue partner of a theology, for whom it is intended, and for whom it is statement and response. What interest does it have? For bourgeois-liberal theology this 'interlocutor' is the non-believer, the atheistic engineer, the university professor, someone in a boundary situation of suffering or meaninglessness – who is usually perceived of as male. By contrast liberation theology has quite another partner in dialogue; it thinks in terms of the non-person whose human nature is denied, perhaps because she is poor, a woman, or not white. The theological dialogue does not take place between bourgeois non-Christians and bourgeois Christians but arises from the victims of this bourgeois culture of exclusion and destruction. Racism, sexism and class society are far more basic boundaries of separation and destruction than the so-called 'questions of faith' which leave this reality out of account. Attractive and beautiful though Harnack's theology seems to me at first sight, it reveals nothing about the poor, those to whom the biblical message is really addressed. Harnack spoke about the infinite value of the individual soul, but not about the colonialism of the German empire or about its militarism. Indeed he was one of the many theologians and intellectuals who rejoiced at the outbreak of the First World War.

The hermeneutical model of liberation theology does not take *just* the text of scripture seriously, as orthodoxy does; it also rejects the liberal thought-model in which scripture and 'modern man' are confronted with each other. Instead, it sets text against context, and does so from the biblical perspective of the 'poor'. The Word of God in the Bible is understood as acting 'from' the poor and spoken 'to' them. Therefore the historical and socio-historical context of the Bible is fundamental.

In theological work with the Bible the decisive factor is not literary criticism but social criticism, an understanding of the context of biblical reality. However, interest in this context does not arise out of an apparent scientific neutrality. The consequences of the biblical stories of believers and the desperate will become clear to me only if I can have a reasonably clear grasp of my particular situation, the particular context within which God's word speaks to us. So there are four different factors in play in the hermeneutical model of liberation theologies:

The biblical text = Holy Scripture
The biblical context
One's own context
The biblical text 'for us' = God's Word.

A biblical interpretation which seeks to find God's Word in the Bible must take account of both contexts. In both contexts it must see reality 'with the eyes of Jesus', which means perceiving it in the light of the victims. Without perception of the victims, the oppressed, there is no perception of liberation.[6]

In the conference of Latin American bishops at Medellin in 1968 a principle of liberation theology was formulated that God loves or prefers the poor in a special sense. In hermeneutical terms, this 'preferential option for the poor' (*opcion especial por los pobres*) means that scripture must be read in terms of those to whom it is addressed. And those addressed by the word of God and thus the deepest concern of theology are, then as now, the poor, the landless masses in Palestine, the wanderers, who have no heritage, no portion of land, no profession, no chance, whom Jesus gathered into his movement: poor who went with him through the land, including a striking number of women. We must really imagine the biblical context in terms of the present-day 'Third World'. In a situation of extreme poverty it is almost the rule that at some point men leave their wives and that a tremendous surplus of destitute women, left alone with their children, are landed with the misery in their own bodies and lives. These are the people to whom the gospel relates. And liberation theology believes that the whole Bible is written from the perspective of the poor: its promise, its promises, are for the poor.[7]

The poor are the criterion for the interpretation of scripture. Latin American theology has not simply taken over the Marxist concept of class but works with the biblical concept of the 'poor', which is not a theoretical sociologial category like the marginalized or the peripheral settlers. The content of the term derives from a concrete outlook and concrete experiences; those involved speak themselves. A mystical component is also involved, because 'the poor' of this theology are not simply thwarted capitalists. On the basis of their situation, their poverty, they have another relationship to life, a deeper need for exchange and communication, a greater hunger for God. We must read the Bible in the context of the poor, in the light of its effect among the poor and the way in which it changes the life of the poor. As we shall go on to see, in the perspective of liberation theology there are links with orthodoxy and elements of liberal theology.

I want to introduce another biblical example to make clear the difference in the interpretations of the different theological traditions. Here I am thinking of the story that Jesus was born of the Virgin

Mary. Orthodoxy interprets the story literally. Jesus was born of a virgin. This dogmatic statement was even made one of the five 'fundamentals' which the American Fundamentalists opposed to the liberal attempt to modify the content of faith at the beginning of this century.[8]

Among Conservative Evangelicals, the doctrine of the virgin birth is made an essential element of Christian faith, without which it cannot be confessed. They do not regard attitudes to war and means of mass destruction as something that determines whether one is a believer or not, but the virgin birth does. Now the liberal critics come along, open the Bible, and state that the most important authors of the New Testament do not know this story or do not mention it. Mark makes his Gospel begin with the baptism of Jesus when Jesus is already thirty, and tells us nothing at all about his childhood. What happened to the virgin Mary was not important for him, nor how Jesus was born. John has Jesus with God from eternity and does not reflect on the birth story, nor does Paul.

With the help of its sideline, the so-called history of religions school, liberal theology compared the various religions in their contexts and discovered that the theme of the virgin birth was a fairly widespread one in antiquity. People were fond of saying that significant men and great heroes were born of a virgin. This peripatetic theme was so widespread that a virgin birth could be reported even of people whose fathers were very well known. For example, four hundred years after his death, Socrates, whose father and mother we know, was said to have been born of a virgin because it was thought that this would express his divinity more clearly. So this was a peripatetic theme which was not native to Judaism but to Hellenism. The Hebrew Bible speaks prophetically of 'a young woman' (Isa.7.14), and then the theme got into Luke's account and so found its way into church history. The undertones hostile to sex and women have no support in the Bible.

So much for the historical origin of this theme and for liberal theology's critical treatment of it. I can remember the doubts about Christianity which I had when I was eighteen; one of the problems which I could not crack (not the biggest, but one of them) was this virgin birth, which I found incomprehensible. I did not know why I should believe it; whether Jesus would be better had he been born of a virgin than if he had had a father. I did not understand what that would contribute to my redemption, to my liberation from sin and grief. I still remember clearly how liberated I felt when I learned from liberal theology that this part of faith was only a Hellenistic interpretation and was not essential to my being a Christian. The liberal paradigm has often liberated people from false stumbling-blocks to faith.

But liberation theology with a Latin American stamp is quite different: here the theme of the virgin birth is not superfluous, but is bound up with the struggle for liberation. It is decisive for the liberator to come into the world from among the poor. The majority of people in Latin America are born out of wedlock; many do not know who their father is. The situation of the young woman who is expecting a child without being able to count on protection or help is quite normal. She gets into difficulties; perhaps she asks an older friend like Elizabeth for advice; she is afraid of being abandoned, of being punished for infidelity. These are all *normal* situations which often happen in our society too. They are incorporated into liberation theology like this: Mary is one of us; she gives birth to the light, the liberator, the redeemer. In the gospel of the peasants of Solentiname, the angel who announces the birth to her is regarded as 'subversive' : 'And Mary immediately also becomes subversive in listening to this message. I believe that she already felt as though she were going into the underground. The birth of a liberator must be kept secret.'⁹ That is a completely new approach to the story; it is quite different when one thinks *from the perspective of the poor*, moreover of the poorest, the wives of the poor. In this sense, the story of the virgin birth is not made superfluous by criticism, but understood in a different way. Here liberation theology takes up the orthodox paradigm, but at the same time understands it differently in the framework of this new exegesis, from the poor/for the poor. It no longer conveys hostility to sexuality and domination, but subversion and rebellion. For liberal theology the virgin birth is a stumbling block which is best removed. For liberation theology it is a piece of bread.

5   The Understanding of Creation

The doctrine of creation within Christian theology can also be bread, life-giving and life-sustaining; but it can also become stone, which cannot express our relationship to reality and therefore gets forgotten. How are we to understand the biblical narratives and statements about creation?

I remember a game from my childhood. We were asked: 'Where is our school? In Raderberg. Where is Raderberg? In Cologne. Where is Cologne? In the Rhineland. Where is the Rhineland? In Germany. Where is Germany? In Europe. Where is Europe? On the earth. Where is the earth? In God's hand.' That's a good game, in which children slowly learn, starting from their small home, how the whole world is 'in God's hand'. Here we have an expression of a bit of creation faith which puts everything, including the whole universe, in God's hand. How great God's hand must be to hold everything! Reverence and trust are the basic relationships which are learned in this game. Starting from Cologne-Raderberg, we cannot fall out of God's hand. 'In his hand are all the corners of the earth, the strength of the hills is his also. The sea is his and he made it; he made the dry land also' (Psalm 95.4ff.).

To be made by God is the deepest cause of our earthly fellowship, not only among human beings, but with all other living beings. With all that is, commonly willed and thus meant as we are, we are part of this earth. 'I have made the earth and created human beings on it; my hands have spanned the heaven, I have ordered all its host' (Isaiah 45.12).

Because we are made communally, our self-understanding must

again catch up with the dimension of collective understanding: individualism does not understand talk about 'God's hand'.

Another quotation from the creation faith on which I want to meditate by way of an introduction comes from the Jesuit scientist Pierre Teilhard de Chardin (1881-1955). He was often accused of overlooking evil and guilt, though more than any one else he thought about the connection between the theory of evolution as a cosmic movement and Christian belief in creation. He replied: 'You are all hypnotized by evil.' And in one of his letters he writes: 'I believe that any thinking has to make a basic choice, a postulate which cannot be proved but on which everything depends. If one assumes that being is better than its opposite, it is difficult to stop on this way and not go towards God.'[1]

So if we really affirm being (and here Teilhard writes in quite Thomistic terms), and if we 'choose' life, as the Bible puts it (Deuteronomy 30.19), in the face of the obvious desperation about human existence and the offers of death, it is difficult to block off these ways and not to go to the ground of being. Both quotations, the children's game and the words of the great palaeontologist and anthropologist, express a movement which comes to rest only in God.

The biblical belief in creation considers three elements together: the creator God, human beings, and the world. I shall again attempt to formulate the common Christian foundations before I go into the different interpretations and accents of the different theological paradigms.

The Christian understanding of creation is concerned to keep the creator God present, to understand created human beings as free and – perhaps the hardest thing to believe today – to regard the creation as good and to love it.[2]

The first statement is that God is the creator and sustainer of the world, the final cause, as philosophers sometimes term it, or the foundation without which nothing is, that is there. The world has a beginning and was not eternal; that is a conception of biblical faith which differs from other religions and which is rooted in its historical consciousness. It has a beginning and also an end, which in the Jewish and Christian view are determined by God. That God is creator is a reason for reverence and trust: this confidence in the world includes awe at the size of creation, at its beauty, at the starry sky above us of which Kant spoke, and at the same time trust, a sense of feeling at

home. Basic feelings of this kind constitute trust in the world. Without
the experiences underlying them human childhood is incomplete and
emotionally impoverished. It is necessary to learn the feelings of
reverence for and trust in creation; they need to be expressed, and
wither on the ground of a purely rationalistic explanation of the world.
Children's songs like 'Twinkle, twinkle little star' are a beginning of
instilling belief in creation. I do not think that 'reverence and trust
must first be directed towards the creator himself', as someone who
heard these lectures objected: I think that this exaggerated separation
of creator and creation is a mistake.[3] We *recognize* the creator in the
creation – where else? We see transcendence in immanence. Trust
does not come abstractly from the otherness of God; it must, for
example, be communicated by the return of the sun in the morning,
of spring after winter. And the 'pantheism of childhood' is not to be
eliminated but to be strengthened.

The second element of Christian belief in creation relates to the
creature and its independent existence; it is made free. Adam and Eve
are free to eat the apple; they are not compelled by destiny; they do
not stand under an absolute necessity. According to Jewish-Christian
tradition, human beings are always understood in terms of freedom.
And freedom also means being capable of evil. Here independence
from the creator, emancipation from parental protection is envisaged,
though at the same time this creature is entangled in the laws of
creatureliness. It lives for only a short time and is bound by the
ordinances of creation, which express themselves as the needs of the
human species for food, sleep, warmth, and so on.

The third element of belief in creation relates to the perception that
creation is 'good'. Nowadays, in view of the destruction which part of
creation, i.e. human beings in industrial nations, is inflicting on the
whole, it is here that the greatest difficulties lie. Must we reckon with
a final end to life on our earth? Have not human beings, at least as
represented by white human beings, who were appointed to 'protect'
and 'preserve' (Genesis 2.15), failed, and irreparably destroyed God's
earth? The Bible tells us that on each day of creation God saw that all
was 'good', and on the last day even that it was very good. What is
there is good, is worth loving and praising. We have no right to regard
the world as evil or, say, to attribute evil to matter – thinking that it
was possibly created by another God. This material world is neither a

chance happening nor an invention of the devil, but the good creation of God.

These three elements of the doctrine of creation – the role of God, the role of the human creature, and the role of creation – have been stressed differently and interpreted differently in the different paradigms of theology. In orthodoxy, God is seen as the creator and sustainer of the world; God has made himself known to all human beings in the creation, and only the disruption of our understanding by sin prevents us from recognizing God's reality. The Bible is not just understood as a book explaining the world, but it *is* understood in this way, and materializes the doctrine of creation in these terms. The creation narrative is taken literally, word for word. The modern church finds itself in a permanent controversy with scientific reason, which declares, 'That's no good, light cannot be there before the sun.' The contradictions in the creation narrative are obvious, even if we make the seven days millions of years. Above all, this controversy gives rise to criticism of a method which is no longer thought to be adequate. It is replaced by the scientific method, which is based on experience and reason.

However, orthodoxy, thus robbed of its foundation, i.e. 'revealed' truth, could still continue for a long time to articulate reverence, trust and confidence in the providence of God, as the expression of a creation-based spirituality, as is evident from the tone of many seventeenth century hymns. But with the growing understanding of the evolution of nature, the picture fades of the Father-Creator who even now cares faithfully for his children; God's power is reduced to initial power. The deistic picture of God as a watchmaker, who has created the masterpiece of a moving world which runs even without God's intervention, indicates this retreat of the creator.

In the framework of the orthodox paradigm, the role of the human being as a creature poised between freedom and bondage to the ordinances of creation becomes increasingly problematical. The doctrine of the 'ordinances of creation' played an ominous role in Lutheran theology, above all during the nineteenth century. In an asymmetrical way it sought to loosen the tension between the freedom and independence of human beings and their createdness, bondage and dependence.

The relationships between man and woman, old and young, rich and poor, authority and subject, were seen as foreordained in accord-

ance with creation, and creaturely freedom was given only to the
superiors. This extremely conservative exegesis certainly has no
support in scripture, which explicitly depicts the rule of man over
woman as a curse of sin, like the barren drudgery of work (Genesis
3.16); but it nevertheless left its mark on social history.

All fundamentalist theologians make the ordinances of creation an
essential part of creation faith and absolutize them. Women belong at
home, fulfil their life through motherhood, by caring for their hus-
bands and serving them. The fixed role-pattern of a particular economic and family order is transfigured into an order willed by God
and given by creation. With a methodologically similar logic, slaves
were understood as those elected by God to serve the whites. Until
well into the nineteenth century, and even today in apartheid, racism
was and is justified.

The condemnation of homosexuality is another example of a rigid,
repressive interpretation of the ordinance. That human beings in
the creation story are of two sexes is exploited in the interest of
heterosexism, the forcible imposition of one form of love; while the
Bible – with its realism and its love of truth! – 'can just as naturally
also speak of the intimate attraction of a man to a man or a woman to
a woman as possible ways of human love; indeed, it openly allows
them as such,' as Willy Schottroff says in a biblical exegesis of the
story of David and Jonathan.[4] Elements of social repression to the point
of trivial matters of fashion, for example the prohibition of trousers for
women, caricature faith in the creation which is made to be good.

The third element of a creation theology relates to the goodness of
creation and the possibility of knowing it, for which God stands
guarantor at all times. Here the motive of sustaining comes into play:
God is concerned for the creation, and does not let it out of his hands,
as a watchmaker does a watch.

Again a contrast can be observed here between orthodox piety, trust
in God with a firm foundation, and belief in the goodness of creation,
which is maintained despite opposition and the experience of suffering
on the one hand, and a narrow theocentric theology which separates
creator and creature as far as possible on the other. The more greatly,
the more remotely, the more sovereignly God is enthroned above his
creation, the less 'he' makes himself known. Orthodoxy prepares for
the desacralization of the reality of the world; it demarcates itself from
all pantheism. Its God supports the tendency to make the earth and

all that lives on it 'subject' to the will of the Lord, which is thought of above all as power.

Liberal theology proves ambivalent in the doctrine of creation. In the controversy between science and faith its starting point is that the truth of scripture cannot be opposed to reason. The old functions of the Bible in explaining the world are abandoned; science occupies the gaps. Over the last three hundred years we can see a retreat of theology, which abandons the positions it occupied earlier and no longer takes part in scientific discussion about the origin of the world. Theologians say: We cannot explain how the world came into being. So we must ask the scientists. First of all only the detailed interpretation – when, what, how creation took place – retreats, and science begins its triumphal parade. Attempts are still made to speak of the creator and to maintain the relationship with him. But the question is whether the basic attitude towards the creator and the world ensouled by him can remain, once the foundation is removed from it. The liberal understanding of creation remains relatively helpless.

The new thoughts ventured by liberal theology appear more in its anthropology. Here there is stress on the independence of human beings, on their freedom. That went so far that idealist philosophers like Schiller said that the Fall, the fact that Adam and Eve ate the apple and were driven out of the garden of Eden, was the happiest event in human history. Only now did that history begin. Emergence from protection, from childhood, liberation from the parental God, is necessity and happiness, as Erich Fromm shows in his interpretation of creation in *You Shall be as Gods*.[5] He gives a critical interpretation of the Hebrew Bible from the perspective of social psychology, with the aim of liberation. This thinking derives from the Enlightenment, which in liberal theology stressed free will and at the same time relativized the alleged orders of creation by recognizing the way in which they were historically conditioned. The dependence of human beings on the whole of creation is replaced by the indpendence of those who understand themselves to be lords and owners of creation.

Friedrich Gogarten (1887-1967) saw the weakness of liberal theology and reworked the dialectic of the dependence and freedom of the created in the conditions of modern times. He explained the role of human beings, not like orthodoxy with the help of the orders of creation, nor in the sense of a liberal belief in progress in which even the word 'creation' is replaced by 'nature', but by the concept of

'sonship', which is a distinctive feature of his writing. His theology of
creation and creatureliness – although extremely androcentric; it deals
only with fathers and sons! – at least expresses the intrinsic difficulties
in creation faith.

The 'son', whom Gogarten explicitly distinguishes from the 'child
of God', owes his life to the father and yet at the same time is
independent of the father, in so far he has entered into the heritage of
the world. He has come of age; he has learned to speak for himself
and no longer needs any spokesman. He no longer needs the father,
i.e. religious tradition, to explain the world. And yet he destroys
himself and the world entrusted to him if he uses it without any link
with the father, if he treats it as a possession, not as a heritage which
he has received and which is to be handed on. According to Gogarten
it is the personal relationship to the 'father' which alone keeps open
responsibility towards the world.[6]

If we understand ourselves as lords and owners of the earth and act
as though we still had a second earth at our disposal – if we deny our
creatureliness – then for us the creation is merely usable material. The
creation is then irrelevant to our relationship to the world in which we
are masters and owners, the world which we have at our disposal,
whether we assume or actually think it true that a world builder, a
demiurge, created everything in a mystical 'beginning'. Our createdness has then lost all existential significance for the present; our
freedom has devoured the bond.

In Gogarten's thinking the roles of God as creator and sustainer of
the world are divided: the Father is the creator, and the free yet
dependent Son becomes the sustainer; in ecumenical theology there
is often talk of human stewardship, of human beings acting as
administrators of the world edifice. From here ways lead to liberation
theology, which above all as feminist theology stresses the cooperation
betwen God and human beings, their mutual relationship.

The third theme of belief in creation, the goodness of creation, does
not play any supporting role in liberal theology. It was very much
suppressed in the triumphal progress of science and industrialism.
While the world was presented as something that could be understood,
at the same time it increasingly became material for human experimentation. Nature became a usable commodity belonging to no one, or
only to the 'natives', who were themselves usable material. There is
nothing holy in it, so it can be used at will.

The sharpest criticism which must be directed at liberal theology on the matter of creation is that it did not respect and press for the sacrality of the created world. When theologians retreated to the point of speaking only of the *fact* of createdness, and not of a creator who was active and present in creation, the world was also increasingly reified as the material at our disposal, with which we can do what we will. As a contrast to the widespread maxim based on Chief Seattle's words, 'Every point of this earth is holy to my people', it must be asserted that *no* part of this world is holy to the white man. Rather, the rule is that whatever is conceivable and possible must be tried out. The experimental character of the modern period does not tolerate any created existence, any creatureliness. We have long since arrived at an ideology of experimentation, the distinctive dynamic of which cannot in principle recognize any limits. Nowadays the beginning and end of human and extra-human life lie in the hands of genetic and nuclear technology. From that perspective we have to investigate another basis for a theology of creation. The debate in liberation theology, which is only just beginning, is taking up elements of the tradition and, particularly through the women theologians of the First World, introducing ecological perspectives into the theology of creation.

The various trends in liberation theology are agreed that the existing world order is hostile to creation, indeed that in its various forms of oppression by class rule, racism, sexism and imperialism over nature it represents an attack on creation. The poor are deprived of their being created in the image of God. Allan Boesak, a black theologian from South Africa, has shown the theological effect of apartheid on human beings: it deprives them of their share in the power of life by making them completely powerless and subjecting them to the total domination of outsiders.[7] The white oppressors in the apartheid state have distorted the image of God in themselves, but the blacks who are oppressed are deprived of their very createdness, their being in the image of God. Against the background of the impoverishment of two-thirds of the human race, within liberation theology God is celebrated not so much as the creator and sustainer, who 'gives the cattle food and his children bread', as a 1783 hymn by Matthias Claudius has it, but above all as creator and liberator. Liberation theology cannot have any great interest in sustaining the present order, but experiences it as present disorder and chaos, in which nine out of every twelve children die. What, then, is the meaning of pious talk like, 'What our God has created he will also sustain, and will rule over it early and late with his goodness' (as a 1673 hymn has it)? Such piety can easily make people cynical. Instead of this it must be stressed that only the God who liberates us is by so doing completing his work of creation. Oppression destroys the essence of being created for freedom!

In the various theologies of liberation there is regularly a description of the way in which the creation is meant to have equality of races, families and classes. In the biblical account of creation nothing is said about black people who are perhaps born as slaves, to serve the whites. We are told of an original couple, Adam and Eve, father and mother of the whole human race. Similarly, feminist theology refers back to the first account of creation (the one which, though it may be later, stands first in the Bible), which articulates the equality of male and female: 'God created the human being in God's own image as male and female' (Genesis 1.27). The story of the rib in Genesis 2 is devalued; it contradicts the first account, which is a clear manifestation of the equality of male and female. It is the two together who form 'man' (in the generic sense). What the image of God is can be conceived of only in terms of both sexes; those who attempt to think of God only as male have not understood who God is; they are confusing themselves with God. Feminist theology stresses that the image of God is reflected in male and female, and not just in half of humankind. By the same token liberation theology, which understands creation in terms of the exodus, reads into God the creator the liberator who seeks the equality of races, sexes and also classes, in accordance with creation. The division of human beings into poor and rich is also overtaken by an equality which God has willed.

In the Middle Ages there was a saying, 'When Adam delved and Eve span, who was then the gentleman?' There was no class distinction; in primeval time all were equal. And the ongoing creation of God even now gives a right to more equality than is realized in class society. Here creation is understood as an act of liberation and is brought very close to redemption. As the Peruvian father of liberation theology, Gustavo Gutiérrez, puts it, the Bible 'does not deal with creation in order to satisfy philosophic concerns regarding the origin of the world'.[8] Therefore it does not describe the act of creation as a preliminary stage, but as an element in the process of salvation. 'Redemption – as an unlimited and unmerited initiative of God and the communion of human beings with God and among themselves – is the inner motive power behind this movement and its definitive consummation, which is set in motion by the work of salvation and in which human beings create themselves.' The creation is incomplete, and God needs us in history to complete it. It is still 'work in progress'.

Thus the role of human beings as God's collaborators in the completion of the original creation is redefined; they are not just involved passively and acceptingly. 'The one who works and changes this world becomes more human, contributes to the formation of a human society – and brings about redemption.' Gutiérrez refers explicitly to a saying of Augustine's: 'He who made you without you does not justify you without you. He who created you without your knowing it, he will justify you if you will it.'[9] From this perspective it follows that human work takes on a new value, and is not only toil and tribulation but continues the creative act of God. The work of liberation, as co-creation, becomes the theme of the feminist theologies of creation.[10] The transcendence of God does not rest in itself, in a creator outside the world, nor is it forgotten in immanentist terms, as often in liberal theology, but comes to consummation in the social praxis of those who as co-creators support the growth of the kingdom of God in the world.

We can only become collaborators with God in this sense if we believe in the goodness of creation, and can also join in the biblical statement 'It was all very good'. It was not chance which gave rise to this world, nor did chaos prove all-powerful, and the future is not determined by an apocalyptic twilight of the gods, the *Götterdämmerung* of Wagner and Germanic mythology. Deep trust in God and faith in God's good creation must lead us, and above all those who are developing a liberation theology within the First World, to develop an ecological theology. We are only at the beginning. There have been a few attempts at reflection where for the sake of creation people are standing out against the destruction of creation.

When we speak of creation, we mean more than nature; at the same time we are expressing the holiness of the earth. There is a poster which depicts the world, this sphere on which we live, with all its rifts and crevasses, a ball in the midst of the universe, crusty and wrinkled and, as the photograph shows, in constant movement, our old earth. Underneath it is the caption 'Love your mother'. That is a new form of spirituality. In the face of the destruction of our world we recall the

creation. That happens in many groups and is an important element
of the liberation theology which is coming into being within the First
World. Hans-Eckehard Bahr and others have written a short book
entitled *Franziskus in Gorleben*.[11] St Francis is the saint who praised
the goodness, the beauty of creation in a virtually unparalleled way,
and Gorleben, where nuclear waste is to be stored, is a place where
creation is being destroyed.

The most important question for an ecological theology seems to
me to be how we can express trust in the creator God and reverence
for creation in our lives. The important thing is to love creation, to
train oneself and one's children to be aware of creation. With my small
two-year-old grandson I have planted bulbs in the earth; I have
explained to him that now winter is coming and first the flowers have
to sleep, and also that the earthworms now no longer come far enough
up for us to be able to see them. These are tiny attempts to achieve a
bit of familiarity with nature and trust in natural return. In a discussion
on love of creation, one of the audience objected: 'I cannot love the
air here in the Rhine-Main district! It is completely polluted. What
do you do about that?!' But if one reflects on creation, one cannot limit
oneself totally to the present moment. Being human also means
knowing what came beforehand and what will develop later. According
to Indian wisdom, for any decision that we make we are answerable
to the next seven generations. I do not just live in this minimal
immanence of my present state and this contaminated air and this
contaminated water. To think in human terms, I must keep in mind
human history and its possibilities, and I am helped to do that by an
understanding of creation and a trust in how it was meant.

I believe that the existential problem over creation is that we are so
overwhelmed by negative experiences that it is hardly possible to have
a primal trust any more. In this situation the Christian task would be
first of all to allow mourning over the death of plants and animals
around us; we should not simply pigeonhole the news of catastrophes
as mere information. We should learn to lament, to make ourselves
sensitive. The liturgy is not an adornment to life but a place for lament,
for the expression of grief. Without compassion for dying seals and
the woods that are wasting away we cannot learn love for creation.
And without this immanence of God in our earth we lose the transcendence of God.

The Understanding of Creation

Orthodox	Liberal	Liberation theology
God is creator and sustainer of the world		God is liberator and creator of the world
The Bible explains and interprets reality	Retreat from the theological explanation of the world	Oppression destroys the equality of races, classes and sexes
Reverence and trust as basic attitudes		
The human creature is dependent	Stress on freedom	The existing order is hostile to creation
Freedom, but being bound to the orders of creation	The orders of creation are relativized	Freedom is the integral liberation of all
Creation can be known and is good	Creation increasingly becomes material without holiness	Ecumenical liberation theology protects the sacrality of creation
Absolute transcendence of God	Immanence of God	Transcendence in immanence

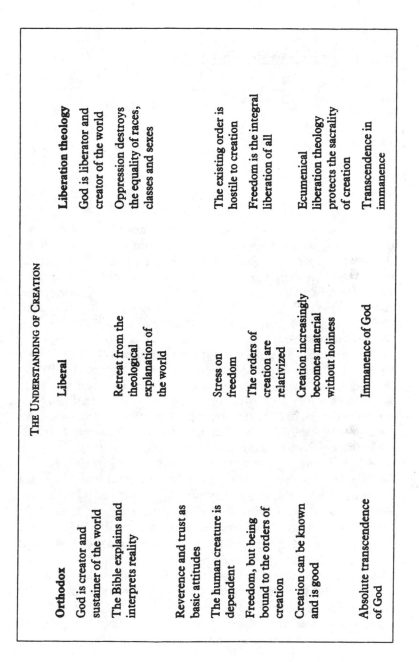

6 The Understanding of Sin

Again my methodological approach will be to identify a basic theological statement and then ask what it means in the different paradigms. Part of the concept of creation is the basic statement that God has created the whole world good. Our question then was: what does this mean from an orthodox, liberal and liberation theological perspective? In coming to the topic of sin I shall similarly begin with the universal Christian statement that sin is separation from God. What does that mean? How is it interpreted?

The Bible tells us a story about how separation from God came about. In Christian tradition this is called the story of the 'fall', but that word does not occur in the Hebrew Bible. I do not want to go into this story here, but before turning to individual paradigms, I do want to reflect on the Christian concept of sin. We misunderstand this concept if we regard it only as a moral concept, if here we think only of the sins which we all commit: lying, stealing, murdering, deceiving. That is bad enough, but what we mean by the singular – *sin*, the fundamental sin, the primal sin – is something else: it is a state, not an action. With a frightful concept which does not occur in the Bible but has played a role in tradition, in contrast to actual sin as the deliberate violation of God's law this primal sin is called 'original sin'. The concept is so difficult because it is misunderstood to be a biological fate, as a result of which one can inherit illnesses or genetic conditions. Not even Augustine, who shaped the Western understanding of sin, meant this. What is meant is that we are born into conditions in which we do not cause sin but already live in sin.

Here I must speak of the experiences of my generation. Without these primary experiences I would never have understood what separates me from God. As a very young woman I went to the Netherlands for the first time and observed that some people did not want to talk to me because I was a German and their relatives had been killed by the Nazis. There it became very clear to me that while I had not 'done' anything – I was too young – nevertheless these others had a right to turn their backs on me and not speak to me because by language, culture and heritage I belonged to a human society which lived in a complex of guilt. I cannot get myself out of this; it just is the case. And this piece of objectivity is part of the concept of sin. Sin is certainly also my decision, my free will, my 'no' to God, but it is also the destiny into which I was born. I am entangled in it through my parents, my teachers and my tradition. Even those born later cannot avoid this reality, and while it is inappropriate to speak of collective guilt, the sense of a collective responsibility for guilt is necessary. I am also responsible for the house which I did not build but in which I live.[1]

It is precisely that which the remarkable doctrine of 'original sin' seeks to maintain. The state of being born in sin does not arise from my personal decision or my will. There is a coincidence of guilt and fate which we must understand 'dialectically'. We must hold together in our thought the two contradictory statements, each of which has its truth but each of which contradicts the other in such a way that in normal logic only one of the two could claim to be true. That is precisely the contribution made by Christian tradition when in the concept of original sin it holds together guilt and fate, which exclude each other. In fact only the person who is free is capable of guilt. But if I am capable of guilt, i.e. am free, that is as it were one side of the coin. The other side is the fate of the sin into which I am born. We do not seek out for ourselves the society in which we live and the place we have in it, but are born into something which is already determined by the structures of sin, of separation from God. We then also affirm this objective constitution in a subjective way. So, put in New Testament terms, sin is a power which rules over us. In an investigation of Paul, Luise Schottroff has worked out very clearly and in a pioneering way for Pauline scholarship this character of the sin to which I feel subjected by birth, time and place, and by my life.[2]

I am already subject to the rule of terror. Paul describes the rule of sin with the metaphors of the Roman empire. Sin rules, subjects, conquers, pays out wages, spreads terror and death. Paul identifies

sin in its context in social history. So 'I' too already, speaking in terms
of the present, live under violent forces: militarism, the wasting of
energy, the consumption of meat, exploitation. If this is understood
as the terror exercised by sin, the question then becomes how I react
to it.

Those are the two elements which we must always hold together.
One element is fate, inheritance, involvement, social compulsion, the
power of sin (the objective element) – and the subjective element is
my will in this, the involvement of my own action, my freedom, my
decision.

Perhaps in the younger generation the experience of being German
after Auschwitz is no longer the only, inescapable, place at which
the individual awareness of innocence founders. But one of the
fundamental insights of the Jewish-Christian religion which cannot
be allowed to be forgotten with impunity is that it must founder, that
given the reality of the world it must fall to pieces because of its
unsuspecting nature, its incredible naivety. People are somehow
wrong right through. We have 'transformed God's truth into lies'
(Romans 1.25). We need forgiveness, reconciliation, the possibility
of a new beginning. In the Christian liturgy the 'Lord, have mercy',
the Kyrie eleison, expresses most clearly this consciousness of sin,
which brings together guilt and fate, psychological and sociological
misery. Only if we learn to pray it with our whole heart do we
understand the meaning of sin.

I come to the orthodox interpretation of separation from God.
Human beings put themselves in the place of God: that is central to
the understanding of sin in the orthodox tradition. It begins when
human beings elevate themselves to the divine level (*superbia*). Human
beings wanted to be like God and to know what is good and evil.
According to Augustine (354-430), who expounds the story of the fall,
Adam was free. He had all that he could wish, but he wanted more,
namely to be independent of God. Adam lived in the garden of Eden.
Everything was there for him. He could have recognized the order of
creation and been happy. But he chose rebellion against God, and any
creature which seeks to fulfil its own being in separation from God
and with no relationship to God forfeits the happiness of oneness.
According to Augustine, creatures condemn themselves to ignorance
and to longings that cannot be fulfilled, to concupiscence, to the lusts
of misdirected love (*Enchiridion* [Little handbook], VII).

Amor sui, self-love, is itself counter-productive: anyone who wants nothing but self-realization and autonomy will lose it. Adam wanted to gain independence from God and live without a relationship to God. In so doing he sinned; he rejected the limitation of being human and denied the creatureliness in which we live. He did not want to be a creature, with the limitations without which being created cannot be interpreted. In this sense sin is disobedience not only against particular commandments but against createdness. Wanting to be like God is the original fault, which is then followed by getting above oneself; in the long tradition of orthodoxy that is also interpreted as pride – Greek 'hybris': presumption, arrogance, self-love. Sin whispers to us that the limitations of the creature should and can fall away; our temporal limitations (we do not have unlimited time), our physical limitations (we do not have unlimited power) and our spiritual limitations (we cannot understand everything) are all pushed on one side, and human beings think that they are their own creators and can do everything themselves.

Reinhold Niebuhr (1892-1971), a great neo-orthodox American theologian, describes sin as pride and distinguishes between the pride of power, the pride of knowledge and moral pride.[3] The idea that power is mine and unlimited, that knowledge is mine and unlimited, and that I am in the right, indeed self-righteous, makes me independent of God and isolates me from my fellow human beings. This is the sin in which we get above ourselves and no longer accept the role which we have as creatures. This original, essential disobedience – once again according to Augustine – results in a blinding of the understanding and a corruption of the will. The understanding is disturbed by the fall, because the balance between reason and passion is destroyed, and human beings give themselves over to transitory delusions and moods. The reason is blinded and no longer sees reality. The will to do good is corrupted, in that the will to power triumphs over the will to good. In the orthodox paradigm God is seen as the one who as creator demands obedience from human beings: disobedience is consequently the nature of sin.

One of the best sources for understanding orthodox thought is the Protestant hymn, the theological content of which is quite strongly marked by orthodoxy and at the same time expresses a living spirituality. For example Johannes Scheffler (Angelus Silesius) writes this about sin:

> I wandered lost and was blinded
> I sought thee and did not find thee
> I had turned from thee
> and loved the created light.
> But now it has come through thee
> that I have longed for thee   (1657).

The place from which sin is recognized as sin must lie beyond sin, and so this hymn – and many like it – speaks about it in the past form, from the perspective of grace:

> I once was lost, but now am found
> was blind, but now I see   (*Amazing Grace*, 1797).

The decisive factor is the emergence from being lost and blind, which is why in Christian teaching sin and grace are always thought of together. But precisely within the orthodox understanding there is a danger which I call the anthropological pessimism of Protestantism. That is a feeling in which sin, guilt, helplessness and despair come together. 'With force of arms we nothing can' is here torn out of the living, militant context of the Reformation period, and 'full soon were we downridden' becomes a reference to the immutability of the situation of human beings before God.

It can be asked what function talk of sin has, and for what it is used. It can be used in order to keep people down, keep them conscious of guilt and helpless, but it can also be thought of as an instrument for analysing the situation, in which the aim remains the overcoming of this separation from the ground of life. Only if we stand with one foot already on the new land of forgiveness and grace do we talk rightly of sin. If, on the other hand, we attempt to belittle and mock efforts at change, steps on the way to conversion, because after all we are all sinners, sin is ontologized and made something eternal – and liberation becomes uncertain. We cannot know anything, we cannot trust ourselves, we cannot do anything – those are the most godless statements of the present, which in apparent humility, apparent obedience, no longer take account of God's action to us and in us.

Many Protestants do not believe in God's gracious acquittal, but only in their own captivity and oppression under sin; they confuse real guilt, which changes us because it can be forgiven, with neurotic guilt-feelings, from which the helpless 'I' sees no release.

Generally speaking, liberal theology defines sin as a lack of love. It is based less on the primal history of disobedience than on the real experience that we all have and that even a little honesty compels us to concede: we do not love one another. That is the case. We fall short of what love should really be. Friedrich Schleiermacher (1768-1834), who formulated his theology in the period of German Romanticism, speaks of the person who tries to live an independent life alone, and who in so doing becomes isolated from the universe and neighbours, limited to self-related interests. Isolation and cutting oneself off from the feeling of 'absolute dependence', which is how Schleiermacher defines religion, is essentially what happens in sin. In his view the nature of piety, which appears in such different manifestations, is 'this, that we are aware of ourselves as absolutely dependent or, which amounts to the same thing, as in relationship with God' (*The Christian Faith*, 2.3).

Any form of purely authoritarian faith is rejected here; we are to accept the truth of being sinners, not because God has commanded it, because scripture says so, because the pope or even the little Protestant popes demanded it, but out of knowledge of the fact that we are dependent on God.

In his *Speeches on Religion to its Cultured Despisers* (1799), Schleiermacher says of Adam in Paradise:

As long as the first man was alone with himself and nature, the Deity ruled over him and addressed him in various ways, but he did not understand and answered nothing. His paradise was beautiful, the stars shone down on him from a beautiful heaven, but there awoke in him no sense for the world. Even from within, this sense was not developed. Still his mind was stirred with longing for a world, and he collected the animal creation before him, if perhaps out of them a world might be formed. Then the Deity recognized that the world would be nothing, as long as man was alone. He created a helpmate for him. At length the deep-toned harmonies awoke in him, and the world fashioned itself before his eyes. In flesh of his flesh, and bone of his bone, he discovered humanity. In this first love he had a foretaste of all love's forms and tendencies – in humanity he found the world. From this moment he was capable of seeing and hearing the voice of the Deity, and even the most insolent transgression of His laws did not any more shut him out from intercourse with the Eternal Being. The history of us all is related in this sacred legend. All is present in vain for those who set themselves alone. In order to receive the life of the World-Spirit, and have religion, man must first, in love and through love, have found humanity.[4]

The liberal concept of sin – cutting oneself off, isolating oneself as a lack of love – is perhaps what seems easiest for modern men and women to understand. Even if I am not convinced that I was conceived and born in sin, that I constantly sin in the sense that I commit actual individual sins, I can realize that love is always greater and requires more than what I am and do. I do not live up to it. My lack of love expresses my remoteness from God. Kierkegaard once spoke about 'the edifying nature of the fact that we are always wrong in the face of God' (*Either/Or*, 1841). One can understand this thought formulated in orthodox terms only if one understands the distinctive concept of love more deeply than is suggested by our world, and recognizes love as the only criterion: only then do we understand how far we fall short of it and do not fulfil it. This is where I see the strength of liberal exegesis, and also its weakness, which lies in the fact that it does not consider love and the need of the human person for relationships radically enough. Therefore sin appears as an individual deficiency, as failure, as remaining in egoism, but not as a structural power which dominates us and destroys us.

Liberation theology first brought out again this objectivity, the compulsion to sin. In 1986 I taught at a Baptist seminary in Nicaragua. The students, male and female, some of them already pastors, had not had particulary good theological training. But when I tried to say something to them about sin, they taught me – very simply and very much in accordance with scripture. While I was still speculating on self-love, power and isolation, a black woman pastor interrupted me and said: 'But it's quite clear. Adam and Eve wanted to have more than others and so they ate the apple, and that is covetousness. Sin is the immeasurable greed of people who want to possess something, and everything else follows from this desire to possess.' I had never thought of it like that before. But it is clear that the poor read the Bible and tradition with different eyes from ours. In a situation of exploitation and under the fearful pressure of those who possess everything at the cost of the exploitation of the masses, it is much more natural also to read the story of the fall not simply as the story of a father-child relationship with prohibition and transgression, but in terms of greed, covetousness, avarice. It is in fact astonishing how one and the same biblical story can be read in different ways. What really is the motive for the action? Why did Adam and Eve eat of the forbidden fruit? Is it true that this is a matter of disobedience, of the individual becoming independent, of an Oedipal conflict, as the Western tradition is fond of assuming? Or is it greed, basing life on having, on possession, which then leads to a state of economic and social injustice? Here we have two different approaches. In the theology which I learned there was never any reflection on the apple, or if there was, at best it was in jest. Thought had a strictly personal orientation: God and the human couple, creator and creature, authority and freedom, prohibition and disobedience, stood in the centre. Latin American theology extracts quite a different side fom the web of symbols: covetousness as what separates human beings from God. For Reinhold Niebuhr, the pride of knowledge, power and morality represent the destroyed relationship, but this 'pride' has its structural side, the privileges based on the unjust distribution of education, the power to exploit others based on private property, the power to discriminate against others based on feelings of superiority. Sin is injustice, and God is understood as justice within the biblical tradition.

I would like to describe in more detail how I came to liberation theology, and in so doing I shall refer to the philosophical tradition of 'human alienation' as it has been developed in the tradition of Hegel and Marx. Paul Tillich took over this concept of human alienation (or estrangement, as he termed it) as a modern way of interpreting sin; at this point his thought develops a reference to a transition to liberation theology.[5] For a rising European theology of liberation this criticism of human alienation, prompted by Hegel and carried through by Karl Marx, is automatically central, because Marx, turning Hegel upside down, noted alienation in the conditions of production in industrialism.

Without an analysis of working conditions we cannot understand the power and rule of sin over our lives of which Paul speaks (cf. Romans 5.12; 7.14; 7.17 etc.).[6] The absence of the theme of work from traditional systematic theology has contributed greatly to a false ontologizing of sin, to misunderstanding it as individual helplessness. Without reflecting on work – the work of women, the unemployment among a growing minority – we can only speak about sin in the detached way that liberal theology does. We then never really get to the Kyrie eleison; we do not get to the bottom of why we need God.

Marx uncovered four different forms of alienation: the working person is alienated from herself, from nature, from her fellow human beings and from the human race. The first alienation, from ourselves, destroys our totality. The worker is alienated from herself because what she is – heart, understanding, many different gifts – is not involved in the process of production, but only a very small part of her: for example two hands, which for hours make only one movement. Here a bit of what a person is is broken off and used; everything else that a person also is is not used, practised. It is not trained, it does not change and so it dies. In such working processes human beings become more stupid, heartless, unimaginative. There are enough descriptions of production in the literature of work which note these phenomena with precision, showing how a spiritual destruction takes place, a destruction of emotional capacities, as a result of which when people get home exhausted, they can only sit in front of the television and drink beer. That is alienation from what we are. Work makes us less than we really should be. It destroys us, alienates us from ourselves. Paul says of the power of sin that I am 'sold under it'. 'For what I would I do not, but what I hate, that I do' (Romans 7.14ff.). In the idealistic tradition of theology we usually think of this as a metaphysical split, but it is the most everyday experience of the majority of people.

The second form of alienation is that of the person next to me, who may not be a sister or brother, friend or helper, but has to be an enemy or a rival. That is also clear from experience on the conveyor belt, where human relationships are regulated by the speed of the belt. If an 'agitator' arrives who speeds it up without the workers immediately noticing, then the relationship between them deteriorates: offence, anger, envy, hatred against one another arise. Charlie Chaplin gave an unsurpassed account of this in *Modern Times*.

There are many other everyday examples of alienation from one another: the isolation of the housewife with small children, her solitude, her helplesness. Our nurture is not focussed on readiness to help but on rivalry. This takes place everywhere; to take the case of the housewife, it is so internalized that she does not attach any importance to herself because she does not do any paid work. The competitive society in which I have to be better, get better pay, perform better, be utterly original and stand out, is an expression of the alienation of a people from their neighbours.

The third form of alienation is that from nature. The balance that makes up good work, meaningful production, the 'reconciliation with nature' of which Marx spoke, is destroyed. What we have is a sheer relationship of domination in which we are lords and masters, 'masters and owners of nature', as the Enlightenment put it, but nature is regarded as dead material. Here, too, it is wrong to ontologize sin, to make it an eternal destiny which then really no longer affects anyone because it has sunk to the banal thought that we separate ourselves from God by the destruction of creation. It is useful to recall other societies which have dealt with their resources in a different way from us. I am thinking, for example, of the Indians, who took only the wood they needed for a fire, who prayed to the river before catching salmon or trout. They understood themselves as part of the whole, not as lords over the whole, in a natural piety which represents the opposite to our isolation and hostility.

The fourth alienation identified by Marx is that from our 'species', i.e. our membership of the human race. We deny our solidarity, we destroy our belonging to other members of the human family and privatize ourselves in our own careers, so that it is regarded as almost unnatural and absurd even to pay any attention to others on whom we dump our toxic waste or to whom we sell our weapons.

I remember a cab ride in New York. It was bitterly cold, and we were driving through Harlem and talking about the cold. I mentioned the fact that the day before, two old people had been frozen to death in a house in which the landlord had cut off the heating; it was thought to be abandoned. The taxi driver looked and me and said angrily, 'This is not your business. What concern is it of yours?' I said, 'These are people. Why do you ask "What concern is it of yours?"?' In this conversation I was struck by the moral assurance with which this man put me in my place and said, 'You have nothing to do with the human race. Mind your own business.' That is a widespread notion among the alienated citizens who are only concerned with their closest neighbours and no longer have anything to do with the community or society, whether in the small town or in the city, not to mention their own country or globally. On the American Right a new insult has recently developed – one worldism, i.e. belief in the unity of the world. This is thought to be Communist.

Sin as separation from God is realized in these different forms of isolation: the lack of relationship to ourselves, our neighbours, to creation and to the human family. Someone who heard these lectures objected that this does not yet say anything about God, and that alienation goes far deeper than Karl Marx thought. In principle I think that this objection is illegitimate, because it thinks of the relationship to God in isolation from other relationships. We are divided from God *in* our living relationships. By living, working, dealing with one another and with creation, we act as the enemies of God. This is not a special religious sphere, as though a quite different, fifth, dimension had to be added to the dimensions of alienation already mentioned; our lack of relationship develops within the dimensions of our alienated reality. Of course one can analyse the dimensions I have mentioned more thoroughly, more comprehensively. But that does not alter the recognition of sin in any way; it becomes living and existential only when we emerge from the servitude of sin. As long as it is our mistress and has absolute power over us, we remain blind. Paul speaks of this condition of ours by calling us 'enemies of God' (Romans 5.10). It is precisely this objective hostility towards the ground of being that is expressed by the concept of alienation. It can at most be criticized for perhaps not bringing out the element of guilt clearly enough and stressing the element of fate too much, so that it could mislead us into thinking of a mechanistic determinism.[7] We are aliens, alienated, not only as those who have been carried off by sin, but also in the sense that we have gone along with it, that exile has now become tolerable, that we have organized ourselves in it.

Having clarified the understanding of sin in the three paradigms, I would now like to make a specific investigation of one form of liberation theology, feminist theology.

The theme of sin was discussed at an early stage in feminist theology, as early as 1962. Valerie Saiving took up what Niebuhr had said about pride, self-righteousness, wanting to be like God, the independence of the separated I. She asked: is this 'imperialistic impetus' common to all humanity, or do the different sexes have different experiences? Is what Niebuhr and other theologians describe, what women also experience as sin? Her conclusion was that, on the contrary, for women self-denial, giving up oneself, not wanting to have any self, is the real sin. The struggle for power and independence, the departure from

SIN: SEPARATION FROM GOD

Orthodox	Liberal	Liberation theology
Separation from God as the basis from which other attitudes follow:	Separation from God as the divine, failing to live up to real human determination	Separation from God expresses itself in social structures and and personal attitudes
Disobedience to God's will	Lack of love	Covetousness
Blinding of the understanding	Egoism	Injustice
Corruption of the will	Isolation from dependence	Alienation from oneself, the neighbour, nature, the human family
Pride, arrogance, hybris		
Getting above oneself rejects limitations and creatureliness		Self-denial 'Wish to be white'

paradise, to eat the apple and then build all kinds of towers in Babel – that is not a women's theme. Women experience themselves quite differently, not in these male categories. Their failure and separation from God comes about in other ways, specifically in the form of self-*denial*. The sin of women is not that we think too highly about ourselves, that we have too much self-confidence, that we develop too much human pride or human hybris, but on the contrary, that we are too yielding, that we practise too much self-denial and obedience, by giving up pride and self-determination. As Valerie Saiving writes: 'A mother also experiences that a woman can surrender too much of herself, so that nothing remains of her uniqueness. She can become a mere nothing, almost a zero, without value for herself, for her fellow human beings or perhaps for God. For the temptations for a woman as woman are not the same temptations as those for a man as man.'[8]

The specifically feminine form of sin cannot be paraphrased with terms like 'pride' or 'striving for power'. Women very often destroy their 'being in the likeness of God', the fact that they are created in the image of God, by obedience, self-denial and subjection to patriarchal role-models. So they do not become human beings at all – in social psychology people talk of the child woman who will never really grow up, and artificially keeps on being a little girl. That often leads to enormous complications in terms of social psychology, in that women artificially take refuge in a role that they really should have grown out of long ago. As women they often make themselves less than they are. Here is an example. As a young girl, to the dismay of my parents I hitch-hiked quite a lot, and as a result also found myself in difficult situations. My main technique for dealing with unpleasant men was to act as if I hadn't a clue; if they dropped hints I deliberately ignored them and talked about the weather. That means that I practised a degree of self-denial to protect myself and presented myself as being more naive than I really was. That's something which women often also do in other situations, for example in flirting. Women live in danger of not making things clear and also not giving way; that is, without real awareness and without personal responsibility. We make ourselves dependent on others and leave to circumstances how things will turn out. We 'wait' as women, in a deep sense, instead of making it clear to ourselves that we personally are also involved and responsible. We rarely take the initiative. These are dangers for middle-class women, a typical result of the way women are brought up in bourgeois society.

In theological terms that means that for me as a woman pride is not really sin, but rather something that I still have to learn. The male conception of the person who rebels against God by affirming himself, by acting proudly, arrogantly and without constraints, is not a woman's concern. Rather, we women are in danger of not developing any pride, of never becoming independent, of constantly remaining within all too narrow boundaries.

As specifically feminine failings which are diametrically opposed to those of men, Valerie Saiving lists: 'Triviality, liability to distraction, talkativeness, lack of concentration and dependence on others for one's own self-determination... Tolerance at the cost of standards... inability to respect the limits of the private sphere..., sentimentality, love of gossip and mistrust of the understanding – in short, under-development or negation of the ego.'[9]

If we really learn to think existentially as women, then we must learn to take our experiences seriously. In what sense are *we* separating ourselves fom God? Feminist liberation theology replies: by taking our place in the patriarchy without resisting, we separate ourselves from what we are meant to be.

In a 'Catechism of Reason for Noble Women', Schleiermacher says, 'You shall not bear false witness for men, you shall not gloss over their barbarism in word and deed.'[10] In the peace movement in the USA I have often met the wives of senior officers who were at precisely this point in their spiritual development and who asked how long they should still go on approving barbarism. Some of them were desperate and were being torn apart; they did not know whether to go forwards or backwards. Others were getting out of situations which they had accepted unquestioningly for decades.

Feminist theology does not claim to have answers to every question, but its aim is for women to find their own voice and not a borrowed one. Of course it is quite natural that this makes separation from God, sin, a clearer and more burning issue. However, it is not a matter of a bland triumphalism towards men, but of women finding their own voice – finally and without distortion. If the Psalms promise that 'God will hear my voice' (Ps.5.4), that also must apply to those who always lacked a voice or had to speak with a distorted one.

7 Feminist Liberation Theology

With the rise of the new women's movement in the industrial countries over the last twenty years, women with a religious concern have increasingly found their own voice. I want to look briefly at the foundations of the feminist theology of liberation, and will be concentrating on three points: new subjects, new objects and new methods.

Who in fact does theology? Now that the doors of universities and church seminaries have been opened to women, now that some churches admit women to the ministry, theology is ceasing to be a purely male concern; historically it has new opportunities to become human. So it is important to ask who does theology, i.e. who is the subject. Who has the power to say what theology is? In other words, what counts as theology? What praxis is reflected in it? Only male praxis? In whose interest is theology done, and who determines the limits of what is theologically relevant?

The anchoring of traditional theology in everyday life was often so nebulous, and there was so little reflection on the context, that it was impossible to ask who really had the power to make decisions here. Women have raised this question again, for example in the rediscovery of one of the finest feminist texts in the Bible, Mary's Magnificat in Luke 1. They have simply asked themselves: Who is speaking there? It is a young woman; she is pregnant, unmarried and poor – a second-class being – and she praises God with her voice, which is at the same time that of the liberating tradition. She names God with the help of the revolutionary statements of the song, which sound like this in a modern translation:

All ages prove that he is there
for those who look to him in earnest.
His power is against the rulers
and he thwarts their plans.
He casts down from their seats those who are on high
and exalts the humiliated;
he fills the hungry with good things,
and the rich go away empty   (Luke 1.50-53).[1]

The Magnificat, or Mary's song of praise, is a basic text for liberation theology. I have never been quite clear who is really singing this song, who is this handmaid of God, a woman who is under so many disadvantages. In scholarly language we call what I am attempting to describe the 'hermeneutical privilege of the poor'. Those who are utterly down, the weak, like this woman, have a priority in the knowledge of God.

This hermeneutical privilege of the oppressed is a central idea for all theologies of liberation. Who really needs theology? Who is looking for it? Who are the subjects of theology? In critical terms, given the Magnificat, women can ask what right a white middle-class person has to define theology. When we hear, 'He casts down the powerful from their thrones and raises up the lowly', by what truth-claims do white males do theology? This question of who calls God by name, the question of the subject, is important for all liberation theologies, but it is important for feminist theology in a quite specific sense. Women who do theology must nowadays constantly go on fighting against the exclusion of women and discrimination against them, against the institutionalized sexism of theological faculties and churches (West Germany is an underdeveloped country when it comes to the patriarchalism which continues in the faculties!). These battles are painful because they do more than put in question the self-glorification of males ('Herrlichkeit', glory, contains the word 'Herr', 'Lord', so that there is a word-play in German which cannot be repeated in English); they are at a deeper level. The claim of theology really to speak of God – and not just of masculine aspects of God which have been split off – puts the truthfulness of theology at risk wherever women are shut out. The interest of women has its own theological roots: it is not just a power struggle in which women also want to become involved; feminist theology grows out of an understanding of the God who is

with the lowly, the disinherited and the offended and who speaks
through them. It is no coincidence that the song of liberation in
Luke 1 is sung by a woman.

For a long time I failed to understand the revolutionary content of
the Magnificat. This song should have been banned from the start! Its
statements are a collection of verses from the Hebrew Bible; when I
studied theology I simply dissected the text in literary-critical terms:
this bit comes from here, that bit comes from there... I now think that
this is a foolish procedure which only distracts attention from the
content. The content, the redistribution of hunger and luxury,
helplessness and power, was not perceived by those who studied it,
either in the socio-historical context of the New Testament or in the
context of their own lives. And the figure of the girl who sings this
song of jubilation suffered precisely the cultural fate that women have
to expect elsewhere: they are made invisible.[2] The biblical realism is
suppressed: a desensualized, pure, exalted Mary bears witness to the
misuse of tradition. The history of the influence of this notion, the
'Ave Maria' with bowed head, extreme humility in her gestures, tells
of this destruction of the biblical reality.[3]

A second point by which we have to make clear to ourselves what
is new about feminist theology relates to its new objects, its new
themes and content. We read the tradition with a specific accent which
women put on the history of women; to use a play on words, her-story
instad of his-story.

What do we learn in the biblical story about woman's story? Where
do women appear? What role do they play there? Where are they kept
quiet about? Here one makes the most amazing discoveries. I always
thought that I knew the Bible very well until I read Phyllis Trible's
Texts of Terror.[4] It is an interpretation of stories from the Hebrew
Bible dealing with women's terror. Jephthah is a general who is
promised victory if he sacrifices the first thing that encounters him on
his return home (Judges 11.30-40). For this fairy-tale theme, he is
perhaps thinking of his dog, but when he comes home it is his
daughter, his only child, who runs out to meet him. This daughter
does not even have a name in the Bible. She meets her friends just
once more, and they celebrate a festival which later becomes a ritual
of the daughters of Israel; and then she is killed. No angel intervenes
as in Abraham's sacrifice of Isaac.

I found it frightening that I did not know this story; it had never come up in my theological education, but people had kept quiet about it. And it is only one of the many stories which tell of terror in dealings with women. I mention it as an example to make clear the shift of interest and subject-matter in feminist theological research. Elisabeth Schüssler Fiorenza has reconstructed the history of a Jesus movement consisting of equals in *In Memory of Her*. Her principle is to read *all* biblical texts feministically, i.e. critically and creatively. It is not a matter of noting women's themes alongside men's themes, women's theology alongside men's theology, and opening up an adjacent area for women in educational establishmnts. Rather, feminist theology offers a perspective on all the traditional objects of theology, which demonstrates oppression and which is therefore one which works towards liberation. In that case the women in the Bible and the stories about them are among the 'new objects', like the denial of a place to women in the history of the church and of theology.

I have already given an example of how systematic theology must change if women think it, in connection with my discussion of the concept of sin. We are normally unaware of the pressure to think in male categories; it is taken for granted that the theological world is a world of men. Because of an unconscious self-trivialization on their part, even women do not perceive what specifically does not correspond with the experience of women in the orthodox determination of the concept of sin. Elisabeth Schüssler Fiorenza suggests as a feminist criterion for Bible-reading 'a critical examination and evaluation of texts to see whether or not they contribute to the wholeness, well-being and freedom of women'.[5]

Here I have already touched on the change brought about by feminist theology, which relates not only to individual fields of theology and their biblical, historical and systematic material, but also to methods. Feminist theology is a liberation theology because it, too, starts from the praxis-reflection-praxis model which I mentioned earlier (5f.). Praxis, reflection and renewed praxis form one and the same theological process. In this way liberation theologies break open that Aristotelian prison into which theology allowed itself to be forced by Hellenization in the third century. It is part of the basic Greek understanding that theory ranks above praxis: the work of the head is regarded as more important than the work of the hands; the work of the husband sitting in the study is more important than that of the wife tied to her household tasks. These patterns of our thought extend

to everyday matters and have led to the development of a conception
of theology which is remote from praxis. By contrast, the paradigm
of liberation theologies is building up a new relationship between
praxis and theology. The theory accompanies us, clarifies matters,
helps us to reflect on what is really at issue: what is decisive is the
living out of faith, its praxis. At this point we see how remarkably
close liberation theologies are to the original Pietism which emerged
as a movement aginst the orthodox church system of the seventeenth
century. All the pietistic terms like *exercitia pietatis* and *praxis pietatis*
already appear in the Dutch pietist Voetius (1689-1676). Almost
throughout the pietistic renewal movement there was vigorous criticism of academic scholarly theology; the mother tongue was preferred
to Latin, 'revival' was required of academic teachers, and philosophy
was rejected.

The parallel which I see is the stress on one's own experience in
feminist theology, the commitment of those who do theology in the
base movement. In an interview Leonardo Boff said: 'I do not
understand theologians in Latin America who have no contact with
the base. Among us you cannot do theology as it is done in Germany,
where it is exclusively taught at the university. We Latin American
theologians are at the same time in the middle of the movement. I
myself work in Petropolis, a poor quarter at the edge of Rio de Janeiro'
(*Publik Forum*, 24 April 1988). That also applies to the feminist
liberation theology which is developing in the first world. Luise
Schottroff writes: 'For many years I did my historical work on the
New Testament in connection with the liberation work in my area. I
suffered from the fact that the Federal Republic of Germany is
a country which has a denser concentration of weapons of mass
destruction than any other country in the world, is a place of violence
and injustice. I took part in the resistance to that and sought to do my
biblical scholarship in the service of the work of liberation. I no longer
wanted to live in two worlds: the world of my desk and the world of
armaments and rocket bases. My historical work seems to me to be
meaningful if it serves the Christian men and women who sit down in
the cold rain to block the exits to the cruise missile bases.'[6]

All contemporary theologies of liberation understand scholarship
not to be obligated to the ideals of neutrality, detachment and balance,
but as partisan support for women, for those at a disadvantage, a

science of advocacy which understands itself as the attorney for the poor, for the oppressed, for women.

These three essential innovations which I have discussed here in connection with feminist theology – new subjects, new objects and perspectives, new methods – apply to all liberation theologies. They have an interest in unmasking traditional bourgeois theology and demonstrating the points at which this bourgeois theology serves the interests of those in charge. The Godhead is seen as that which achieves justice for the people allied to it in the covenant. The essential gift of the Jewish people to the human family is the insistence on justice founded in religion. The prophetic tradition of the Hebrew Bible constantly criticizes religion detached from righteousness: festivals and celebrations (cf. Amos.5.21-24; Hosea 6.5ff.; Isaiah 1.14ff.), its priests and rituals (cf.Jeremiah 6.13ff.; 7.4-11; Isaiah 58.2ff.), in order to point to the will of God, to doing justice.

> With what shall I go before God,
> how shall I show honour to the Most High?
> Shall I come with burnt offerings,
> with one-year-old calves?
> You have been told, man, what is good!
> He requires only one thing from you:
> do justice and be there for others,
> match God in your life   (Micah 6.6-7).

The 'right to practise justice and to love good', as the Zurich Bible translates it, is also a central theme for feminist theology. The first thing that this theology discloses is that sexism is unjust and against the will of God. God has not made us slaves and dependents, objects of men, but as one of these two earthly beings, man and woman (Genesis 1.27), in his/her image. Everything that falls short of this created freedom offends against the basis of biblical thought of God, which is a thought of justice. The emancipation of the Christian community from patriarchal structures and androcentric conscious-ness is suggested here. By 'androcentric' I understand the linguistic confusion of human being or 'man' with the male which dominates our language, and the practical confusion which is manifest in the structure of society.

But precisely here there is a difference between Latin American and feminist liberation theology which is relevant to method. The task of feminist theolgoy is more difficult because patriarchal oppression also stamped the biblical tradition deeply. The Bible is written in a languagage dominated by men; it lives above all by androcentric images. There are only a few feminine images for God.[7]

The whole approach of the Bible is androcentric. The confusion or identification of human beings with the male is found in the Bible, and in this sense the Bible is also a document of the patriarchate. So we cannot use it as directly as it is used in many base communities. Feminist theology attempts to discover other historical traditions within the Bible which support the full personhood of the woman and in this sense really express liberation.

Some women have concluded from the great difficulty that the document to which Christianity refers, namely the Bible, is a patriarchal document, that they should put this document aside and depart from this tradition. Here I am referring to the post-Christian wing of feminist theology which is breaking away from the Bible. The most important representative of this line is Mary Daly, who has left the Catholic Church and broken with Christianity because she regards it as hopelessly, unchangeably patriarchal. Others, who in West Germany include Luise Schottroff and myself, represent a more moderate Reformation wing. We too see that the Bible is an androcentric and patriarchal document, but at the same time we discover in it a fundamental opposition to these traditions; we read it as a book of justice, aimed at liberation from all the bonds that enslave us. 'Cast out the old leaven, so that you may be a new leaven' (I Corinthians 5.7) – such hopes are still alive in the women's church which is coming into being today. We are attempting to work out the contradiction within the biblical traditions more clearly and to bring them to consciousness, so that we do not have to leave the house of the church; but we want to purge it of the traces of patriarchy.

The position of feminist liberation theology does not amount to exodus, to departure, to celebrating the goddess, but is concerned to remain true to the Godhead (to use a term from Meister Eckart) of this tradition, so that its justice ultimately becomes visible as a humanitarian one.

That constantly brings us into conflict with the patriarchalism of the Bible. We cannot be without the Bible, nor do we want to be – and yet it is the book in which women are often humiliated and hurt. The Bible speaks of God – and at the same time it distorts God. Of course I feel humiliated when I read what I Timothy says about women: 'Let a woman learn in silence with all submissiveness. I permit no woman to teach or to have authority over men; she is to keep silent. For Adam was formed first, then Eve; and Adam was not deceived, but the woman was deceived and became a transgressor. Yet woman will be saved through bearing children, if she continues in faith and love and holiness, with modesty' (I Timothy 2.11-15).

I breathe a little sigh of relief when I learn that these statements do not come from Paul but from one of his pupils. But the massive obstacles to the liberation of women within the Bible and posed by tradition cannot be denied. We must confront them and work through them. And those men who do theology cannot avoid this task either.

But my personal experience is that my confidence has grown through work on the liberating character of the Bible, and my hope in God as the God of justice, which I understand also to mean sexual justice, has grown through intensive critical attention to the Bible. And that has happened precisely when I have had to criticize particular parts of the tradition radically.

Work in the liberation movements for peace and reconciliation with creation have made me more hungry for a good use of the tradition. It has relieved me of my biblical relativism suggested by the Western culture deriving from the Enlightenment and has grounded me more deeply in the human traditions of the Bible. I do not feel excluded or homeless as a woman, and I think that an increasing number of women feel the same. It is not we feminist theologians who betrayed the tradition with our criticism of the personal and institutional sexism of the church when we began the exodus from the hierarchical and patriarchal culture of Egypt, but that part of the male church which continues to identify the Golden Calf of capital, violence and phallic power with God.

In this learning process on the part of many thinking Christian women it became clear that we have to reject a literalistic understanding of the Bible in which every word is said to be the word of God. We take up the Bible as partners in dialogue; in it speak people who have responded to the call of God but who – as males of their time – have missed, denied or perverted the call of God to justice. Theological reflection helps me to recognize that the author of the Letter to Timothy is furthering patriarchy and that the passage I have quoted is thinking about nothing but patriarchy. Martin Luther said that the important thing is whether the Bible 'urges Christ'. The biblical authors often did not 'urge Christ' but patriarchy. So what is the criterion? Who is interpreting the Bible correctly? Paul betrays what he proclaimed elsewhere, justification by faith, when he declares that women are not justified by faith but by bearing children and being obedient. If one reflects on Paul's theological thought and the strength of his polemic against the works of the law and his championship of faith, then it seems almost incredible how women here are made exceptions and subjected to a law. One can only regard this position as anti-Christian. There are such parts of the Bible, passages which 'urge patriarchy'. If we want to do feminist liberation theology, we must find criteria for identifying the point at which the Bible 'urges Christ'.

Elisabeth Schüssler Fiorenza has called for a critical examination and evaluation of biblical texts in terms of whether or not they 'contribute to the biblical sense of salvation and wholeness... Therefore, according to this criterion biblical revelation and truth can today be found only in those texts and traditions that transcend and criticize the patriarchal culture and religion of their times... only the non-sexist traditions of the Bible present divine revelation'.[8]

As women, we read Romans 8 like this: 'We have not received the spirit of slavery so that we have once again to fear, but we have received the spirit which is given when we are accepted as children. In this we cry God, Father and Mother. This very spirit bears witness to our spirit that we are children of God' (Romans 8.15ff.).

8   The Understanding of Grace

Sin and grace, both words which in our everyday language are usually used only in trivial contexts, are extremely closely connected in theological reflections. In retrospect I want once more to sum up what has really changed in the understanding of sin in the paradigm of liberation theology:

individual ───────────────▶	collective
personal ───────────────▶	social
ontological ───────────────▶	historical

The individual aspect of sin is being increasingly related to the collective aspect in a radical understanding of sin. Particularly in the Hebrew Bible, sin, like grace, is not primarily related to the individual but to the community, the people: the word describes the orientation of a community. That does not mean that the guilt of the individual is therefore less, or that we can no longer sing, 'Oh, my sins have smitten thee.' It means that we read, assess and experience this guilt in respect of our world, and not just in respect of our inner life and our private relationships. Here the paradigm shift is particularly clear. This social understanding of sin in the singular, and not just sins in the plural, is also slowly establishing itself within the church. Where there is reflection and prayer, where sins come to be confessed, where this theme emerges within the liturgy, the talk is increasingly no longer simply of the egoism of the individual, and compassion is put above hard-heartedness. Rather, solidarity is set against blindness. The question becomes: In what social structure do sin and forgiveness find expression? Where do they become visible in our common life, in the treatment of immigrant workers, of our water, in the Third World, and so on? Connected with this shift from the individual, often individualistic, understanding to a collective, communal action is a systematic theological reflection which does not so much describe sin in ontological terms, what human nature is, as seek to think of it in terms of the historical situation. Racism is sin, as the World Council of Churches has constantly demonstrated, just like sexism and the oppression that the class society brings about. Statements of this kind sound almost like truisms to us today, but we must remember the long history whch has led to such insights. The historicization of the concept of sin is at the same time its concretization; we are indeed 'all sinners', but this insight only becomes concrete when we see, for example, the collaboration of European banks with present-day South African companies. In that case 'Racism is sin' means that we who are involved with these businesses and thus derive advantage from them are separating ourselves from the love of God. We despise it; it does not interest us.

Just as in sin we separate ourselves from God, so God reconciles himself with us in grace. That is the basic Christian affirmation. God's turning to us is grace, which removes the obstacles to the relationship between God and human beings. If sin means separation, segregation, isolation and alienation, then grace is the reunion of the living with the origin of life – and thus precisely what God wills. It is simply the happiness of no longer being separated. The wish for reunion is one of the deepest human wishes, and it is precisely for that reason that separation is so destructive. To be with God means no longer to be separated.

In the legends about Francis of Assisi there is a story about Francis and Clare: the two have to separate and cannot bear to do so. It is a story of separation and reunion. One day Francis and Clare were walking from Spello to Assisi in great agitation. The people looked at them maliciously and whispered about them, and they had to put up with insinuations and jokes. So they walked on in silence. It was cold, and the landscape around was covered with snow. Francis said, 'Have you understood what the people around are saying about us?' Clare did not say a word. Her heart seemed to be being squeezed with pincers. She wept. Finally, Francis said, 'It is time for us to part.' Then Clare went down on her knees in the middle of the road. After a while she pulled himself together, got up, and went along the road with bowed head, leaving Francis behind her. The way led through a wood. But all of a sudden she no longer had the strength to go off in this way without consolation or hope, without a farewell from him. She waited. 'When shall we see each other again?' she asked. 'In summer, when the roses bloom.' Then a miracle happened. It was as though a mass of roses blossomed in the snow and on the frosty branches. Clare plucked a branch and put it in Francis' hands. From that day on Francis and Clare were never again separated.

I tell this story to make it clear that grace is not just a counterpart to sin in the moral sense of the word; grace is more than acquittal before the judge, and we might wonder whether the concept not only uses the framework of legalistic thought but also bursts it. The full meaning of grace can most simply be expressed in an everyday word, 'happiness'. Any authentic great happiness in our experience has the character of an unmerited gift. Something has happened to us. The roses begin to bloom in the middle of winter. Unexpected, beyond our control, undeserved – these adjectives appear in the theological description of grace. Grace is 'God's personal condescension and absolutely gratuitous clemency to man,'[1] as is said by Karl Rahner – the person to whom we perhaps owe the most important theological statements of our time about grace.

Of course the forms in which theology has reflected on this unmerited turning of God to human beings have changed with the different theological paradigms. Orthodox thought is shaped by the objective need for the reconciliation of God with human beings. This can only happen if expiation is made. Anselm of Canterbury (1033-1109) deeply influenced Western Christianity in his assumption that God's honour and justice had been violated by human sin, so that satisfaction had to be offered before God could forgive human beings and they could be declared righteous. But because no sinner can offer adequate penance, this is fulfilled by the God-man Christ. He assumes the burden of human guilt and the punishment which follows from it, namely death, and so makes it possible for God to be God, in other words, to exercise grace.

So God has the possibility of letting grace prevail, and this is expressed in two forms: forgiveness and participation in divine life. It is important to hold on to these two aspects of grace – justification and sanctification. The real difficulty in systematic reflection on grace lies in this twofold development of what grace brings about. The Protestant tradition insisted very one-sidedly that grace must justify sinners before it sanctifies them. Particularly within the German tradition, there is hardly any mention of the sanctification in which Catholics and the Eastern churches experience God's living grace. The doctrine of justification is known to many Christians as a legacy of Luther, but the other side of grace which goes with it, its healing power, hardly plays any part, or even becomes theologically suspect as merely doing good works, mere actionism, just politics. In such arguments remnants of the orthodox paradigm are suddenly conjured up even by liberals. The *sola gratia*, 'by grace alone', is then cut down to the pronouncement of a God who is still just conceived of as judge in the last judgment. All the other qualities of the Godhead, that it heals, makes the blind see and comforts the anxious, that it seeks what is lost as the woman in the Gospel seeks her coin (Luke 10.8), are blotted out. Grace is halved, it reaches only the innermost heart of sinners who feel guilty, but not the reality of their lives, their bank accounts and their relationship to others. Grace is robbed of its power really to change us, to unite those who are separated. It is no longer *gratia transformans*. This half grace is what Dietrich Bonhoeffer in the Nazi period called 'cheap grace'; he used this expression to criticize his church, which was afraid of conflict, and took advantage of the Reformation heritage, the '*sola gratia*', to shut its ears to the call of God, and to keep quite when it was time to speak.

However, in the great Christian tradition the person under grace is not just the person who has received acquittal before judgment, but the one who has in fact been freed from the compulsive character of sin. The Greek church fathers – very boldly, as we feel in our intimidating tradition, which takes things by halves – spoke of the 'divinization of man' and in this *deificatio* (*theiosis*) expressed the transforming power of grace. Paul Tillich calls grace the 'new being, the reunion with one's true being, the unmerited state in which love is effectively present to us'.[2] So grace is not only a point like being released from prison, but a really new beginning. It hallows. It breaks down the prison. 'Be perfect, as your Father in heaven is perfect' (Matthew 5.48). The Bible speaks of our participation in the divine nature (II Peter 1.4) or of the fact that we are members of the body of Christ (I Corinthians 12.27), or in the Gospel of John: 'Whoever remains in me and I in him, he brings forth much fruit' (15.5).

In the New Testament and even more in the tradition there are a great many different pictures which express this power of grace, justifying and sanctifying power. How do people become free from servitude to sin? According to Christian doctrine, this comes about through the death of Jesus, which opens up grace to us. The images in which we are told of grace all derive fom the ancient world and we cannot simply take them over as they are. Nevertheless they have a power which provokes us to reflection. Here I want to mention five different images which play a role in classical theology.

> The acquittal of the accused person before the court
> The redemption of the prisoner or slave
> The sacrifice of the innocent for the guilty
> The purification of the polluted
> The healing of the sick.

That God is the judge of the earth and proclaims justice on the peoples (see Psalm 9.9) is a primal image of the Hebrew Bible. So too in the New Testament human beings stand before the judgment seat of Christ (Romans 14.10; II Corinthians 5.10), and the acquittal does not take place on the basis of proven innocence, but because we are 'justified by his blood and will be saved from the wrath to come' (Romans 5.9). We are 'justified and have peace with God' (Romans 5.1).

In the case of the picture of redemption we must recall ancient legal practice in which prisoners of war or slaves could be redeemed. As I Peter says, 'You know that you have not been redeemed from your life of vanity with transitory things, with silver or gold, but with the precious blood of Christ' (1.18ff.). Christ gave himself as a 'ransom for all' (I Timothy 2.6). In this picture, above all the inescapable character of the all-prevailing power of sin becomes clear. Christ pays for our freedom with his blood. The people who used such images to speak of redemption must have felt betrayed and sold, in a hopeless situation, perhaps like an Asian woman sold into prostitution in Frankfurt, who sees no way of escaping. How great is the promise of redemption for the desperate! That Christ gave himself as a 'sacrifice and gift for God' (Ephesians 5.2) takes up the sacrifice attested in the

Old Testament, which the high priest offered once a year for the sins
of the people.

Excursus on the relationship between Judaism and Christianity

The notion of the priest who sacrifices himself has been handed down
above all in the Letter to the Hebrews, in an argument over the
understanding of sacrifice and priesthood in the old covenant in which
old and new keep being compared, to the disadvantage of the former.
Just as the sacrifice of the high priest could only become effective with
blood (Hebrews 9.22), so too Christ brought about purification from
sin through blood (9.14) – however, this is not alien blood (9.35), but
his own (9.14), and it is not offered often (9.25), but once for all
(9.26,28: 10.12).

This contrast in which old and new are compared, to the disadvantage of the old, belongs to one of the darkest and most difficult chapters
of Christian theology, its relationship to Judaism. 'Instead of gifts and
sin offerings' (Hebrews 10.8), Christ offers himself – and in so doing
robs all former means of sacrifice of their force. The underlying pattern
of 'old' and 'new' which we find here – along with the false historical
assertion that the Jews were responsible for the death of Jesus – is one
of the main roots of Christian anti-Judaism. The old is 'surpassed' (as
scholars put it, tending to veil the brutality of the procedure); it is
abolished and replaced. So, too, the Hebrew Bible is surpassed by the
New Testament, which is thought to be on a higher religious level;
in the Christian perspective the Hebrew Bible becomes the 'Old'
Testament, with all the negative connotations which this expression
contains. God's covenant with Israel becomes the 'Old' covenant, and
finally God himself, as a 'Jewish' God full of vengeance and hatred, is
contrasted with the bright God of Jesus. This catastrophic historical
opposition has consequences which extend down to the present,
when feminist theologians attempt to support their criticism of the
patriarchate with the traditional anti-Judaism of Christian exegetes
and historians.[3] However, in so doing they are only following the
dominant traditions of exegesis.

There is a rationalistic objection to these conceptions, which says, 'That's all very well, but if *I* have sinned, what is the use of Jesus dying for it? My sin is my sin. The death of someone else really cannot change this in any way.' This objection indicates the modern difficulty that we have with this idea of the sacrifice made so that others can become free. Such ritualistic conceptions have no roots in our culture. For us, the person, understood as the individual, is responsible for his or her actions. There is no one else who could intervene. Just as each person dies for himself or herself, so also each individual is responsible for himself or herself. For this way of thinking, the concept of grace remains irregular and absurd.

In fact it has a specific ambiguity, which can perhaps be made clear by means of the primal model of the Christ who sacrifices himself. Like almost all the basic theological concepts, grace too has a liberating function and one which eternalizes slavery.

Productively, present-day Christians in the United States interpret the sacrifice of Christ in this way: because Christ has given himself as a sacrifice, any further sacrifice is an insult to God. The sacrifices of blood which North American imperialism requires in El Salvador are directed against Christ himself, as though his sacrifice had not done enough, as though human sacrifices had to go on. As though any further bloodshed, even of the supposed enemies of God, the Communists, were not a meaningless and faithless act in the once-and-for-allness of the sacrifice of Christ.

Negatively, this same basic theological notion, the 'once for allness' (Hebrews 10.12), has a tranquillizing function: Christ has already put all things in order; all is well with us. Thomas Müntzer (c.1490-1525) already criticized Luther because he allowed Christians 'to chalk things up to Christ', in other words, cheerfully to go on running up a bill in the tavern of sin because Christ has already paid for everything. In this sense Müntzer understood the problem which arises from half grace, from cheap grace which separates justification from sanctification. The image of purification from pollution or uncleanness appears in many religions. In the Psalms we read: 'You will purge me with hyssop and I shall become clean; you will wash me, so that I become whiter than snow' (Ps.51.9). In the New Testament we often find the image in connection with blood. The Book of Revelation speaks of those 'who come out of the great tribulation and have washed their garments and made them white in the blood of the Lamb'

(Revelation 7.14). The basic notion is that only blood can wash away
what separates us from God.

The purification of the polluted and the healing of the sick are two
images of grace which have their origin in the Hebrew Bible. However,
for early Christianity they are shaped by the Jesus tradition in the
Gospels. In the Gospels, with one exception (Matthew 5.8), Jesus'
healing of lepers is spoken of in terms of purification, being pure,
cleansing. Now these are central to his activity, for they are seen as a
sign of the coming of the one who is expected. 'The blind will see' and
the lame walk, lepers will be cleansed and the deaf hear, the dead will
be raised and 'the good news will be brought to the poor' (Matthew
11.5). Jesus purifies those who have become cultically and socially
unclean through leprosy. The lepers were not part of the community
of God and his children and are rehabilitated by the action of Jesus
and his followers. Everything that is written in the letters, the
doctrinal texts of the New Testament, about purification from sin and
unrighteousness, is to be understood in this context. Both leprosy and
injustice attach themselves to a person, and grace consists in making
the unholy holy again. 'If we walk in the light, as he is in the light, we
have fellowship with one another, and the blood of Jesus his Son
cleanses us from all sin' (I John 1.7). The leper (Matthew 8.1-4) is to
go to the priest and have his purification confirmed; in this way, after
an interval, he can take part in the cult again: 'Draw near to God and
he will draw near to you. Cleanse your hands, you sinners, and
purify your hearts, you men of double mind' (James 4.8). Here the
purification of the hands, the departure from transgressions and the
hallowing of hearts, becoming single-minded, are seen together. God
forgives us our sins and 'purifies' us fom all unrighteousness (I John
1.9). Purification and healing are acts of grace, and in these images it
becomes particularly clear how the power of God is nothing that
degrades us into becoming mere recipients. The commission of Jesus
to his disciples, female and male, goes against all dogmatic constriction
which seeks to reserve power, healing, change – in short, miracle – to
a God who intervenes vertically from above. The sending out of the
Twelve makes a clear statement here: 'Heal the sick, raise the dead,
cleanse the lepers, drive out demons' (Matthew 10.8). According to
the biblical conception, the female and male disciples of Jesus are
involved in healing, driving out, purifying. God does not want to

hoard grace selfishly but to distribute it in such a way that there is more of it.

There has been a basic and long drawn out dispute in the history of theology about the involvement of human beings in their redemption. Are we involved in redemption, as the synergists think, or do have we to rely completely on the divine action, as monergism taught? I would like to clarify the two possible answers by a model from a Hindu religion, Bhakti. A distinction was made there between the 'ape-grip' school and the 'cat-grip' school. If a mother ape is in danger, she holds her young tight, and saves them by leaping away. The mother indeed acts, as God acts in our salvation, but the baby ape collaborates by clinging on to its mother. Cats are quite different: if danger threatens, they take their young in their mouths; the little ones are passive and do nothing to rescue themselves – all co-operation is excluded.

Perhaps in the West the Catholics belong to the ape school while the Protestants belong more to the cat school.

From the perspective of liberation theology the collaboration of those who are to be freed is indispensable; indeed, one has to say that God's action without us is a misunderstanding. God wants us to be involved in God's activity, which is more than merely distributing grace. Becoming involved means allowing participation, and God would still be conceived of as an autocratic authority if he kept his power to himself. The mutuality of giving and taking, needing and being needed, is necessary for love. To this degree liberation theology has a certain anti-Protestant focus and yet goes beyond the ape-grip school towards collaboration between God and human beings.[4]

I have enumerated the various images of reconciling grace here – which are far from being complete – in order to make it clear that a dogmatic reduction of this abundance to just one picture, for example that of the self-sacrifice of Christ, is not in accordance with scripture. The wealth of images does not call for a simplification, as in scientific language, but it opens us to the mystery which needs language and imagery if it is to be expressed at all, and yet which continually transcends language and images. How do men and women emerge from the despair and the emptiness of sin to another life? That is the question to which the doctrine of grace responds.

I am often afraid that in theology we give answers to questions which no one is asking. We cannot simply insist on and repeat Luther's question, 'How do I find a gracious God?' On the other hand, the

feeling of living in a world without grace has certainly grown with
the increasing mechanization of society. Many people feel that our
architecture, our school system, our prisons, are graceless.[5] Therefore
little is done to resolve the images of grace in a rationalist direction or
to declare that the role of blood in these images is necrophilic and
morbid. Perhaps, rather, our task is that of adding new images to
tradition – our own, mediated by our own experience.

Liberal theology, too, has attempted to work on this. It has
subjectivized the process of the giving of grace, understood in objective
terms, and stressed that grace is concerned with a forgiveness which
represents a change of heart. Without this change of heart, it doesn't
matter how much you wash and sacrifice; that doesn't make any
difference if it does not touch you, does not make you free, does not
allow you to love yourself and accept yourself. I believe that acceptance
of self belongs in this context. And, to put it in the language of the
eighteenth century, reconciliation is really a form of education. In a
short philosophical and theological work, *The Education of the Human
Race* (1780), Lessing arrived at the following solution to one of the
basic problems of the Enlightenment, that of the relationship between
human reason and divine revelation, which according to Reimarus
were quite irreconcilable. He assumes that God has an 'educational
plan' for human beings within which the truth is first of all merely
revealed, to be wondered at and to be believed, and is later taken over
and made clear by reason. He shows how God slowly draws human
beings step by step within history closer to himself and away from
guilt, sin and ignorance. The education of humanity in this idealistic
sense is a basic conception within liberal theology. Revelation continually gives a new 'directional impetus to human reason', and in this
sense God draws human beings slowly to him. Human beings are
forgiven, and in so doing are brought up. These are modern conceptions which emerge in liberal theology in order to express the mystery
of the gift of grace, that we can become free from sin. The thought-
model of liberal theology attempts to think of the liberation from sin
which, as we have seen, is understood as egotism and isolation, as
education which brings us to God. The overcoming of separation from
God through grace takes place as a change of heart.

The liberation theologies, like the Black theologies, the feminist
theologies and the Latin American theologies, think of the grace of
God as a liberation which takes place within the socio-cultural and

GRACE

JUSTIFICATION AND HEALING

justificatio et sanctificatio

Orthodox	Liberal	Liberation theology
Atonement	Reconciliation	Liberation
Satisfaction	Forgiveness	Change of social relationships and personal life
Acquittal	Change of heart	
Images of grace:	Education	
Ransom	of the	
Sacrifice	Human race	
Purification		
Healing		

socio-political context. That does not necessarily mean just material change – the concept of liberation in liberation theology has many sides. But it does include real changes in life. The picture which is used time and again is the story of the exodus, of the liberation of the children of Israel from slavery. In Egypt they suffered economic oppression (Exodus 1.11-14). They suddenly had to make the same number of bricks without being given more material for them, and even had to look for the straw themselves (Exodus 5.6-18). They were politically oppressed. They had no voice; they did not have their own administration, but were under Egyptian law, under pagan law. They were oppressed culturally: they could not sing their own songs or celebrate their feasts (5.1-4). It can be demonstrated from this primal history of oppression and liberation that liberation always has these different dimensions. It is not, as a superficial right-wing criticism all too easily assumes, 'just' a political or 'just' an economic liberation; this economic liberation from forced labour is at the same time a spiritual and cultural liberation. Liberation is a total concept – and by total I mean one with different physical and spiritual dimensions. Where liberation takes place, one can see how people change: in their bodies, in their relationships to one another, in their social relationships; how their neighbourhood, their streets, their schools, take on another appearance. In this sense liberation is a change of the whole of life, of life-style, of behaviour.

In this context liberation theology – above all Latin American liberation theology, but also others – stresses the need for struggle. *Liberacion es lucha*, 'liberation is struggle', is written on houses and churches. The word 'struggle' should not immediately once again conjure up the thought of violence and make this the one prevailing force. One of the greatest social struggles in history, namely the freedom movement among industrial workers in the last century, was based on a non-violent principle, the strike, a great means of struggle for the unarmed. When the workers kept talking about the 'struggle', they did not mean weapons. That was the language of their masters, who had weapons, and if need be could draw on the police and the military. The oppressed were unarmed, and for that reason had to find other, non-violent, means of fighting.

But the fighting spirit, the militancy, as people are fond of calling it in the Romance languages (I, too, like using this word, but have contantly been subjected to fearful attacks as a result) – a clear, resolute fighting spirit – is part of the history of liberation; it gives up the constant toleration of injustice, this helpless, self-pitying 'We can't do anything about it' position.

Liberation is always related to oppression and cannot take place unless it identifies the oppressors. I have to be clear about who or what produces this oppression where and how. I stress that, because this is by no means clear in the context of the middle class of the rich countries; the oppression experienced, above all that of women, often produces only dissatisfaction, frustration, guilt feelings and in no way the analysis of reality which is need to achieve a real awareness of sin. To demonstrate once again how oppression as sin is to be associated with liberation as grace, I want to interpret a text of Paul along the lines of liberation theology.

> Let not sin therefore reign in your mortal bodies, to make you obey their passions. Do not yield your members to sin as instruments of unrighteousness, but yield yourselves to God as those who have been brought from death to life, and your members to God as instruments of righteousness. For sin will have no dominion over you, since you are not under law but under grace (Romans 6.12-14).

The context of this passage is that the Christian has 'died' with Christ through baptism (6.2,4,7), our old nature has been 'crucified with' it (6), we have been 'acquitted' from the rule of sin (7): we are dead to sin, but alive to God (11). The inner connection of the text with Paul's thought is provided by the basic pattern of 'formerly' and 'afterwards'; here too Paul is looking to the time when we were 'enemies of God', as was said earlier (5.10), back from the time of grace which now prevails. I want to read the text in these two directions – the meaning of sin and the meaning of grace – and begin with the first difficulties which confront the modern reader. They relate to the anthropological statements which are here bound up with the word 'body'.

We live in a 'mortal body' (6) or, more correctly, we 'are' body. We can connect the word body with 'have' or 'be', and Paul does not think that the connection which I have to my body is like that of an owner to his or her machine; I 'am' body, and that means above all that I am dependent. Paul uses the expressions 'body', 'members', 'instruments' or 'weapons' and 'yourselves' in parallel. Here they mean the same thing. They are not some kind of ingredient of the human organism but human existence as a whole. Existence means corporeality, being bounded, being conditioned. The biological process in itself conditions our existence.[6] No one is asked whether they want to be a boy or a girl. Paul's language reminds us of our lack of freedom, of our dependence. All men and women are dependent on food: hunger, exhaustion and age are phenomena which belong in this context and remind us of our bonds and lack of freedom. But we are dependent not only on biology but also on the dominant features of our time, its culture, its ideas and its laws. As Ernst Käsemann put it in his commentary on Romans: 'Corporeality is standing in a world for which different forces contend and in which each individual is caught up and drawn into their struggle, belonging to one lord or the other and representing this lord both actively and passively.'[7]

So this deep dependence is relevant not only biologically but sociologically, and also psychologically and culturally. I am dependent on prevailing ideas. Here is an example to clarify this. The shame that most women in our culture feel at menstruation is an attempt to deny a physical dimension. We conceal it. We internalize our anxieties and in so doing, even if we do not want to, we represent the male order which is hostile to creation, which treats menstruation as a disruptive factor or makes fun of it as an embarrassment. I am dependent on the prevailing ideas about my 'body'; even in my dreams I am dependent on the culture in which I live. Even my wishes are directed by others, and they destroy me because they function as 'instruments of unrighteousness'. 'Do not yield your members as instruments of unrighteousness' (13). I explain it to myself like this: my desires for consumption, which are brainwashed into me by our consumer society, contribute to the impoverishment of others. So by eating meat we see to it that cattle are fed by grain with which people could fight hunger. But ideology dictates to us that a certain amount of meat is part of a proper diet. My wishes are dictated from outside and destroy me, because they function as an instrument of injustice, of exploitation.

Let me give another example from Latin America, where over the last fifteen years an increasing amount of agricultural land and pasturage has come into the possession of foreign businesses which use the land for their export produce. On it they plant strawberries or produce orchids, which are therefore cheaper for us to buy. The practical consequence is that people can no longer grow their beans and their grain. Their subsistence is no longer secured by the world trade model of the free market. Our economic order is an order of exploitation, which produces hunger and destruction. 'Do not yield your members to sin as instruments of unrighteousness.' Of course Paul is not referring to my historical context, but he thinks that my dependence, my anxieties, my false wishes, are being used by the power of sin to maintain sin and to perpetuate the conditions in which we live. That means that my wishes function objectively as 'instruments of unrighteousness'. Moreover the state of the economy on which I am dependent can well be matched up with the mythological pictures which Paul presents of the power of sin. Sin springs to life, seizes power, and dominates. And that is precisely what happens within a closed economic situation which does not function for human needs but for the profits of the owners. Sin, namely this unjust system under which we live, has the demonic features of which Paul speaks. We do not understand it; it is frightfully complicated, it is uncontrollable, and we can do nothing about it – those are the assertions which we constantly repeat and under which we take shelter. In this way we deny the injustice of the system and our share in it. All this is what I mean by 'demonic features'. Looking outwards, we deny our part in production and business; looking inwards, in the desires mentioned by Paul we have a wealth of denial mechanisms at hand. Our 'desires' and our production match and form a system of injustice: an omnipotent system in which sin has power over us.

So I am not reading this text from the perspective of the hostility of Christianity to sexuality. Living in a body means being dependent. It is a feature of biblical anthropology that it understands that we are not already 'born for freedom'; first of all we find ourselves in social dependence, in which sin directs and manipulates us. I believe that we live in a world in which above all things inner direction by sin, i.e. the functionalization of our wishes and desires in the direction of the needs created by capitalism, is tremendously important. That goes with a denial of the real needs which we have in common as human beings, i.e. the need for good air, drinkable water, better schools, alternative forms of transport, and so on.

If we put our capabilities as human beings, our potential, our capacity for thought, our commitment – and Paul includes all these things in this remarkable term 'your members' – if we put them at the disposal of the injustice which dominates us, then we are dead or, as

Paul puts it, when we lived like that we were dead. We held 'truth captive in injustice' (Romans 1.18). Sin, unrighteousness, ruled over us as a queen. Through our bodies, through our participation in this world, through our conscious or unconscious support of this world, we belonged on the side of death. According to Paul it is impossible to be neutral under the domination of sin. There is no neutrality, because we always already live in the mode of belonging and participation: 'Corporeality means that nobody, fundamentally speaking, belongs most deeply to himself alone.'[8] Part of Pauline anthropology is the understanding that because we are body, related to one another, relational beings who exist only in relationships, this question of who has power over us and who rules over the earth is decisive.

The bourgeois pigeonholing of 'religion' and 'politics' makes the theologians who are dependent on it incapable of understanding even one basic thought of the apostle Paul. Christoph Blumhardt (1842-1919), pastor and socialist member of parliament, whom I regard as a father of liberation theology, wrote in the 1890s: 'We should not ask subjectively, "Will I be righteous before God?", but, "How does God's righteousness come over me?" In the Bible we never have "The righteousness which stands before God"; that is just the way Luther translated it because he had the wrong idea of it. The Bible had to bow to that. In the Bible we always find "God's righteousness".'[9]

If I ask, 'How does God's righteousness come over me?', then I am focussing on an objective basic experience, though one which relates to the subject, which in liberation theological terms I would formulate as the transition from despair to praxis. In injustice, under the rule of sin, the most sensitive of us are desperate, as can be seen from the steadily increasing number of those with psychological illnesses. One can demonstrate from many other phenomena how the rule of sin under which we vegetate drives people to despair. So the question is not, 'How do I become righteous before God?', but, 'How does God's righteousness come over me?' In that case the grace of God means what is promised to us in the transition from despair to praxis. There is no neutral ground in life between despair or sin on the one hand and praxis or faith on the other. There are no ways out, as though some people did not need grace. Luther's expression 'righteousness which stands before God' reflects this in connection with the person under judgment. But 'God's righteousness' in fact means the transition which holds for the material body and the whole earth. 'God's righteousness' means that the earth ceases to be a place where life is rejected, a place of exploitation and injustice. Justification and sanctification belong together.

In this short text Paul says here that we are *capable* of righteousness *in Christ*. In Protestantism that is difficult to learn, because traditional Protestant thought is disfigured by an anthropological pessimism which attributes all that is bad to human beings and nothing that is good. In a television broadcast a churchman was asked what the church's attitude was to the new armaments. He spent a long time discussing strategic needs until the reporter became impatient and said, 'Now tell me as a theologian, what you think about this?' The reply was, 'We are all sinners, with or without bombs.' For me that was a particularly striking instance of the absence of grace. It is as though middle-class people of the rich world did not believe that in Christ we are capable of righteousness. They do not believe in liberation or redemption. They believe in sin in a deep, honest sense, in the tragedy of human existence. Faith in Christ, the liberator, is unknown. They do not know what it means to become free, and indeed many people believe that the more they believe in the hopelessness of sin and achieve this subjection to sin, the more Christian they are.

In this text Paul says that we can put our members – once again, our capacities, our riches, our beauty, our potential, our dedication – at the disposal of life. We can make them 'weapons of righteousness'. We can become 'instruments of peace', which again implies that if we are not instruments of peace, we remain instruments of war. That is what I mean when I say that there is no neutral ground, nothing in between. We can become instruments of peace whom God uses. We would no longer be standing under the compulsions which dominated us, whether we were Christians or non-Christians. According to Paul, being subjected to the powers only applies to the time before grace, 'when we were under tutelage, subject like slaves to the powers of the world' (Galatians 4.3). Now that we live in the time of Christ, we are called 'not to cast away grace' (2.21).

We no longer stand under the laws of the imperialistic structure of exploitation, but under grace. We no longer stand under the compulsion of sin but under grace. We must not go on living as we did before. We can exchange the dependence on sin for a new, different kind of life. And in this life we are in fact fighting for space in time for this other life. Paul calls what grace does with us conversion. We are 'redeemed' (Galatians 4.5), God has 'sent the spirit of his Son into our hearts' (4.6). Grace is what brings us from the despair of dependence on the ruling powers to praxis. Grace is the New Being, to use Tillich's words, and reunion with our *true being*, which is concerned to live for union, not for separation. Our body and our life are then there for righteousness. Justification and sanctification coincide.

A fine term in this Pauline text is 'yield': 'Do not yield your members to sin as instruments of unrighteousness' (Romans 6.13). The Greek term *parhistanein* means 'put at the disposal of'. Do not give what you are to sin, do not put yourself at the disposal of this power, but put what you really are at the disposal of God's justice. In a parable of Jesus this invitation is phrased, 'Earn interest with your pounds' (Luke 19.11-27). Life is an obligation on us to increase what has been given us in accordance with creation: grace liberates us for this. The words 'put oneself at the disposal of' also have erotic connotations: 'yield' is an expression of love. To surrender oneself to God for something, to put oneself at God's disposal, to make oneself available, *disponible*, as the French worker priests kept saying, is the goal of grace. In great dedication I enter an obligation, a commitment, which changes my real life, my body. I know what I am living for. In that case the place where I live will look different, the time which I devote to certain things will change, my priorities can no longer be dictated by 'this' world. I no longer spend my money, consume, in the same way. To be 'in Christ' means to practise this surrender, to which Christ calls us in grace.

Let me quote from the 1970 Taizé Easter Message: 'The risen Christ will prepare us to give our lives so that one human being is no longer the victim of another.' That is in direct continuity with this text of Paul, which I shall now paraphrase once again: 'Therefore the system of injustice shall no longer determine your way of life so that you run after false dreams. Do not put your capabilities at the disposal of capital. It uses them as weapons for exploitation. Give yourselves to God as those who are no longer dumb and powerless but have come alive. Put your desires at the the disposal of life as a weapon of righteousness. For the system of injustice will not be able to break you; you are not under its compulsions, but under grace.'

Sometimes I hear the objection that my theology paints Christianity in too beautiful colours, and does not bring out its anti-human and destructive features clearly enough. It is certainly true that my interest is not so much in the tolling bells which ring out in the centres of power. The prayer breakfasts of the American presidents and the solemn masses in which General Pinochet takes part are indeed necrophilic. But I think that in the liberation theologies and base movements that are coming into being all over the world we have begun a new chapter of church history. It is indeed the shamed, those deprived of their rights, who – despite all Marxist predictions – understand religion as their cause and not only make God their sanctuary and refuge but also proclaim God as their liberator. It can hardly be denied that Christians nowadays play a particular role in the battles of the Third World against injustice: in Sri Lanka and South Korea, in South Africa and Latin America, and among women throughout the world. The argument that Christianity has always made pacts only with the powers of the time, with patriarchy, with capitalism, is untenable in this form. As well as Pope Innocent III there was Francis of Assisi, and this clash between the Christ from above and the Christ from below can be found at every stage of church histroy.

Of course I am ashamed of the stories of terror within the history of Christianity. But it is necessary to read history other than through the eyes of the rulers. There is a criticism of Christianity which is so fixated on authority that the oppressed history of the Christian masses, the poor, the women, cannot be seen at all and history as the negative counterpart triumphs once again over her-story, which is put to silence. We should know where things were otherwise and where they are otherwise today. In this sense it is very important to me to present Black theology as another, radical, form of liberation theology. The history of the Afro-American slaves and their descendants cannot be understood without Black religion. Indeed it was the 'African' side of the religion of the Blacks in Africa which helped Black Christians to go beyond what James Cone calls the 'white caricature of the gospel' and to understand the liberation of the oppressed as God's will and work.

My own first personal encounter with this theology, or, more accurately, with Black reality, took place in a church in Chicago in 1972. There the Blacks were organizing people to sign up on voters' lists. The Black Civil Rights Movement centred on Martin Luther King had made this registration an important element in the liberation struggle; people were encouraged to go in, register and vote. I was at a gathering of this kind; the church was completely full, with Jesse Jackson standing at the front, and then it all began with a liturgy, an exchange between pastor and congregation. The pastor said, 'I am', and the congregation replied 'I am'. Then he said, 'I am black', and everyone, including my husband sitting next to me, responded:

I am black
I am beautiful
I am to be respected
I am to be honoured.

The whole congregation, perhaps three thousand people, was involved. I was sitting next to an old black woman, with wrinkled, work-worn hands. And now this old woman next to me said, 'I am beautiful.' I think that for the first time I then understood what beauty is: this feeling of worth, of strength, of knowledge, of being grounded in human worth. I have often reflected on beauty, on the conditions of aesthetics, within literature too. What is it that we call beautiful? And this old cleaning woman who, as I then saw, also had no teeth and certainly no money to buy false teeth, said that she was beautiful. She knew it. 'I am a child of God' was the foundation of this liturgy of liberation. It was so fascinating that my husband cheerfully repeated, 'I am black.'

James Cone, one of the leading black theologians in the USA, says, 'There will be no peace in America until white people begin to hate their whiteness and ask from the depths of their being, "How can we become black?""[1]

I did not know his remark at that time, but on that Saturday morning in Chicago I got to know the feeling. Cone then talks about what it means to be black: 'To know God means to be on the side of the oppressed, to be one with them and to have a share in the goal of liberation. We must become black with God.' If God is on the side of the oppressed, then God cannot be 'white', just as he cannot be 'man'. In that case, we must think and speak about God in a different way. In that case we must become black with God, become woman with God. When Cone says that we must become black with God it is clear that he is not just referring to skin colour: he has that already. He is saying this to himself and to his race, his people. To say that we must become black with God is to talk about a becoming, not a being, the accomplishment of liberation and not just a skin colour, a bit of biology. That is a dynamic of our spirit, our conscience, our existence, and not a state of our skin. And each of these statements can be transferred to feminist theology or other models of liberating theology: we must become woman with God, become poor, become black, become old, and recognize God in the many faces of the oppressed.

There are two important presuppositions to these theological statements within Black theology. First, the soil in which such a theology comes into being is the suffering community. The language of theology challenges social structures, because it is inseparable from the suffering community. A theology which does not articulate the suffering community, does not speak from it, think from it, feel from it, is *de facto* a theology of oppression. Theology cannot be neutral or avoid taking sides with either the oppressor or the oppressed. We have already touched on Cone's second presupposition, namely that blackness is an ontological symbol of oppression. Blackness in the sense of our 'standing by the blacks' is a symbol that we are taking part in God's action. If we can become black, then we can participate in God's liberating action.

At this point I shall add some thoughts about the method of dealing with witnesses to the tradition. If we want to know in what sense a particular element of the Christian tradition, for example a prayer, a biblical statement, a devotional custom, or whatever, really expresses the liberating character of the gospel, we must ask, 'For whom was that written? For the oppressed or for the oppressors? Who has something of this history, of this narrative?' Frank Crüsemann has made an interesting investigation into the book of Ecclesiastes, from which I have learned a good deal in terms of method.[2] He shows how the sceptical world-weariness of 'all is vanity' (Ecclesiastes 1.2) is a mood which derives from comparative satiation. It comes about in the rich, aristocratic upper classes. It is not the mood of the oppressed. The text articulates the nihilism of the members of the court in Jerusalem. I have learned from this article to take seriously the question of those to whom the text is addressed: For whom? In whose interest? With what instructions for action? In clarifying these questions, James Cone pointedly said that the Christ event is a Black event.

We can distinguish various phases of the history of Black theology. It began in the late 1960s. The new theological reflection came into being from the Civil Rights movement: Martin Luther King is the most powerful symbol of this unity between the Civil Rights movement and the Black church. This liberation movement has deep roots in the Black church and religion and yet is active and works 'on the street'. It embraces millions, and in this century has become one of the most important of the movements struggling for freedom. With it, the subjection of the Black church to the norms of white Protestantism came to an end. Previously Blacks had learned from white teachers and had studied white theology, at any rate academic theology. The Civil Rights movement caused a break. The significance of Martin Luther King, Jr, for Black consciousnesss and Black theology cannot be overestimated, though as late as 1987 Cone still had to note: 'The fact that many white theologians can write about American religion and theology without mentioning him shows the tenacity of racism in academic circles, and there is an evident tendency to limit theology to the academic work of a small group of professors.'[3]

Martin Luther King associated the political, democratic tradition of freedom with the biblical tradition of justice and redemption, as this can be found in the story of the exodus of the people of Israel from Egypt and in the prophets. He then fused these two traditions with the New Testament conceptions of love and suffering which are manifest in the crucifixion of Jesus into a theology which challenges all Americans to build another society. On 4 April 1967, in Riverside Church, New York, packed to the last seat, against the advice of many of his black and white friends, King made a prophetic accusation. He condemned America as 'the greatest perpetrator of violence in the world today'. He proclaimed God's judgment on America and stressed that God would break America's back unless this nation brought justice to the poor and peace to the word.[4] A year later he was murdered.

In the early 1970s, Black theology entered a second phase and became more strongly academic. A relatively small group of scholars began to embark on theology and write books, like James Cone. Black theologians attempted to find their own language. But we must keep in mind that this phase of reflection is the second stage, and that the first stage of Black theology also had a human starting point. The story about the liturgy with which I began this chapter ('I am black, I am beautiful') is the initial experience, the faith, the praxis of the self-organization of Black people by means of Black culture, shaped by church piety. Then comes theology, which reflects on it and brings it into contact with the biblical tradition. Black theologians attack the racism, the individualism and the materialism of the American economy. Readiness to make the struggle international developed under the increasing influence of the Latin Americans and the independent theologians from Africa. Here, from 1977 onwards, we can note a third phase in Black theology, in which it recognizes its own cause in other liberation struggles of the Third World.

Black theology uses Black experience, history and culture as sources. These experiences are associated with revelation: there is a self-revelation of God in Black experience as the subjective side of oppression – in Black history as the struggle for liberation from slavery and the recollection of it, and in Black culture in its music, literature and religion. The biblical revelation would make no sense if it were separated from these other sources of theology. Revelation as a Black event takes place in experience, history and culture, and not beyond them. In this way a real dialogue developed between Blackness and the biblical message, and while intellectual use is made of other theologies – Cone mentions that of Karl Barth, which was a factor in shaping him – they are rejected existentially, since they lack the central experience.

This central role of experience is also characteristic of liberation theologies of another kind. Feminist theology, too, is based on the experience of women, the history of women and the culture of women, and engages these elements in dialogue with revelation. Here experience, history and culture become an important foundation for what theology really means. We call this process 'contextualization', and it takes place in all theologies, though unconsciously in the theology of the white man, who confuses himself with human beings generally.

From the black experience of his black people, James Cone says: 'Sin is the desire to be white.' That hits the nail on the head. It is a harsh, existential statement. To give oneself up, to deny one's people, to dream false dreams, is alienation and separation from God. By analogy we can say, 'Sin is the desire to be rich and powerful.' As women we can say by analogy, 'Sin is the desire to be male or a kind of male substitute'; it is denial, trivialization of our experience, history and culture. This clarity of the thought of black theology in the context of racial conflict produces a quite different existential depth from any that would be conceivable were it merely to take over white theologies. Christology, too, is rethought in this perspective: a white redeemer cannot help us. Christ was black. Unless we think of Christ as Black (Black theologians say), as a brother of the Black, we are not thinking of Christ, but of a symbol of domination. The redeemer cannot have the same colour as the skin of the oppressor. As a European woman theologian of course I have difficulties which are connected with the historical Jesus: I assume that he had dark, but not black, skin. But the living spirit in the Black church shows itself to me in the very fact that this historicity of Jesus does not play the central role that it had in my theological education. It is Christ, really the Black Christ, who takes form here. That has always been the case in Black culture: we need only recall the spirituals. There Christ appears as the fellow slave who hangs lynched on the tree, and as the liberator of slaves, beyond the deep river. There slaves sing of heaven as the place where they can go around freely: 'There is nobody to turn me out.' There are descriptions of heaven here which can only be understood on the basic presupposition of a contrast between the oppressors and the oppressed.

Martin Luther King often referred at the end of his sermons to a Black hymn which goes back to a lamentation of the prophet Jeremiah. Jeremiah saw how the evil were successful and the good had to suffer. 'Is there no balm in Gilead?' he asked, 'is there no longer a physician there?' (8.22). Cone writes:

Centuries later, it was our enslaved forebears who experienced the injustice of life, and who day in and day out expected nothing but the whip of the overseer, endless cottonfields, and incredible heat; but in this situation they did something quite astonishing: they looked back a few centuries and transformed Jeremiah's questions of his time into a sign of rebellion. Now they could sing:

There is a balm in Gilead
To make the wounded whole
there is a balm in Gilead
to heal the sinsick soul.[5]

To my understanding of sin and grace, the word 'sinsick' speaks volumes. Sin is disgusting, and one has to vomit if one lives in it without grace. It is a disease, like an addiction; but there is balm in Gilead, and even the sick can be made 'whole'.

10 Who is Jesus Christ for Us Today?

According to Christian doctrine Jesus Christ is the redeemer of the world. The Greek technical term for teaching about Christ is 'christology', the Logos about Christ. I add the words 'for us today', which frequently occur in the ecumenical world, to the question 'Who is Jesus Christ?' in the awareness that not all Christians agree on the 'today' or the 'for us'. Many concentrate on the eternal Christ; indeed they use Christ to distance themselves from their own history. So historical awareness is one reason why Christians in the ecumenical world, which keeps open a kind of world conversation between the Third, Second and First Worlds, have chosen this formulation. The second reason is an awareness of solidarity: in saying 'for us', Christians in the ecumenical world want to go beyond those who would only accept a 'for me'. To understand that, we must keep in mind the fundamentalist trends in Protestantism which make their central theme 'a personal relationship to a personal Saviour and Redeemer' and cultivate a spirituality in which the question what significance Jesus Christ has for me completely swallows up the other question: what he means for the whole created world, conceived of historically.

I do not think that individualism as a horizon is sufficient to express the significance of Jesus Christ. The individualist understanding says, 'Jesus Christ is my personal saviour, my redeemer.' That presupposes that as an individual I am alone and that the depths of my spirituality are touched only when this redeemer, Jesus Christ, puts me in a personal relationship to himself, which then becomes the most important thing and defines my being a Christian. My questions to this kind of piety relate to the way in which my personal tie to Christ is bound up with my economic, political and sexual life.

I want to demonstrate that once again by using my national identity as an example. One of the factors governing my life is the history of my people. Belief in Christ concerns our whole life and does not draw us out of history into a private salvation history, but connects us more deeply and unavoidably with the others around us. Christ encounters me in the dimensions of my life. What has been done to other people in the name of Jesus Christ by my people also affects the way in which I am a Christian. It is clear that Auschwitz would not have been possible without Christianity. Christian anti-Judaism and modern antisemitism are part of my heritage. In this responsibility for what I have inherited and for what I am handing on I understand my life. The acceptance of Jesus binds me to others, and the 'for me' becomes 'for us'.

One of the catastrophic consequences of capitalism is what it does to rich people at the heart of this economic system by reducing humanity to the individual. One can see how American commercialism presents all items as being 'quite personal to you', even if millions of them exist. Your initials must be on your T-shirt, on your ball-point pen, on your bag – and on your Jesus. He too is quite personal to you. The spirit of commercial culture is also alive in this religion: for fundamentalism, which is massively effective, Jesus is 'my quite personal Saviour', and really no more can be said than that. The confession of 'Jesus Christ – my personal saviour' brings no hope to those whom our system condemns to die of famine. It is a pious statement which is quite indifferent to the poor and completely lacking in hope for all of us. In the light of this individualistic reduction we must put the question of christology ecumenically and ask about Jesus Christ 'for us today' in the age and the place in which we live.

One of Bertolt Brecht's Keuner stories goes: 'Someone asked Herr K whether there was a God. Herr K. said, "I would advise you to ponder whether your conduct would change in any way depending on your answer to this question. If it would not change, we can drop the question. If it would change, then I can at least help you by saying that you have already decided that you need a God."'[1] This insight equally applies to Christ and our relationship to him. If our behaviour is not changed by our relationship to him, we can drop the christological question. If it would change, we 'need' Christ. In what sense?

Here I want to adopt a different method from that used in the earlier parts of this book. So far I have been describing theological themes in the framework of the three great paradigms which govern the present discussion. I have stressed the differences and deliberately neglected what the paradigms have in common. I wanted to prompt a sense of the difference between present-day theologies. I have not paid much attention to the overlaps and the theological approaches which are difficult to fit into the basic scheme I have suggested here, although of course I am clear about the relativity of such a division, which is deliberately not that of 'theology' but of a variety of theological paradigms. Here I want to begin with a testimony to Christ which derives from a concern with the theme 'Who is Jesus of Nazareth – for me?' (Perhaps this text can be heard or read in light of the question of the theological paradigm to which it is closest: it is a mark of the quality of particular theological texts that they transcend the schools of thought and opinions from which they come.). Helmut Gollwitzer was one of a hundred contemporary figures who replied to the question in a book: his answer is quite personal, but not in the least individualistic.

I will say what Jesus means in my life if I understand the invitation correctly. In other words, I am not to sum up what is most important in what I hear of him through the mediation of the Christian tradition, but how this has influenced my life, to the extent that I have been aware of it.

The most important thing, from which all the rest follows, is that through hearing what can be heard of him I have never been alone. Certainly, like anyone else, I have often enough felt alone, abandoned, helpless, but he has spoken to this solitude with his 'I am here.' I spoke to him, asked him, heard very clear words which he said to me, had to take account of them – and the spell of solitude was broken.

He gave me – still gives me – things to do. He is involved in a great work, the greatest here on earth: the revolution of the human race, the individual and all people, for a new life, for real, fulfilled humanity. That is what he is involved in, that is what he is winning for his disciples. To become involved in that is already to participate in the new life oneself. Even without him we have all kinds of things to do: all kinds of things that we want to do and all kinds of things that we have to do – for a great variety of reasons. The dust of transitoriness, an ultimate meaninglessness, constantly lies on them.

The connection with Jesus' great work gives an eternal significance even to the most unlikely things: nothing will be lost. A joyful meaning enters into all action.

That he wants me to be involved in this is a daily cause of amazement. Every day I experience the limits of my willingness to serve, of my readiness for sacrifice. My involvement in his work is usually a quite lamentable compromise between what this work needs and what I think I need for myself. I do not want either to give up the collaboration or to stop doing things on my own account. I have not got that far with revolutionizing my own life. Nevertheless he does not give me up. When I was a young man, I was preoccupied with the heart of the Lutheran doctrine of justification, the 'justification of the godless', and that has never left me since: he accepts those who are useless and promises every day to make them useful.

He makes people dear to me. Some of them are dear anyway, and many others are not. He tells me that he loves those who are alien, indifferent or even unattractive to me. In so doing he helps me to behave in a different way, to be capable of talking, listening to others as openly and seriously as I would like them to listen to me and take me seriously, never writing anyone off, never pronouncing a final judgment on anyone, always attempting new things with them in hope. In this way he extends my horizons towards those who are further afield: to those outside my milieu, to the needs of society, to the Third World. They all become my neighbours.

In this way he disturbs me. Because of his intervention I cannot behave as I wanted to at first. Of course, unfortunately I often enough do just that. But he does not leave me to my inclinations and moods. He struggles with me, there are arguments, and sometimes he prevails. To be disturbed in this way is the healthiest thing that can happen to us. I cannot find the experience of calling him 'Lord' oppressive. He does not restrict my freedom; he is not a despotic superego against which I have to fight to come to myself; on the contrary, the more I allow myself to be governed by his intervention, the freer, the more open, the more friendly and the more joyful I become.

The first time I was in a Gestapo prison I repeated to myself verses from old hymns. In them Christians say that Jesus' is everything and that it is good to commit everything to him. I did not find myself in a position to do so. I was anxious and I loved my life. I scratched

the name Jesus on the cell wall with a bit of wire. Whenever I looked
at it, it said to me everything that I have written here. Then things
were not as bad as I had feared, but even if they had been worse –
as they were for many other people! – he would have been right.
He will be right in what he says to me and to everyone.[2]

Christology is the attempt to grasp the mystery of Jesus. What is
there special about this man from Galilee who was tortured to death?
Why could he not be done away with? Why is he still present and
effective, as he is in this text? Gollwitzer's answer to these questions
is deeply rooted in the orthodox tradition, and I chose his text precisely
to do justice to the strength and life in this tradition, which often
seems to us to be formal and a thing of the past. The first thing that
Gollwitzer says about Jesus is a reference to what Jesus has done for
him: 'I have never been alone.' That is a description of the function
of Christ or the 'works' of Christ. For the theologians of the
Reformation, the significance of Christ is not to be read out of his two
'natures', his divine and human modes of being, but out of his 'works'
or his 'office', as Luther was fond of saying. One Reformation principle
runs: '*Hoc est Christum cognoscere, beneficia ejus cognoscere, non... ejus
naturas*' (Melanchthon, *Loci Communes*, 1521). To know Christ is to
know his benefits, not his natures. That is a move away from a
speculative christology, a shift to a christology orientated on praxis.

Christ breaks the spell of solitude and 'gave and gives me things to
do', as Gollwitzer puts it. That means that he involves me in his work,
the revolution of the human race, which means real, fulfilled life for
all. This work of Jesus is indeed seriously hindered by my sin, which
Gollwitzer calls 'the limits of my willingness to serve', but it is not
done away with. 'Nevertheless Christ does not give me up,' says
Gollwitzer, and in so doing links christology as the doctrine of how
Christ involves me with Luther's doctrine of justification, which
develops the way in which God takes up 'the useless' and daily
promises to make him useful and to hallow him.

In speaking of the work or the benefits of Christ, at the same time
Gollwitzer indirectly articulates what the old tradition called the two
'natures' of Christ, his manhood and his Godhead. How can one think
of the two in such a way as to maintain the unity of the person? That
is the question to which the church's Council of Chalcedon (451)
responded with the formula 'true man and true God' (*vere homo, vere*

deus). It is important to understand that the recognition of the 'natures' of Christ remains subordinate to the acceptance of his 'work' that he does for us. The third strophe of the hymn 'A great and mighty wonder' expresses that clearly:

That blossom so small,
that smells to us so sweet,
with its bright shining
drives out the darkness,
true man and true God,
helps us from all suffering
and saves from sin and death   (1844).

First of all there is a focus on what Christ does. There is mention of the fragrance of the rose, which is an old image of Christ – as opposed to the great 'stink of the world', with which the Middle Ages were so familiar; then it is said that Christ drives out the darkness, in which human beings perceive nothing, and only then does the christological formula appear, used almost like a prayer.

If we want to understand the significance of Christ in a theological text it is a good method to see what it says about the human and what it says about the divine. In Gollwitzer, the statements which refer to God in Christ are as follows: Christ does not give me up, he struggles with me, he disturbs me, he is no despotic superego, he makes me more free, more open, more friendly and more joyful and – in an eschatological phrase – he will prove right. In this text Gollwitzer has avoided the traditional images of Christ and his significance with the help of verbs like disturb, struggle, make more free, prove right. This kind of talk moves away from dogma towards narration, narrative. However, he has also justified an image in the tradition, the word Lord, which many people today find objectionable.

Excursus on neo-orthodox theology

The background to Gollwitzer's thought is the theological school of Karl Barth (1886-1968), which in Europe is usually called 'dialectical theology', whereas in North America it is classified as 'neo-orthodoxy'. This terminology indicates the nearness of Barth and his pupils to classical orthodoxy. On the other hand, in some respects Barth's theology clearly points towards liberation theology as it subsequently developed outside Europe in the 1960s. In this sense the theology of Karl Barth and his 'left-wing' pupils (H.Gollwitzer, G.Casalis and F.W.Marquardt) is diametrically opposed to the organizing principle of this book, which distinguishes between three contemporary theologies: orthodox theology, liberal theology and liberation theology.

However, the dialectical theology of the 1920s is clearly a radical break with liberal theology. Liberalism produced a self-confident union of Christianity and culture, the 'Christ of culture' of which Richard Niebuhr speaks. History appeared as gradual progress: the idea of Herder and Lessing, repeated down to Harnack, that the human race is slowly but steadily being 'educated' by God to greater humanity, lay at the heart of liberal Culture Protestantism. This optimistic perspective collapsed with the outbreak of the First World War. The lights went out in Europe; a slaughterhouse came into being in the midst of civilized men with a humanistic education who, fired by an ideology of the Fatherland which destroyed any world citizenship, set on one another with the most brutal weapons (including poison gas). Behind the façade of industrial and scientific culture there suddenly appeared the barbarism of imperialism, of militarism, of contempt of the foreigner.

It is perhaps a feature of the greatness and clear-sightedness of Karl Barth that more than anyone else he was affected by the fact that in August 1914 all his revered teachers were jubilant about the First World War. He writes: 'A day at the beginning of August of that year impressed itself upon me personally as the *dies ater* (black day) on which ninety-three German intellectuals made a public statement on the war policy of Kaiser Wilhelm II and his advisers. Among them, to my dismay, I discovered the names of almost all my theological teachers whom hitherto I had faithfully revered. Having been led astray by their ethos, I noted... that for me at any rate the theology of the nineteenth century no longer had any future.'[3]

Barth had been a young pastor when he experienced the contrast between the workers and cultural-liberal Christianity in Safenwil. He had come to experience the class struggle and in this helpless situation had had to ask himself: what shall I preach? Where do I belong? What side am I on? He understood that this culture was not a harmonious progress but stood under a judgment, a crisis. Judgment and crisis are important terms for this new theology: we are subject to God's judgment, not to an increasingly refined divine education. History is not a history of progress but a history of catastrophes and judgment.

The dialectical theology which was founded by Barth and his friends Brunner, Thurneysen and Gogarten was an attempt to restore Christian faith on the basis of the revelation of God in scripture. Barth went back to forgotten truths of orthodoxy: revelation stands over against religion. It does not tell human beings what they can tell themselves. It is the alien, the other. There is a sharp polemic in dialectical theology against religion, which is seen as the way human beings take to God in vain. It is not we who seek God, but God who seeks us. God comes down from above, breaks into our world from outside. It is not our striving for God but God's search for us that we experience in revelation. Religion is unbelief (cf. *Church Dogmatics* I.2, §17). Only the revelation of the 'wholly other God' points to an Archimedean point outside what is given.

The same is true of Holy Scripture, which has absolute validity over against historical relativism. We must first orientate ourselves on scripture; the construction of academic thought is secondary. That too is a Reformation principle which old orthodoxy put forward: *sola scriptura* – only on the basis of scripture – do we know the *solus Christus*, Christ the sole Saviour. With this is connected the move from the individualism of liberal spirituality, which puts God and the individual soul at the centre, to the church. Barth changed the title of his *Christian Dogmatics* to *Church Dogmatics*; this appeared from 1932 onwards and represents his life's work (it is in thirteen volumes).

God is now the wholly other, the alien one, the incomprehensible Lord who is unknowable by us and who makes himself known exclusively in a free act of his grace. God's transcendence, his beyondness, is decisive. Whereas liberal theology stressed the immanence of God in nature and history, neo-orthodoxy with great solemnity stresses God's otherness. What we feel and think, experience and detect, has nothing at all to do with God, but is a projection of our wishes and dreams. The reality of God transcends our concepts *and* our feelings. It is not we who know God, but God speaks to us in his word, i.e. in Christ. In him, Barth writes in his 1922 *Commentary on Romans*, 'God becomes veritably a secret: He is made known as the

Unknown, speaking in Eternal silence; He protects himself from every intimate companionship and from all the impertinence of religion.'[4] In a later work Barth uses the same term 'impertinence' against the mystic Angelus Silesius: here he is attacking the theology of Culture Protestantism which, speaking of the infinite worth of the human soul, assumed a natural closeness between God and the soul.

Christology is the theme in which the contrast between liberal and neo-orthodox theology appears most clearly. It is no coincidence that Harnack can sum up the gospel without Jesus Christ appearing at all! 'In the combination of these ideas – God the Father, providence, being a child, the infinite value of the human soul – the whole of the Gospel is expressed.'[5]

So Christ is not one of the essentials. For Barth, Christ is 'the plane which lies beyond our comprehension. The plane which is known to us, He intersects vertically, from above.'[6] 'Vertically from above' is one of the images with which Barth constantly depicts God's intervention, God's claim, God's revelation.

Neo-orthodoxy versus liberal theology	
Revelation *solus Christus*	Religion
Holy Scripture *sola scriptura*	Historical relativism
Church	Individuality
God's transcendence and unknowableness	God's immanence in nature and history
The 'wholly other' God	Transfiguration of culture
Man as sinner	The infinite value of the human soul
The understanding of history as discontinuity, judgment, crisis	Development and education

'God is in heaven and we are on earth' is another often-repeated basic thought. If liberal theology sees something of God in human beings themselves, neo-orthodoxy sets the wholly other God above us. A synthesis of the 'God above' and the 'God within' seems impossible.

I now return to christology as the attempt to grasp the mystery of Jesus. Wherein lies the power of Jesus, his power to change and shape life? The various theological paradigms have used various images and symbols for Christ. The traditional answers to this question in the dogmatic language of orthodoxy are: Jesus of Nazareth is the anointed, the messiah, the Lord, the Kyrios, the Saviour and Redeemer, the true King of Kings, the Son of God, true God and true man. He appears as Rex, Victor, Cosmocrator, and also as the Lamb, the Logos, the Mediator. These symbols for Christ come from a variety of ancient traditions. The word 'Messiah' comes from the Jewish sphere and denotes the thousand-year-old hope of the Jewish people for the messianic time and the Messiah who will come as judge and ruler of the world to bring justice and peace. The word 'Christ', the anointed, is the Greek translation of the title Messiah. 'Lord' is an expression from Hellenistic religion: the Kyrios was the powerful Lord who brings salvation, and the word has retained a place in the liturgy, in which we still sing 'Kyrie eleison', 'Lord, have mercy'. The honorific title 'Lord' was applied to many other deities and heroes in the syncretistic world of Hellenism. The earliest Christians took over the word and transferred it to their Lord, Jesus of Nazareth; they worshipped him as the Lord who has power over all rule in the empire and in the cosmos.

This process of fusion and renaming is not unusual. Almost all the predicates which are applied to Christ also appear in the cults in the environment of the earliest community, which testify to the Saviour (*Soter*), the Lord (*Kyrios*), the Son of God, and also the resurrection of Attis and Adonis and many others. Alongside Judaism and this syncretistic, religiously pluralistic world of cults, late-Greek philosophy with its cosmology and metaphysics played a central role in the formation of dogmatic formulas, which culminate in the statement that Christ is Son of God, 'conceived by the Holy Spirit, born of the Virgin Mary', as we read in the Apostles' Creed.

The intrinsic difficulty in the theological doctrine of Christ is how to express the fact that he is from God without giving up his humanity. Depending on whether the divine nature or the human nature stands in the foreground, theologians talk of a 'christology from above' or a

'christology from below'. In the former the stress is on the event of
Easter; in the latter it is more on the cross. The danger of orthodoxy
was always that it developed a christology from above in which God
sends his Son into the sinful world and he takes the form of a man,
indeed of a slave; however, he really belongs on the side of God, as
then becomes evident in his miracles, his resurrection and ascension.
This danger that Christ only 'looked like' a man, only played the role
of a man for a short time, is called 'docetism', seeming.

Docetism extended so deeply into the tradition that for example
Augustine could not bear the fact that Christ cried out in despair on
the cross, 'My God, my God, why have you forsaken me?' (Matthew
27.46). He reinterprets what seemed to him to be all too human a
statement as though it were not Christ but only his human nature
which cried out in this way; of course this puts in question the depth
of the humanity of this Son of God. Christ's suffering becomes a
semblance if it does not affect his awareness of the nearness of God.
The decisive point of his nearness to us, that he 'took the form of a
servant and became in the likeness of human beings and was found in
appearance as a man' (Philippians 2.7), is not sustained. This is the
danger of any christology 'from above'. But given the historical reality
attested in the Gospels of the poor man who could do no miracles in
Nazareth (Mark 6.5) because they did not believe in him, even
orthodoxy could not finally take off; it could not deny the bitter earthly
reality. So it attempted to maintain the duality of the natures in the
unity of the person. As the victorious Messiah, Christ belongs on the
side of God: I recall Handel's oratorio *Messiah*, which attests so clear
a christology 'from above', from the power and glory of God – in
contrast to Bach's Passions, which celebrate the suffering of an
innocent as the place where we catch sight of God.

As I have already said, the Reformation broke with christological
speculation. Luther calls the theologians of the early church 'sophists'
and mocks:

> So the sophists have depicted him, as he is man and God, count his
> legs and arms, mix his two natures marvellously together, which is
> just a sophistic knowledge of the Lord Christ, for Christ is not called
> Christ because he has two natures – what concern is that of mine?
> But he bears this glorious and comforting name by virtue of his
> ministry and work; that which he has taken upon himself, the same

gives him the name. That he is by nature man and God is his own character, but that he directed his ministry hither and poured out his love and becomes my saviour and redeemer, that takes place for my comfort and good; it is important for me that he wills to free his people from sins. In the first chapter of Matthew it is shown by the angel Gabriel that he is to be called Jesus. Not because he is God and man, but because he is to have this office and to go to work to help the people from sins and death. That makes him a man, and that is what we too must hold him to be, that he is head and supreme Lord of Christianity and of all divine bliss (WA 16, 217f.).

Referring to the doctrine of the early church, the Reformers described the task of Christ as a threefold office: Christ is the prophet who proclaims salvation, so that we can assume that he is 'teacher and master' (according to Matthew 23.8-10); he is the priest who offers himself as sacrifice (*satisfactio*) and intercedes for us (*intercessio*); finally he is the king who exercises lordship over the world. We find traces of this doctrine of the prophetic, priestly and royal ministry of Christ in many Christian testimonies, hymns and prayers.

By contrast the modern, liberal model thinks subjectively. The question who Jesus is for me is answered in personal terms: my redeemer, my friend, my saviour, 'Jesus is my confidence and my saviour in life' (1653). Appeals to this comforting, healing helper can be found in many hymns. Jesus is seen as physician, as teacher, as traveller on the way. It is interesting to investigate the christological statements and images in hymnbooks. In them one can note how subjectivism becomes increasingly strong in the modern tradition, both in pietism and in the liberal tradition. 'So take my hands and lead me to my blessed end and eternally...' (1862) is an expression of this worship of Jesus which is wholly fused with trust in God. The spirit of 'I am not alone' still blows here, and has given the hymn its tremendous popularity, but at the same time all the disruptive, disturbing elements which raise questions, and which appear in Gollwitzer's text, are filtered out; nothing is left of the Jesus of the biblical tradition.

If we look at the paradigm of liberation theology, we find there an understanding of Jesus which strives for neither the objectification of the mystery in dogma nor for a subjectivizing in personal appropriation. The liberation theologies mention the mystery of Jesus in his historical existence. They say of him that he was poor, hungry, forsaken, subversive and 'out of his mind' (Mark 3.20); that he was a worker, a nobody without papers, a carpenter, unemployed, a political prisoner, tortured. They attempt to begin where Jesus began, where he lived, where the poeple met him – not in churches but in everyday life, and that means in misery. He is not recognizable by his halo.

Latin American liberation theology makes a unique identification with the poor Jesus of the Gospels and the life of its own people in wretched settlements. Just as at that time Jesus was one of the overwhelming majority of those living on the margin of a minimal existence, so 'for us' he is the Christ of the poor. Here at last a christology 'from below' is taken seriously. The Spanish-European ruling culture celebrated Christ as the 'salvador del mundo' and at the same time identified itself with the oppressors. The poor man now takes the place of this glorious Kyrios: the child born out of wedlock, the fugitive without possessions and power, the rebel who is regarded as a criminal. He belongs to the country people who do not earn a proper wage and mostly have no job; he is a manual worker, one of the country sub-proletariat. He does not count. Jesus is like a poor woman who comes to the authorities and is sent away ten times and even then does not get what she needs. He is a cipher; he has no real kin; he has no title like 'Doctor' to put before his name; he has none of those things which can protect one in life, make an impression on others. In this sense he is a 'nobody', a 'non-person'. He is thought to be crazy, out of his mind; that is how his family regards him: he is an idler, he breaks the law. In the language of the prevailing system he is a 'terrorist', a *subversivo* as they are called in Latin America, who is made to disappear, is tortured and killed. A mass from Nicaragua, the *Misa campesina nicaraguense*, celebrates this christology from below from the experience of the suffering and struggling people. There Jesus is the 'God who sweats on the street, the God with the sunburnt face, who looks and feels as we do, the *Cristo trabajador*, Christ the worker'.

> I have seen you in a village shop
> and in an inn on the road;
> I have seen you at a lottery stall
> and you were not ashamed;
> I have seen you at the filling station

testing the tyres of a truck;
and even on the street patrol,
in overall and leather gloves.[7]

Here the theological danger of the docetism which is rooted in Western theology is really overcome. We are still far removed from it within the rich world. To some degree the exaggerated and steep christology of the tradition pays the price in post-Christian modernity; among us Jesus is largely seen as a heavenly being who never lived. For popular atheism the only power and glory he symbolizes is that of the institution – as though he had never been, or had been only a phantom on earth. The consciousness of the First World hardly knows any other christology than that 'from above'; the heresy of docetism dominates the extinct religion of the masses.

The intrinsic difficulty of Christian doctrine consists in remembering that Jesus was a real human being like everyone else, who talked, sweated, was hungry, was anxious – and of whom at the same time we say that he gives life, shows the way and lives the truth (John 14.6). Let me quote once more from the Nicaraguan mass, which articulates the true God and true man in its own way.

I believe in you, comrade,
Christ man, Christ worker,
victor over death.
With your great sacrifice
you made new people
for liberation.
You are risen
in every arm outstretched
to defend the people
against the exploitation of rulers;
you are alive and present in the hut,
in the factory, in the school.
I believe in your ceaseless struggle,
I believe in your resurrection.[8]

In the context of the revolutionary struggle it is evidently possible for Christians to overcome the difficulties which allow the Christianity of the old world to get bogged down in docetism.

Are there also liberating christological statements within the framework of our First-World culture? Gollwitzer speaks of the Jesus who does not leave me alone and who interrupts and disturbs me. For many years I lived with Bonhoeffer's formula which called Jesus the 'man for others'. Because he was there for others and not just for himself, he produced a different form of relationship to God for us all. Today Bonhoeffer's formula sounds too idealistic, particularly for women, who are emerging from an enforced being-there-for-others, since it suggests that Jesus was the one who always only gives, is always only there for others. In discussions of this christological formula of Bonhoeffer's the objection is that talk of 'being there for others' does not express the mutuality of all human relationships. Real love is always a giving *and* taking, a reciprocal relationship.

Orthodox theology sought to express that by seeing Jesus as one with the Father and thinking of the Spirit as proceeding from both. The Spirit itself expresses this mutuality, and to some degree it is a godless notion to imagine Jesus as only the one who gives and loves, without knowing anything about receiving. Jesus gives because he has received – like every loving soul. In this context God can really be thought of only as Word, as a calling into being and being called by us. For this reason another objection which is often made to a christology of liberation, that Jesus appears only as a lawgiver, one who makes demands, falls short. It seems to me that Jesus' demand that people should follow him (Matthew 16.24) is at the same time an invitation to grow into love. Precisely when we understand the 'law' in the Jewish sense as way, as Torah, it is at the same time gospel. Jesus makes possible what he requires: he entrusts us to God. That is what Paul means by the expression, 'He was the firstborn among many brothers and sisters' (Romans 8.29). Such a christology is interested in drawing us in, and only by stressing that he was as we are can we say in what respect he was not as we are: in respect of sin. In fact we do not live for others but exploit others; we live for ourselves. But that does not distinguish us in a physical or metaphysical sense from Christ, but in an existential sense. Starting from his historical existence we know that, 'He was as we are.' Just as he did miracles, so he accepted that his disciples, too, could do miracles (Mark 16.17; Matthew 10.7f.). In just the same way he sends us out to do miracles, to feed the hungry, clothe the naked, call the dead to life. Really to believe in miracles means to do miracles oneself. Luther said, 'One must draw Christ into the flesh'. Unless you 'draw him into the flesh', far from the great formulae of christology, you fail him. You may perhaps admire him, but you will not be following him. You imagine him as cosmocrator, as light-being, as redeemer, but not as a bent human being with a peasant's face, with all the traces of torture on his body, as Matthias Grünewald painted him. The Christ from below looks like the other peasants who were hanged and impaled at that time; today, too, Christ is portrayed as a *campesino*, often with Indian features.

The charge of docetism is as old as Christianity itself and is most clearly expressed today in liberation theology. But there is also another danger, that of seeking him as the 'mere man', and overlooking God's power in him. If we say he was just as we are, we can be led into a lack of commitment. Unless I hear God's voice in him, unless I see something sympathetic, helpless in him – if I think that there are of course many idealists who wish the world well – then I have got no further than admiration and remain uncommitted. And this lack of commitment brings no comfort, because it cannot really save and involve me: I am like someone who has attempted the impossible.

I recall a long conversation with an enlightened non-believing Jew about Jesus: 'Why do you have anything to do with this Jesus? He wasn't successful! He changed nothing. He's completely uninteresting because he didn't change the face of the earth. He founded a religion which has almost nothing to do with him, which reintroduced precisely what he wanted to do away with: hierarchy, power, oppression, exploitation. What's the point in calling on him, since he had no success!'

This criticism again confronts us with the question of belief in Jesus. Why should there be more to Jesus of Nazareth than this solitary dreamer? What is the meaning of this 'more', this hope, this other relationship to life, which is not subject to the criterion of success? We shall discuss this question when we embark on the Christian understanding of God. Here I just want to add a few personal comments, speaking for myself, on why I need this Jesus.

Sharing in his dream, I call myself a Christian. My understanding of reality is shaped by the Jewish Christian tradition. In it life means involvement, living in relationships, living by and for relationships. I could even say that the more the relationship, the more the reality; the less the relationship, the more death there is. This character of life as relationship also means that we always already live with, by and under 'images', former pictures of life or pictures handed on to us by others. We hear stories; we identify ourselves: each person has a world of pictures, and it is inconceivable that we could be human without images, pictures, forms and voices which speak to us. There is no life without images; we are always already in relationships which make demands on us; we always already live with and under images which comfort us and promise us meaning. The question is really only what comfort, what promise, these pictures offer us. The photograph of a beautiful young woman in a swimming pool in the springtime garden of a luxury villa is also an 'image' in this shaping, educating, attractive sense: I can make it my goal, my life's dream. However, from a Christian perspective this picture is an idol which promises human beings hope and meaning and life, and for which they offer great sacrifices. The images of our advertising are icons of the religion of consumerism. The image of Christ is also an icon, but of quite a different life.

The author J.D.Salinger, who wrote *The Catcher in the Rye*, has an image in one of his novels which communicates what I mean; he calls it the Fat Lady. He depicts a family with highly gifted children who appear on radio broadcasts. The older brother Seymour explains to his brothers and sisters who are taking part in a radio programme called 'Wise Child' that they have to shine their shoes for the Fat Lady: 'He never did tell me who the Fat Lady was, but I shined my shoes for the Fat Lady every time I went on the air again – all the years you and I were on the program together, if you remember, I don't think I missed more than just a couple of times. This terribly clear, clear picture of the Fat Lady formed in my mind. I had her sitting on this porch all day, swatting flies, with her radio going full blast from morning till night. I figured the heat was terrible, and she probably had cancer, and – I don't know. Anyway, it seemed goddam clear why Seymour wanted me to shine my my shoes when I went on the air. It made *sense*.'[9]

A sister in this family who was similarly told about the Fat Lady by her brother says: 'I didn't ever picture her on a porch but with very – you know – very thick legs, very veiny. I had her in an *awful* wicker chair. She had cancer, *too*, though, and she had the radio going full-blast all day! Mine did, too!'

This image of the Fat Lady is now contrasted with the world of television, and a 'goddam Broadway theatre, complete with the most fashionable, most well-fed, most sunburned-looking audience you can imagine'. ' "But I'll tell you a terrible secret," says the older brother in a telephone conversation. "Are you listening to me? *There isn't anyone out there who isn't Seymour's Fat Lady.* That includes your Professor Tupper, buddy. And all his goddam cousins by the dozens. There isn't anyone *any*where that isn't Seymour's Fat Lady. Don't you know that? Don't you know that goddam secret yet? And don't you know - *listen* to me now – *don't you know who that Fat Lady really is?* Ah, buddy. Ah, buddy. It's Christ Himself. Christ Himself, buddy."

For joy, apparently, it was all Franny could do to hold the phone, even with both hands. For a fullish half minute or so, there were no other words, no further speech. Then, "I can't talk any more, buddy." The sound of the phone being replaced in its catch followed.'[10]

I think that the hostility to religion in our time is connected with our fear of images that really change us. We do not want to see the Fat Woman because she disturbs us. One has to look for a storyteller like Salinger to make clear the connection between the Fat Woman, Christ, and all of us.

Such a christology, mediated by poetry, brings together the 'below' and the 'above'. Christ is indeed present in this the least of my sisters (Matthew 25.45). Christ appears here in this mystical image of the Fat Woman. He disturbs and reconciles, he causes anxiety, just as the ugliness, stupidity and suffering of the Fat Woman disturb people and make them anxious. At the same time this Christ draws me into the mystery of God. I am steeped in love. That is precisely what Salinger tells us. The brothers and sisters of the older brother who speaks here emerge from their desperation. 'It made sense' to shine one's shoes; it makes sense to live.

11 Cross and Resurrection

The Christian God is not a little Chinese god of fortune (the praise he got from Brecht), a god in whose kingdom it would be possible to live without want and suffering. Jesus, multiplying loaves and healing the sick, could also have had all this. Instead, Jesus identified himself with the sufferers and was afflicted by their diseases. For the sake of the sufferers he was made to suffer, and to overcome death he entered into death. To go the way of Jesus means finding a different relationship to suffering from that of avoidance and denial, which is customary for us.

It is a particular feature of Christianity that the cross, this sign of death, stands in its midst. As far as I know, in no other religion is there such a strong stress on suffering and dying, whereas myths of revival, the return or the resurrection of the dead occur frequently. Do we have to draw the conclusion from this comparison of religions that Christianity has a fixation on death, is necrophilic, obsessed with suffering and death? This very old criticism of Christianity, made openly, for example, by Goethe, has been accentuated in our century by psychoanalytical investigations into the sado-masochistic areas of the human soul. Is it the enjoyment of tormenting and being tormented that made this ancient tree of torture the central symbol of the Christian faith? Does a perverse love of suffering motivate Christians to worship a tormented God?

Of all the objections to the Christian religion, this objection related to the cross seems to me to be the most radical. The difference from, say, the charge that Christians have a naive and pre-scientific belief in a creator is that here, in the conflict over the significance of the cross of Christ, the whole of Christian faith is at stake. So we must ask how the various theological paradigms interpret the fact that Jesus Christ was crucified and rose from the dead. In this chapter I want above all to go into Latin American liberation theology, since I think that its most important contribution is the interpretation of the cross in the everyday life of the poor: here a new kind of *theologia crucis* has come into being.

In *orthodox* theology the main accent is on the question of the meaning of cross and resurrection, on the Father and his will and plan to redeem the world through the death of the Son. God has himself resolved to surrender Christ for the salvation of all. Different theological theories articulate this mystery of the 'plan of salvation'; here I shall lump together up all the pre-modern theologies as 'orthodox', without going more closely into their various tendencies: the differences relate to the question whether God is actively 'reconciling himself with the world' (II Corinthians 5.19) through his struggle and victory over death, or whether reconciliation with Christ is offered to him – as recipient. For both variants, the will, plan and action of the Father stand in the centre. A Good Friday hymn by Paul Gerhardt (1607-1676) runs:

A lamb goes and bears the guilt
   of the world and its children;
it goes and atones in patience
for the sins of all sinners.

In a dialogue between God and Christ which probably takes place in heaven, certainly before the passion of Jesus, God prays:

Go, my child, and take to yourself
the children whom I shut out
for punishment and the chastisement of wrath.
The punishment is severe, the wrath is great;
You can and shall release them,
through dying and through blood.

And Christ replies to him with that deep inner surrender to the will of God which is characteristic of this kind of spirituality:

Yes, father, yes from the bottom of my heart;
impose and I will bear it for you;

my will hangs upon your lips,
my doing is what you say (1647).

We shall meet the basic theme of Christ's 'yes' to the will of the
Father again in the interpretation of the cross in liberation theology.

The orthodox mode of thinking finds radical expression in the
theory of satisfaction developed by Anselm of Canterbury (1033-
1109). Here God is presented as a king whose honour is violated by
human sin. God himself is not in a position simply to allow grace to
prevail or 'to close his eyes'; his honour calls for either punishment
which would destroy humanity or satisfaction which humanity cannot
supply as such. Only the God-man Christ can accomplish the necessary
expiation.

This is a model of the need for the incarnation envisaged in juridical
terms: Christ as the innocent victim submits to the will of the Father
and thus reconciles the Father with us. Sometimes this notion is
associated with the symbol of the blood which washes us clean. Only
blood can wash away transgressions. That the punishment we deserved
is laid on the person of Christ then runs right through the whole of
the orthodox Christian tradition. We should really have been punished, but we were acquitted. Jesus Christ was punished, since he
bore the suffering, the punishment, the damnation, indeed even the
curse that we were under vicariously for us, and in this way redeemed
us.

It is difficult nowadays to get to grips with this thought construction.
It sounds absurd to us, but in our time it has undergone a significant
revival, which possibly helps us to understand what it is really about.
Here I would like to recall the Black civil rights movement in the
United States and Martin Luther King, Jr (1929-1968), who was
deeply convinced that unmerited suffering, undertaken voluntarily,
has a saving power for society, which he believed to be sick. King
thought that the participants in the civil rights movement would get
into difficulty as a result of their non-violent protests and actions.
They would have to suffer humiliation, loss of prestige, unjustified
fines and imprisonment, and indeed lynching and judicial murder.

King, a Baptist preacher, stood within the orthodox tradition of the
Black church, though in his study he had come to know the power of
the liberal paradigm, for example in the form of Paul Tillich. He
believed in the healing, reconciling power of suffering undertaken

voluntarily. He saw the power which lies in 'the blood of the lamb'. In this way he freed the orthodox tradition from its reified worship of this redeemer who died at an earlier point; over against a 'christolatry' (Mary Daly) in which Christ is revered as an idol, in his life and preaching, and even more in his dying, he pointed to the inner power which a movement gains when it voluntarily takes on itself avoidable suffering for the sake of the reconciliation of a whole sick society. 'There is power in the blood of the lamb.' This interpretation of King's takes over the notion of necessary sacrifice and voluntary suffering from orthodoxy but – very much in line with the liberal heritage – does not so much see God as the one who needs to be reconciled: what needs to be reconciled is society, which is torn apart and is destroying itself.

The liberal paradigm which developed after the Enlightenment thinks of the cross in terms of Christ's action. Because God's love is always unchanged, there is no need to make God change his mind. Christ, rather, is the one who reveals this nature of God, his fatherly love. According to Schleiermacher, his 'activity of reconciliation' consists in drawing believers into the 'power of God-consciousness', making them part of the 'community of his undisturbed blessedness'.[1] Jesus loves us so much that he sacrifices himself for us and our brokenness, and overcomes our alienation, so that we become free and certain that we ourselves are children of God. According to Ernst Troeltsch, Jesus' unity with the Father is not a 'unity of being' but a 'unity of will'.[2] Christ wills what God wills, and thus becomes the teacher and educator of the human race.

We look in vain for a deeper interpretation of the cross of Jesus within the liberal theology of Schleiermacher, Ritschl, or Troeltsch.

Only the theology of liberation and its conception of the cross and resurrection points to a new way of thinking about this content of faith. In recent years the significance of the cross has dawned on me anew personally as a result of encounters with Christians, men and women in Latin America, who interpret the cross in a different way from us, against a different background of historical experience. One presupposition is their understanding of the cross as a realistic event and not as a symbol. In our world the cross has become an empty symbol; it is worn as a golden ornament and regarded as a religious sign. We do not know a great deal in our culture about its real historical significance, as an instrument of execution used by the Roman empire against rebels and insurgents.

But the cross is understood only when one becomes clear about this objective function of crucifixion as an instrument of power politics in the service of the rule over, and oppression of, subject peoples. Those who dedicated themselves to justice among men and women in a world of brutality were tortured to death slowly and in public. We can read from the passion narratives how the state power used crucifixion: the cruel punishment of the ringleaders, the destruction of the group as subversives, and the public deterrence of possible sympathizers. The cross was very appropriate for these three political aims. Many Jewish martyrs before and after Jesus were executed in this way. Women too, like Jesus, died a martyr death. The Romans were afraid not only of armed rebels but perhaps even more of people like Jesus who preached and lived out the kingdom of God and his righteousness in the midst of a world of exploitation and brutal subjection. 'The kingdom of God' meant that ultimately people should be able to live in a way which accorded with God's creation. Luise Schottroff writes: 'The Jewish people groaned under hunger and political oppression. Jesus died as a martyr for his people and for God's righteousness. The Romans understood that the physical embodiment of God's justice in the world is subversive, and threatens the powerful.'[3] This subversive Jesus had to be eliminated.

The objective function of the cross, its real-political significance, its status within the social history of the oppressed, has long been misunderstood by the mainstream churches. The cross was spiritualized and became purely individualistic; it was interpreted without reference to the kingdom of God and its righteousness. Today that is most clearly understood by those who in their own lives experience blows, persecution, infringements of rights, mockery and exclusion, and finally torture and judicial murder, which are legitimated or tolerated by the state. A woman friend from Argentina told me how she was arrested and, though not directly tortured, was interrogated for two nights under humiliating conditions. They put a blindfold over her eyes and she was interrogated for hours by a group of men who were unknown to her. At one point she said, 'I am a Christian,' and one of the men who were interrogating her began to laugh crazily and said, 'Why are you telling us that? I too am a Catholic.' He took her hand and put it on his bare chest where a cross was hanging; then he gave her the cross to hold and laughed himself silly at the thought that particular views about life and commitment to the poor went with her claim to be a Christian. It was a profound shock for my friend that a man, a sadist, a torturer, should devalue the cross, rob it of its original significance, and claim it for himself and for the 'national security' which he served, by saying, 'I too am a Christian.' Such are the different ways in which the cross can be understood: as a symbol of desperation, humiliation and torment, and as an instrument of domination!

We need a deep realism if we are going to reflect on the cross. Without an understanding of history, without involvement in history, we only arrive at a timeless symbol and lose sight of the event, which can be given a precise location. Christian faith thought in historical terms from the start, even in the Apostles' Creed. How else did Pontius Pilate get into the creed? Liberation theologians are often accused of confusing politics and religion. 'Stick to religion,' people say. 'Why do you have to keep on talking about South Africa?' To this standard objection we can gently reply, 'In our creed we have "He suffered under Pontius Pilate, was crucified." That is historical, political information. Here we have mention of the Roman empire and its power structure. Christ and Pilate – this connection is not just an invention of the Marxists, but is the reality of the world in which Christianity came into being and without which we betray its truth.'

So what is the cross – as understood by liberation theology? I shall begin with a lecture which I heard in Latin America, given by the Foreign Minister of Nicaragua, Miguel d'Escoto, who is a priest and member of the Maryknoll Order. He led a 'way of the cross' during Passiontide. The way of the cross, *via crucis*, is a traditional form of devotion, in which believers follow Jesus' way of suffering through fourteen stations, singing, praying and meditating. People went on this *via crucis* from north Nicaragua to Managua; they stopped at the fourteen stations of the traditional way of the cross, sang and prayed there, heard the individual stages of the passion of Christ and meditated on them, and in so doing brought their own life and the fate of their land before God. They went the way of the cross, with Miguel d'Escoto unarmed and unescorted in their midst. At one point he met a young soldier who was carrying a small New Testament with him in his ammunition pouch. 'That's my best defence,' said the young man, and the book had been read so much that it was falling apart. A journalist asked a woman with two small children, who had had to carry them alternately, why she was going along in the heat. She told him that her husband had been murdered by the Contras four months earlier and that she had to go along to pray to God for the war finally to cease.

Miguel d'Escoto came to the small Baptist seminar at which I was teaching and spoke to us about the significance of the cross. I tried to write down this lecture as literally as possible, and to catch his simple, popular tone in the translation. This is what he said:

We all know the expression 'bear one's cross'. For example, when a wife has a husband who drinks, that is her cross. It is too hot for another – that is her cross. The tortilla is burnt, that is a cross. In other words, all kinds of things are a cross. Now of course that does not mean that not even the smallest sufferings – far less the big ones – can be brought to the Lord and accepted by him; they too have a value. But that is not the cross. The cross is the unavoidable consequence of doing the will of the Father. And what is the will of our Father? To put it simply, for us all to be sons and daughters of God. We recognize that by living as brothers and sisters. Unless we recognize that we are brothers and sisters, we do not recognize that God is our Father. The decisive thing is to live out this community, this solidarity. But that leads us to make prophetic accusations against everything in society which prevents us from living as brothers and sisters: exploitation, injustice, racism, machismo, contempt for women. All that human beings invent to dominate others and take advantage of them, in order to set a group or an individual above others, is directed against God's will.

In a society of brothers and sisters we are all partners. We all work at the same task, and no one exploits others. If we see it as our task, clearly and categorically, but in a Christian way, i.e. in a non-violent way, to accuse anything that is contrary to God's will, then we become the objects of aggression, of the hostility of others who have an interest in maintaining the old order. All reprisals, all persecutions which are inflicted on us as a consequence of our attempts to create a brotherly world – that is the cross.

We sometimes believe that we can outwit the Lord, that we can do the will of the Father without people persecuting us. We want to be cleverer than Christ. He may have been very good, but he was rather naive. That's what many people think, even if they don't say it. The gringos say that 'You can get to heaven in a Cadillac,' but that's not really true. You cannot get redemption without a cross.

Today we have a situation in Nicaragua in which to be a Nicaraguan and a Nicaraguan Christian means to be condemned to heroism and martyrdom. For us there can only be heroes and martyrs out of loyalty to Christ – or renegades and traitors. There are no other possibilities. One could say that life is unfair. But what is life? It is a series of trials, demands and possibilities. And so one life begins to differ from another, depending on how we use our opportunities, offers and temptations. For what? To allow God to become visible in us.

We are always like the man who went to Jericho, and on his way had an opportunity in the form of the bloodied man who had fallen victim to robbers. What do we do? Do we keep on with our engagements, rush on to Jericho... and forget our brother? The demands are like those in an examination: one person gets a difficult examination because it calls for more; another a relatively easy one. There are people who can succeed in being good people simply because they do not have to live in Nicaragua at the moment, and who even as good Christians have a different opportunity. Not everyone is presented with idols; not everyone is told, 'Offer incense to the idol or we will kill you!' But that is what we are told in Nicaragua – not only individuals, but the people. There is someone here who says that we are to fall on our knees, someone who says, 'Your will be done, because you are strong and have great piles of nuclear weapons and because you have lots of money. So your will be done!' That is what they want, and that is even what they say. The whole people, with the human weaknesses which everyone has, argues for a more just, human society. The people goes on, although it knows that it will be forgiven if it sacrifices to the idols of imperialism. But the people says, 'I am not offering any sacrifice to idols. I shall go on trying to create a new society.'

Some go on because they believe in Christ, and they deliberately do so out of loyalty to him. Others feel called, though they do not know where, as for example the good Samaritan who was an atheist. But he heard the voice. So he too is in our company. We have many good Samaritans in our people! And so in this project we continue to bear our cross not just as individuals, but as a people. And that is what we should be particularly thinking about at Passiontide. I have often said that not even ten per cent of us Catholics, priests included, are real Christians, for to be a Christian means to acknowledge Christ, and the only Christ is the crucified Christ. Not to accept the cross means to reject Christ. We do not accept being nailed with him to the cross, and that means that we do not accept him. Generally speaking, the church does not accept Christ, any more than his Jewish contemporaries did. They did not accept him because they did not want this kind of redemption.

I would like to tell you something personal: a prayer which occurred to me many years ago. For a long time I have had a picture of Martin Luther King in my office. For me he is the greatest saint of our time, and certainly a person who has influenced my life more than many others. Not that he has changed me as much as I would have liked, but he has still influenced me. I was a missionary in Chile and was in contact with Martin Luther King, arranging for him to come to Chile. The National Church Council was in process of dealing with the formalities, but King was killed, so nothing came of it. But I still have a photo of him in my office and in my room. Many years ago, at the beginning of Passiontide, I was sitting in my office in New York; it was the Tuesday before Ash Wednesday, and everyone was already going home, but I stayed in the office to think about what I was going to do that Passiontide, sunk in contemplation of the picture of Martin Luther King. One Passiontide after another people had said that they were content with my work, but I was not content. And as I looked at the picture of Martin Luther King I suddenly felt ashamed. I saw him as a person who made himself free of everything and did what the Lord asked of him. I said to myself, 'He is somehow a special person, and thank God there sometimes are such people.' But I noticed more and more that the special element is the grace of God in a person, for he too was afraid; he too had his human limitations. The most important thing is the grace of God which changed him into what he was.

So that day I kept on reflecting, until finally a prayer occurred to me. It went, 'Lord, help me to understand the mystery of your cross. Help me to love your cross, and give me the power, the grace, to take it upon myself as you offer it to me.' And I can tell you that this works. I am someone who is afraid even of the dentist, and yet there came a moment when I could say, 'Lord, my life is yours. Do what you want with it.' That's a long time ago now, and a wish came over me to do something which in prayer and after discussion in a group of brothers and sisters, we regard as what 'doing the will of God' now means at the place in which we live. If we have this readiness unconditionally to be there for the will of God, we put our lives at God's disposal, so that God becomes visible through us. The important thing is for us to be available to God now. For unless we are at God's disposal, our intellect develops to the point of being our own downfall. In that case we are like a tiny computer. If anyone begins to make a proposal before we have finished the phase of meditation, the head already begins to analyse and recognizes what the danger is if we accept the proposal. In that case I am no longer listening to it, but am already rejecting it. I see it as a danger. To free us from this fear, so that we can be real instruments of the Lord, capable of making a new world, a world of love and freedom, so that we can really live by this divine message of love, we first need personal liberation. Unless we are free, we cannot be instruments for the liberation of anyone else. And what prevents us from being free? Anxiety. Liberation is a problem which first begins within us, of not having any anxiety about the consequences. We can have anxiety, but we must control this anxiety. It is anxiety in the sense that we recognize the risk; otherwise it would be blind.

Jesus knew, when he was going to Jerusalem, what would happen to him, and he told this to Peter. And Peter replied: 'Don't go. They'll capture you.' But Jesus retorted, 'Depart from me, Satan.' The Lord knew where he was going. And we are often like the community after the death of our Lord, before the Holy Spirit, full of anxiety behind closed doors. So we must pray that the Lord will liberate us from the fear of the consequences of doing his will; that he will liberate us from fear of the cross; that in the cross he will show us, not death, but an invitation to new life.

The supreme gesture in life is that we should become accustomed to contemplating even the cross with joy, because life is love. If I look at the cross for a long time, I sometimes see it as Moses in the wicker basket. May the Lord free us from paralysing anxiety and ground us in this love, this passion for justice, this fire, for he said that he would bring fire which would be kindled in our hearts. That is the fire of his divine transforming love which purifies us. As we said in the *insurrection evangelica* (that was this crusade), 'We pray for this fire to seize us.'

That is what Miguel d'Escoto said that time in Managua. Let me stress once again three characteristic points in this exegesis of the cross. The first is acceptance of the will of the Father, which we must see as the decisive characteristic of christology. It is the great 'yes' to the will of God, the 'Yes, Father, yes from the bottom of my heart', which occurs in the passion hymn, the unity of Christ's *will* with God instead of the speculative unity of *being* of their natures. There are two objections to this possible 'yes' to the will of God. The first says, 'That's all very well, but we don't know what the will of God is. It is unfathomable, and it would be sheer arrogance to want to know it.' This conception is one of the typical remnants of a religion which has otherwise died out, and by which we are poisoned as though by parts of a corpse. The prophetic tradition of the Bible and the proclamation of Jesus leave no doubt about what is the will of God. 'He has showed you, O man, what is good; and what does the Lord require of you but to do justice and to love kindness, and to walk humbly with your God?' (Micah 6.8).

The other objection to the great 'yes' to the Father's will comes from a false idolizing of Jesus and says, 'Jesus could indeed accept his Father's will, but am I Jesus? Am I not just a weak human being?' Here too an apparently pious, humble, self-deprecating position is used to escape God. The wisdom of Jesus is manipulated in order to increase the distance between him and us as though it were in Jesus' interest to keep us as far away from God as possible. This danger of putting Jesus forward so as not to have to follow him is an old one. As we saw, Thomas Müntzer called it 'chalking it up to Christ' and Mary Daly has called this danger 'christolatry': Christ becomes an idol which prevents people from growing up, being capable of love or saying 'yes' to the will of God. The interest of liberation theology lies in precisely the opposite direction, in making God visible in us so that we ourselves no longer stand in the way of the God-in-us.

The second point in d'Escoto's argument relates to the 'unavoidable consequence' of saying 'Yes' to the will of the Father: the cross. Confrontation, struggle and suffering are unavoidable. The supreme goal is not the preservation of harmony but God's will for justice for all. Influenced by the lifestyle of bourgeois Christianity, people are largely unaware of this consequence of the great 'yes': the avoidance of suffering is one of the supreme virtues accepted quite as a matter of course in our culture. Things were quite different for the Jesus movement in its origins, and where today it endorses the great 'yes'. The centre of faith was not marked by the avoidance of suffering, a fear of conflict, a desire for harmony, but by the love of God which calls for justice. Of course Jesus, too, could have avoided the cross, as could have Martin Luther King or Oscar Romero. The Gospels stress that he went his way of his own free will. In conversation with Jesus, it proves that Peter, his best friend, still wants him to avoid confrontation (Matthew 16.21-23). Who would want to become the 'object of aggression'?

There were in fact enough reasons not to go to Jerusalem, just as nowadays there are also very good reasons for business people and technicians not to stay in Nicaragua but to go to Miami and avoid the harsh trial of which Miguel d'Escoto speaks. Jesus went to the cross of his own free will and in awareness of what was awaiting him. He could only demonstrate the will of God voluntarily as the attempt to live by a relationship to God.

The consequence – suffering, the cross – certainly clouds Jesus' certainty of God, as can be seen in his cry of despair on the cross. But this night of faith, the 'My God, my God, why have you forsaken me?' (Matthew 27.46), at the same time contains light from Easter morning.

The third decisive point in Miguel d'Escoto's interpretation of the cross is the dimension of resurrection which becomes visible in the cross itself. It is no coincidence that here, at a moment for his country which is very close to that of the historical Golgotha, he resorts to the expression of a mystical affirmation of the cross as it has developed in the tradition of Spanish mysticism. 'Accepting' the cross as a consequence goes over into 'loving the cross', because it is an expression of unity with God's will, which cannot be destroyed or deterred even in dying.

This indestructible unity of love, this 'Yes, Father, Yes', is at the same time the step beyond the death which the objects of aggression have to expect. The resurrection of Christ, too, must be thought about in the real conditions of social history; otherwise it becomes an empty symbol, a divine rescue for Jesus. Here once again is Luise Schottroff, on the resurrection:

The Romans did not succeed in destroying Jesus living with their whole army. Jesus' death on the cross was not the end of his career, but the wonderful beginning of the kingly rule of God over this world. The mustard seeds of righteousness now emerged quite rapidly all over the Roman empire.[4]

For me it is still the simplest, as it were demythologized, non-miraculous formulation of the resurrection to say that they could not do away with him. They simply could not succeed in destroying him. That is resurrection. What his life meant, what his spirit was, what his disciples did, this 'yes' to God's will lived, and lives today, and this life appears in the cross. Redemption without the cross is not the redemption in which we become one with love. That becomes clear when we keep in mind the occasion of d'Escoto's speech, the *via crucis* of the Nicaraguan people.

The foundation of the new spirituality of the way of the cross is given in Jesus' presence in the least of us (according to Matthew 25.40). The suffering of the poor and of the people is related to the suffering of Jesus. The time of the passion is the present. The causes of the suffering of Jesus and his kin are identified as social and political causes: as exploitation, hunger, military rule, terror. The places of suffering (prison cell, torture chamber, child labour, etc.) are shown in pictures or conjured up in words. In the First World, in whose ecumenical base movements similarly symbolic actions, like ways of the cross and pilgrimages, are becoming increasingly important, these places of crucifixion are often sought out and visited: for example, in the USA, institutes of military technology, test stations, recruiting offices, banks; in West Germany, nuclear power stations, former concentration camps and institutions of mass destruction as at Mutlangen. The instruments of suffering are related to the suffering of Christ: the crown of thorns with the picana, which is used for electrical torture; arrest by the cars of the secret police which have no number plates, and which make people 'vanish'. Thus in religious meditation and in prayer before God there is awareness of who suffers, when, why and where. A new element of testimony in addition to the naming of the station is the testimony of individuals, which are followed by meditation and prayer.

For the spirituality of liberation, the new ways of the cross are a living form of the appropriation of the tradition, which in Christian understanding is always the depth of historically imposed suffering. In addition to the memory of the suffering, the *memoria passionis*, however, the Latin American ways of the cross also have a fifteenth station of the cross which celebrates the resurrection of Jesus and his brothers and sisters. 'We are now taking the steps which you once took. We experience your resurrection in any brother who raises himself up. Help us, so that the whole people can rise up in a new Guatemala...' – so Christians prayed on a *via crucis* of the people of Guatemala in 1988.

The Christians in Nicaragua, also, anticipate in prayer and waiting the fifteenth station of the way of the cross. I believe that with us, too, there are experiences of a similar kind when we do not understand faith as flight into a whole world but learn to love the cross as the tree of life. Our experiences are more invisible, because the difficulties with which we have to cope in our everyday and professional lives are normally not those of martyrdom, of the cross. We are not invaded by a great power when we attempt to organize a juster life; but Christians must count on encountering difficulties today. Becoming a Christian at the end of this millennium is becoming more difficult and more costly.

Really living like Christ will not mean reward, social recognition and an assured income, but difficulties, discrimination, solitude, anxiety. Here, too, the basic experience of the cross applies: the wider we open our hearts to others, the more audibly we intervene against the injustice that rules over us, the more difficult our lives in the rich unjust society will become.

Women, particularly in small places, sometimes say to me: 'I cannot commit myself publicly to the peace movement. I cannot do it, otherwise I shall be down the drain.' That was said to me by a woman who taught religion for a few hours in a small village as an unaccredited teacher. We were at a blockade, and she came by night and brought us tea; it reminded me of Nicodemus, who did not go to Jesus by day, because he could not bring himself to do that (John 3). 'I can't do it,' she said. And yet this woman did good; she allowed herself that bit of justice and concern for others without which we cannot become human. There are people among us who do the truth, who stand up for the victims of violence, who cause disturbances, whereas force seeks to keep everything under control. A great inner freedom goes with loving the cross, and I also find this spirit of freedom in what

Miguel d'Escoto said. We misunderstand the cross if we make it a necrophilic, death-seeking symbol. We are not sick on the cross. We are free to avoid the cross. The offers of most new religions are in the direction of avoiding suffering; they promise happiness, rapid fulfilment, but they avoid the reality of history. They interpret the will of God as private fulfilment; in other words, they attempt to creep round the cross. Our society offers hundreds of possibilities of this. In the apartheid of the middle class we can easily avoid the cross. Or we take it on ourselves with all the difficulties with family, profession, society, that we find ourselves in when we commit ourselves seriously.

Love has its price. The cross expresses love to the endangered, threatened life of God in our world. It is no longer a question of a biophilic embracing of life which spares itself the cross. The more we love God, the threatened, endangered, crucified God, the nearer we are to him, the more endangered we are ourselves. The message of Jesus is that the more you grow in love, the more vulnerable you make yourself. You have fewer securities and weapons. You can be attacked if you become visible or if 'that which is of God' shines out in you. If you share out your life instead of hoarding it, then the great light will become visible in you. Sometimes that will make you lonely, and you will lose friends, your standard of living, profession, career, but at the same time you will change yourself. In this process the cross, this sign of isolation, of shame, of abandonment, becomes the tree of life without which you cannot exist any more. The dead martyr wood begins to shoot. Then all at once you know where you belong. Not with those who shout, 'They're all crazy anyway. They're all Communists.' Nor with those who declare with a sad smile, 'But we have no alternative. What is truth? We live under the pressure of events.' These Pilates, whom one meets so much in the middle class and who always say, 'What is truth? You can't really know. It's much more complicated', relativize justice and truth in the interest of their strategy of avoiding suffering.

It is one of the encouraging recognitions of feminist theology that at the passion of Jesus there were women who remained with him after all the men had run off. They stood under the cross from afar. As the hymn has it:

> Ah, keep my heart thus moved
> To stand thy Cross beneath,

> To mourn thee, well-beloved,
> Yet thank thee for thy death.

Today, too, women stand under the cross. They sit by the crosses on Greenham Common or in the Hunsrück in front of the institutions of killing. They explain to the supermarket staff and to their sisters who buy from them what the Outspan oranges from South Africa taste of – blood. They do not arm themselves or get into tanks. They weep. Nowadays throughout the world we see women who have just had enough of hunger, the military and big business at the expense of our mother, the earth. There are women for whom justice is more important than their finger nails, who choose life in the face of the fantastic offers which death constantly makes us, this rising death, this silent death, this automobile death by which we choke. 'Choosing life' means 'embracing the cross'. The mystical undertones in what Miguel d'Escoto says sound strange, indeed crazy. But it is not so crazy to love life so much that we love even the cross as a consequence of saying 'yes' to the will of God. Then we know that our love is greater than anything that this world can do to us. We can take into account the cross, the difficulty, the lack of success, the anxiety... Christianity has never promised us a bed of roses in the sense that one could simply creep back into paradise. Christianity says: 'The way to the bed of roses goes through the cross.' It is no coincidence that the cross in the rose was Martin Luther's weapon. In this instrument of torture Christians have seen a rose blossoming, a sign of the love of God. 'Embracing the cross' now means growing into resistance. And the cross will become green and blossom.

12   The Kingdom of God and the Church

Jesus proclaimed the kingdom of God. And what came? What became of it? Disappointingly enough, the church. For most non-Christians, and indeed for many Christians, the theme of the church is ambivalent or even has quite a negative significance. They experience the church as a great institution which publicly administers the traditions of religion, fulfils an external role by organizing certain rituals, and represents a factor of political power within the Western world. It sounds strange and incomprehensible that one can 'believe' in the church, as the Apostles' Creed puts it, that one can even 'love' it like a mother, as Catholic Christians have often attested. The structure which is often designated the established church, the official church, or the 'church from above' is perceived with mistrust or indifference. Nevertheless, even in indignation and anger at the arrogance of the official church, there are still glimmerings of the great expectation, as if people still knew that the church really has other values and tasks than those of a great enterprise which controls money and power effectively. Even those who are alienated from the church have some inkling of the mystery which makes the church alive without its existing purely nominally, and on the basis of certain privileges guaranteed by the state. This mystery of the church is its relationship to the kingdom of God. The title of this chapter is deliberately not 'Church *or* Kingdom of God'; an 'and' maintains the tension between the two entities. Something is promised and expressed which at the same time is the inner criterion of the church as an institution: participation in the historical liberation of God with a view to the kingdom. Without the shining forth of the kingdom of God the church is an association like any other, structured in hierarchy, imposed by blind pressures and misuse of office. But the widespread attitude of 'Yes to Jesus, no to the church' remains inconsistent. In reality a yes to Jesus which does not want to have anything to do with the church is weak and superficial. For being a disciple of Jesus is related to the kingdom of God; it is a response to the message that the kingdom of heaven has come near, and from the beginning it was made in society. The task of the church is orientated on the kingdom of God, and that means that the church belongs 'between the times'. It recalls its origin, the time of the original Jesus movement, when the kingdom of God was proclaimed and took form in Jesus – and at the same time it lives for the other time at the end of all time, when the promise of the kingdom is fulfilled and it is realized in 'abundance of life' for all (John 10.11).

Justified as criticism of the official church and its compromises with state, industrial, economic or military power may be, we have to learn that the deep, anxiety-ridden mistrust of organization and constitution, of the institutionalization of the Spirit generally, does not spring from a greater proximity to the Spirit, but only from the extreme individualism which dominates our culture. It is easy nowadays for us to be blind to the need to go on the way of the kingdom of God together, and not as mere individuals. It is all too idealistic to play off the Spirit against the institution. The church always realizes itself in a twofold sense: as event – the grace of God – and as institution – in space and in particular spaces, in time and at agreed times, in 'ministry' and in the necessary divisions of tasks, though these must not quench, must not 'grieve' 'the Spirit' (Ephesians 4.30).

The criterion for what the church is remains the kingdom of God; the church arises out of its proclamation, and organizes itself in its direction. Participation in the historical liberation of the people of God by God is and remains the criterion by which we can distinguish the church from a mere apparatus of power. In an ecumenical document which seems to me to be fundamental to the present understanding of what the church means, Philip Potter says: 'The church is the people of God which has been created and hallowed through the exodus in the death and resurrection of Christ. It is called to participate in the suffering of Christ for the redemption of our torn and divided world.'[1]

Wherever God acts in a liberating way in and through human beings, there is participation in the liberating action of God, involvement, allowing oneself to be drawn into the process of liberation; there 'church' appears in the full sense of the word, related to the kingdom of God. By the expression 'historical liberation of God' I mean, first, that God also brings the people out of Egypt today, and then that God's own self is liberated. The hidden God becomes visible, tangible, audible. He does not remain hidden but becomes knowable; it is possible to taste the goodness of God (Psalm 34.9).

The concept of the 'kingdom of God' stands at the centre of the original proclamation of Jesus. This kingdom, of which Jesus speaks mostly in parables, i.e. telling stories about it rather than defining it, is understood as God's nearness to men and women which is experienced in justice, peace, and above all joy. It is also true of the kingdom of God that it is closest to those who are farthest removed from it. The proclamation of the kingdom is addressed to the poor and the wretched: 'kingdom', when portrayed in narrative and pictorial form, expresses the social and political character of liberation more clearly than concepts like 'salvation' or 'redemption'.

> Thy kingdom come! on bended knee
> The passing ages pray;
> And faithful souls have yearned to see
> On earth that kingdom's day.
> The day in whose clear-shining light
> All wrong shall stand revealed,
> When justice shall be throned in might,
> And every hurt be healed.

The correct translation of the New Testament phrase *basileia tou theou* is 'kingly rule of God'. There are many views about how this expression should be rendered. The 'kingly' rule of God is part of an androcentric (male-centred) language, as is the word 'Lord'ship. English-speaking feminist theologians have attempted to talk about 'queendom of God' instead of 'kingdom of God'. Others have attempted to understand the kingdom of God as the 'commonwealth of God', a term which I feel well expresses the communal benefits of salvation in which all human beings share, but which (like 'Reich' in German) has too strong historical connotations. It is a daily difficulty for all who do theology that the basic concepts are overburdened, destroyed or worn out – a difficulty which we shall probably always have to cope with.

Over and above these linguistic difficulties, the term 'kingdom of

God' poses a problem of content which at the same time is what gives it such productivity and depth. The difficulty here is that the time of this kingdom is understood in two ways. On the one hand the kingdom is 'at hand' (Mark 1.15), is described in the present as 'dwelling within you' (Luke 17.21), and on the other it is regarded as a future reality. 'Repent, for the kingdom of heaven is at hand' (Matt.4.17). What is the meaning of 'at hand'? Is God's kingdom there or not? The kingdom of God is 'already there'. The technical term for this experience which the friends of Jesus had is 'present eschatology'; by contrast, when the kingdom is expected only in the future, the term used is 'futurist eschatology'. The two tenses contradict each other: what is there need no longer be expected. And yet they supplement each other in a paradoxical way: only what is already present by being foreshadowed, anticipated in loving expectation, needs confirmation, fulfilment, realization. So the kingdom of God is among us and before us, fulfilled and unfulfilled, already known and tasted, and yet still to come. Paul expresses the same thing when he says, 'But if we have died with Christ, we believe that we shall also live with him. For we know that Christ being raised from the dead dies no more; death has no more dominion over him' (Romans 6.8f.). 'Already there' and 'not yet' represent a complex structure, a 'both-and' which cannot be grasped within positivistic logic. They represent a dialectic, an indissoluble and necessary contradiction in which the church on the way to the kingdom of God shares.

We can see how both the 'already there' and the 'not yet' belong together if we think of relationships between human beings, which must necessarily be different from relationships between people and things. Things can be got by having, acquiring, owning. Actions like acquiring, buying, taking over, lead to a having – in the present. But relationships between human beings are more complicated, and in them the present 'having' destroys the future being. For example, if I think I know someone completely, if I think that by loving him or her I utterly possess him or her in the present, expect no more of him or her, if his or her reactions are predictable, then present security has completely swallowed up future expectation. The eschatology of love destroys itself in a pure present without expectation.

When transferred to the church, that amounts to a self-destruction which begins when the church feels sure of the present Christ and thinks that it 'has' him in word and sacrament. The present possession of the Spirit has then swallowed up the incalculable future of God. If Christ has become completely the possession of such a community, if there is no longer anything unknown, dark, mysterious, about him, then the Christness is stamped with a false triumphalistic certainty, the boundaries are drawn clearly between within and without, church and world, us and them, and God becomes a household object to make use of.

The kind of enduring and all-embracing loving relationship in which we need both the 'now already' and the 'not yet' must be paralleled by the relationship between the church and the kingdom of God. If its relationship to the kingdom of God is the intrinsic criterion for the church without which it becomes an association for the cultivation of religious life, then this dialectic must also be applied here. A church which is stuck in the 'now already' will revolve, above all, around itself; it will no longer expect God. It has become self-sufficient. The immigrant children in its area remain invisible, and the more distant South African children in prison have nothing to do with its banking arrangements. That Christ will finally come again and finally ransom all captives, that the hungry will be filled, is no problem for it in its own satiation. Thus its comfort becomes shallow fellowship, its supposed nearness to God a cutting itself off from the griefs of others, though these are the birth-pangs of the Messiah.

This self-sufficiency of the church of the rich world, its essential interest in self-preservation, contradicts the message of Jesus, which points the disciples towards a greater expectation of festival, of joy, of laughter for all. There is a kind of churchliness which avoids taking account of the theological working out of the 'not yet' and has forgotten all connections with the original Jesus movement. That the first Christians were awaiting the return of Christ as scattered groups with no legal and social status, that they saw in their visions 'a new heaven and a new earth' (Revelation 21.1), without tears and hunger and war, is at best appropriated as a private hope – and is regarded by conformist theologians as wishful thinking trapped in a pre-scientific world. By contrast, the living church, the assembled people of God, which can occasionally be found even among us, is specifically the expression of a waiting for God, a longing for the heavenly Jerusalem. And just as a love without longing becomes stale and boring, so too a church without a hunger and thirst for righteousness becomes superficial, dispensable, accidental.

If this relationship between the kingdom of God and the church remains a 'between the times', a being on the way, then the form of this church of the 'now already' and 'not yet' cannot be defined more closely. According to the New Testament conceptions which gradually become established its task is a threefold one: kerygma, diakonia and koinonia, i.e. proclamation, service and community. All three elements are indispensable and interconnected; where one is missing, the others are also in danger and threatened with ossification.

Kerygma is the Greek word for the proclamation of the Gospel. It means both the act of proclamation – preaching, teaching, instruction – and its content, what is proclaimed, the assurance that the time of salvation promised by the prophets has come and has become visible in the life, death and resurrection of Christ. However, the kerygma is not simply a particular doctrine aimed at the understanding, but a call to new life and to conversion. Those who hear the call and accept the new life are promised the comforting and encouraging spirit of God in the kerygma. They have desperate need of this spirit, because living out the kerygma is always a matter of bearing witness, testifying to the truth. The *martys*, the witness, is part of the proclamation, as its testimony, the *martyrion*, which in certain historical circumstances becomes the testimony of blood, i.e. martyrdom. Diakonia means serving or service. The church is the community of those who are there not to rule but to serve. Church institutions, like Christian Aid, point to this substantial function of the church in offering disinterested service to others – not only to fellow-believers but to all in need. Paul uses the word *douleuo*, to serve in the attitude of the slave (Romans 6.18, 22); in the Gospels the word *diakoneo* appears in the sense of 'perform a personal service', especially at table (e.g. John 12.2). Serving as the attitude of the early community has its foundation in Jesus himself, who has come to serve his own (Luke 12.37) and to wash their feet (John 13.1-20). Service means not just the individual good deed but self-offering, indeed the sacrifice of life. 'The Son of Man also came not to be served but to serve, and to give his life as a ransom for many.' Diakonia was the new element in the first assemblies of the people of God which was terrifying to the pagan environment, and it remained the decisive characteristic of the disciples of Jesus. 'The kings of the Gentiles exercise lordship over them; and those in authority over them that are called benefactors. But not so with you; rather let the greatest among you become as the youngest, and the leader as one who serves. For which is the greater, one who sits at table, or one who serves? Is it not the one who sits at table? But I am among you as one who serves' (Luke 22.25-27). In this context, to serve does not just have a therapeutic or even cosmetic significance, but rather contains criticism of all rule and radically does away with oppression.

The third element of the church is koinonia, communion with God and communion between its members. The koinonia grows out of the church's message and diakonia. Paul uses the word where he speaks of the participation of Christians in God's grace (e.g. I Corinthians 1.9). Now already – in the not yet of the kingdom of God – the church is living the new life, the new lifestyle; in communion with God men and women trust one another, share their resources, find a different way of dealing with one another from that offered to them by 'this' world of rivalry and anxiety about one another. The great pietist Count Zinzendorf (1700-1760) said: 'I do not hold to any Christianity without community', without a community supported by the spirit of Christ, which in practice behaves in a different way. There is no living church without lived koinonia, shared life. Its clearest and most tangible expression is the liturgy: in praise and prayer, dance and music, celebration of the eucharist and baptism (to mention just the Protestant sacraments), the people of God celebrates its community and its being on the way.

Where there is a living church, kerygma, diakonia and koinonia appear together as its basic elements. We can read church history, asking which of these three functions was most important and which was neglected at a particular time. We can also think through our own church experiences by means of these three dimensions: where have I encountered kerygma, where have I learned something for my life? Where has diakonia come alive for me? Where have I been helped and where have I been used? Where have I met koinonia, where was I supported and felt myself 'inside'?

When I think of the experiences with the church which have become important to me in recent years, what come to mind are some services which have been held not in houses but in the open air; not in churches, but before the cathedrals and walls of death in our country, in Mutlangen, in Brokdorf, in the Hunsrück.[2] At these services of prayer I could hear the gospel, the liberating message, or at least its promise. Here witness was given, simply by people going to such a remote,

The Three Dimensions of the Church

Kerygma	Diakonia	Koinonia
Proclamation, preaching, teaching	Service, serving	Communion with God and with the rest of the community
Communication of the message by word and sacrament	Offering help to people in need	
Concretion of the will of God	Social and political diakonia instead of theocracy	Building up the community
Bearing witness to the life of Christ	Being there for others	New lifestyle
		Praise and celebration
Martyria	Orthopraxy	Liturgy

Characteristics of the Christian community (according to Potter)

Kerygma	Diakonia	Koinonia
Participation	Sharing	Unity of the churches
Confessing	Healing	Expectation of the kingdom of God
Learning	Reconciling	

strictly controlled and totally supervised place. Here everyone was entrusted with a political diakonia, in that they went on to explain what they saw and heard. Those on whom we are now already inflicting famine through our bombs were present in our prayers. Above all, however, here I experienced community, a solidarity of those who share their anxieties and hopes, their tea and their shelter. When we prayed 'Thy kingdom come' before the great wall which in the Hunsrück even now separates the medium-range rockets from the people living around, everyone knew what the prayer meant. We had become one in the face of the overwhelming power of military technology, the police and soldiers, 'one in Christ'.

One of the main dangers of Protestantism lies in its excessive stress on the kerygma, or more properly, on the kerygma reduced to preaching. The church is regarded as the place where preaching is done. Church takes place between ten and eleven on Sunday morning. The two other functions of the church disappear from view and hardly affect the ordinary members of the congregation. As it is usually only the women in the local communities who provide diakonia for the old, sick and lonely, the whole community is not involved in diakonia. Nothing is said about the diakonia of women and it is certainly not understood as perhaps the better preaching. Moreover, in any division of work, diakonia is assigned to diaconal works: the necessary political diakonia of peace groups, Third World groups and ecology groups is at best tolerated on the periphery.

If church *de facto* consists in sitting still for an hour on Sunday without getting to know anyone else, the unity of kergyma, diakonia and koinonia is destroyed. How can any life develop which deserves the name 'church', in the sense of the assembled people of God?

I think that a preferred place for the experience of the church today is the ecumenical world. Fellowship with Christians who come from other traditions, Christians, for example, in the United States who have many democratic features in their worship, helps us towards an exodus from the widespread weariness, boredom and staleness with church. In his Vancouver report, to which I want to refer again here, Philip Potter refers to eight criteria for the 'house of living stones' (I Peter 2.5) which we call the church. The first three, participation, confessing and learning, relate to the kerygma. Sharing, healing and reconciling relate to diakonia. And koinonia arises in the unity of the churches – which is to be built up – and their expectation of God's kingdom.

Real proclamation arises in a 'fellowship of participation'. All are called to an egalitarian community which Reformed doctrine speaks of as the 'universal priesthood of all believers'. Participation is the opposite concept to hierarchy, the holy rule of priests over laity, men over women, old over young. 'It must not be so among you,' said Jesus (Matthew 20.26). I Peter attests participation in the bond with the expression 'be yourselves built into a spiritual house, a holy priesthood'. But this original 'royal priesthood' of the community (2.9) to which all are called 'has degenerated over the course of history into a kind of individualistic, pietistic religion'.[3] Hierarchy then replaced participation.

Furthermore a fellowship of confessing, of bearing witness, goes with proclamation. But confessing does not mean asserting in season and out of season that Christ has redeemed us, as some fundamentalists believe; above all it means, rather as in the Quaker tradition, speaking the truth to the powerful. 'Speak truth to power' is the task of any Christian and of the community. A church publicly confessing the faith in this way is at the same time a community of learners. In the Bible learning is a process in which people develop a relationship to God and his way of truth, justice and peace, so that they can follow this way obediently in their relationship to one another and extend it to all peoples. Moses says: 'The Lord said to me, "Gather the people to me, that I may let them hear my words, so that they may learn to fear me all the days that they live upon the earth... And the Lord commanded me at that time to teach you statutes and ordinances, that you might do them in the land which you are going over to possess"' (Deuteronomy 4.10,14). The prophet Isaiah prays to God: 'My soul yearns for you in the night, my spirit within me earnestly seeks you. For when your judgments are in the earth, the inhabitants of the world learn righteousness' (26.9).

To many people the formulas of the kerygma sound all too timeless, all too distant and remote. Is proclamation really always the same unchanged and unchangeable message of God's love? But what kind of a love would it be which in such repeated assertions trickled down from heaven without any concern for the real situation of the recipients? Kerygma, precisely if we keep in view the event, the act of proclamation, cannot simply always be 'the same dish'.

No one has seen that so sharply in this century as Dietrich Bonhoeffer, to whom we owe the best ecclesiological statements (i.e. statements related to the church) in German. After a short period working both in a theological faculty and in the pastorate, during the time of the Church Struggle Bonhoeffer became wholly involved in the church. In his book *The Cost of Discipleship*, which first appeared in 1937, he took issue with his church (the Church of the Old Prussian Union), a church of 'cheap grace', which isolated the kerygma of the justification of the sinner from the discipleship of Christ. Over against a universal kerygma, which is always the same because it is not binding, Bonhoeffer recalls the concreteness of the word of God. 'The church must be able to say the Word of God, the word of authority, here and now, in the most concrete way possible, from knowledge of the situation. The church may not therefore preach timeless principles, however true, but only commandments which are true today.' According to this insight of Bonhoeffer's the Word of God is not simply a correct principle, the repetition of an established truth – that would only be powerlessness, which parrots previous bad developments. Real proclamation cannot take place without risk. It is bound to a participatory community of those who confess and those who learn. 'For what is "always" true is not true today in particular. God is "always" God to us "today"... Can the church preach the commandment of God with the same certainty with which it preaches the gospel? Can the church say, "We need a socialist ordering of the economic system", or, "Do not engage in war", with the same certainty as it can say, "Your sins are forgiven you?"'[4]

Bonhoeffer answers this question not with self-assurance, but with a reassured yes. His questions to the church as to whether it may legitimately adopt a political standpoint are as topical today as they were in the Nazi period. Even today, Protestant church leaders and conservative theologians are fond of evading this question by playing off the Lutheran conception of 'law' as God's threatening, demanding, punishing words against the 'gospel' as the forgiving, gracious word that brings men and women happiness. The church may preach only the second, the good message, in confidence and security. All that it says in criticism of society is merely 'law', and not really the message of the church. This common division between law and gospel leads to the absurd weakness of the church, which sets about forgiving sinners their sins, but no longer dares to mention sin itself. Because we live in a pluralist world and cannot clearly recognize what is said to us about nuclear power and the economic order, there is no injunction to recognize the will of God today. In this way the church separates message from discipleship and in so doing destroys the original sense of kergyma, which is bound up with *martyria*, testimony.

This tendency to celebrate 'proclamation as a substitute for discipleship' becomes terrifyingly clear in the latest statement from the Seventh Synod of the Evangelical Church in Germany, in November 1988: 'The nature of the church is certainly not defined by what human beings bring about in it. It is not described as an ideal society, nor are Christians described as better people. Rather, the nature of the church consists in men and women hearing the word of Jesus Christ and as sinners appropriating salvation in proclamation and in the sacraments, and handing it on.' This is precisely what Bonhoeffer calls 'cheap grace'. Christians in the Nazi period conformed with the Nazis, and Christians today are economic conformists, even if this conformity involves the destruction of God's creation. Such a church separates the kerygma from discipleship. 'Of course,' the synod text goes on, 'in this definition it is always presupposed that God's word also brings forth fruit.'[5] The 'also' in this statement is treacherous: the application of faith to life is understood as a second step, which can also be lacking. Orthodoxy is separated from orthopraxy. 'The church has always been a mixed entity and will remain so. Only God knows whether or not one believes.'[6]

The pious tone only obscures reality; whether Hitler or Pinochet 'believe' anything is irrelevant to the victims of both of them, and to the people of God. Real faith cannot be detached from love any more than the message of testimony and discipleship can.

I return once again to Bonhoeffer, because this teacher of the church saw very clearly that any retreat to the supposedly 'pure' gospel without discipleship goes against the spirit of Christ. He pleaded that the church should take the risk of setting out to proclaim God's commands as being valid today, 'as concretely, exclusively and radically as can be conceived'.[7] He thought that the church had to keep silent until it could formulate clear positions. His understanding of the gospel was not ethics-free. The church can in fact speak in concrete terms about armaments, inflicting famine and destroying the creation, because for itself it believes in the forgiveness of sins. That we are fallible people and can make mistakes did not lead Bonhoeffer to withdraw from the world of action. The spirit of relativism and 'anything goes' which characterizes the 1988 synod paper was alien to Bonhoeffer; the church may not avoid drawing on the full extent of its knowledge so as then to be able to say concretely and clearly, 'Do not go to war and do not prepare for it!' Bonhoeffer refers to Luther's admonition *pecca fortiter* (sin clearly and boldly). In *The Cost of Discipleship* he writes: 'The only answer to the difficulties of ethical conflict is God's commandment itself and thus the demand to stop discussing and at last to obey. Only the devil has a solution to ethical conflict to offer, and that is: keep on asking questions, and then you won't have to obey.'[8] These sarcastic comments of Bonhoeffer's reflect a controversy with a church which has 'replaced simple action... by ambivalent thought'[9]. The *orthodox* tradition has put proclamation and kerygma so much in the forefront in Protestantism that there is hardly any theological reflection on the two other elements which keep the church alive, diakonia and koinonia.

As Lutheran orthodoxy understands it, the church is based on the 'unfalsified preaching of God's word in law and gospel and the celebration of the sacraments in accordance with Holy Scripture'. In the Reformation view there are only two marks (*notae*) of the true church: sound doctrine and the celebration of the sacraments, as the 1530 Augsburg Confession put it (Article VII). Thus tradition as a source of revelation, the hierarchical structure of the church, the apostolic succession, and other elements of the Catholic doctrine of the church are declared to be inessential. This positive formula is remarkably arid: against the fullness, riches and beauty of the Catholic tradition the new beginning had to reflect on central issues: the Reformation understood itself above all as a process of purification, reduction and concentration. Nevertheless, as the place where preaching is done the church is a caricature of this tradition: people go to the liturgy without really participating in what goes on, and the experience of worship means being put utterly at the mercy of an authoritarian communication structure.

Liberalism changed this very little. Here, too, diakonia played a subsidiary role and kononia increasingly faded away. The role of the church was reduced within the division of church and state: the church limited itself to the inward and transcendental content of Christian faith and left out the socio-political dimension. Diakonia then simply becomes charity, help given to the victims, without a prophetic criticism which goes to the roots and without social change. The building up of the community, the element of koinonia, is neglected on the basis of individualism. Participation in being a Christian takes place through participation in the kerygma, not in diakonia and koinonia. That is a definition of bourgeois Christianity!

Two great counter-movements against such an understanding of the church were pietism and the revival movements with their stress on the community which arises out of the gospel. But even they could not alter the fact that the church did not take the most important demands of social and political life seriously. Here I might mention industrialization, the formation of the proletariat, colonialism, militarization, the emphasis on war. These are the central demands to which the church largely reacted only in the affirmative; it went along with them and howled with all these wolves. Its diakonia was reduced to the micro-social level of the community. We can again learn what diakonia really means from Dietrich Bonhoeffer, and then from the ecumenical movement. The idea of a church without privileges, a 'church for others', runs right through Bonhoeffer's thinking; in prison he sketches a vision of the church which we must not forget:

> The church is the church only when it exists for others. To make a start it should give away all its property to those in need. The clergy must live solely on the free-will offerings of their congregations, or possibly engage in some secular calling. The church must share in the secular problems of ordinary human life, not dominating, but helping and serving. It must tell men of every calling what it means to live in Christ, to exist for others.[10]

These requirements anticipate liberation theology. In this vision diakonia becomes social diakonia to the poor. The Brazilian cardinal Paolo Avaristo Arns describes the church in these terms: 'The church exists to defend the life of the poor people. It exists to speak the truth. It exists to further justice.' By putting itself on the side of the poor, the church risks losing its privileges. By interceding for those who have disappeared and those who are tortured it takes the side of Christ. By – like Cardinal Arns – mentioning the debt crisis which has arisen in the interest of the rich and is to be paid off by the poorest, it is not just proclaiming a merely temporal word of the 'law', nor is it going beyond its competence, as people are so fond of saying, but is moving from mere orthodoxy into the sphere of orthopraxy. The gospel for the poor, the good news for them, is at the same time intrinsically *dys-angelium*, a threat, to the rich. Cardinal Arns says:

> We must stop giving the blood and misery of our people in order to pay the First World... My conviction is that everyone in the First World who has faith must stand up and say: the peoples of the Third World will die if they have no money, if they have to pay even the interest on their debts. They are our sisters, our brothers; they are the children for whom we in the First World are responsible.[11]

Such remarks by a church leader – and corresponding praxis in communion with the poor – clarify the image of a church without privileges which is envisaged in the ecumenical world today. According to Philip Potter, the 'living stones' which form a habitable house represent the community of the church from the perspective of sharing, healing and reconciliation. A fellowship of sharing is a community which practises sharing, first of material and technological resources, but also of the 'gifts of the Spirit'. In this kind of sharing Potter also has in mind persecution, torture and death, which are a consequence of discipleship for many Christians in Latin America, South Africa, the Philippines and other parts of the world. The church should also share the 'gifts for the life of the world', which are often the sacrifice of life, in the sense of a community of prayer and action. To mention a simple example of this praxis: in many countries the day of the murder of Archbishop Oscar Romero (24 March 1980) is commemorated and celebrated in services. In this way the communion, koinonia, of the whole body of Christ is built up.

Other definitions of the community of the church are its capacity to heal and to reconcile. 'Heal' here is used in the original sense of physical and spiritual healing of members of the body of Christ who are separated from one another. The stronger are mobilized to support the weaker. But the term also includes all the healing action that we perform towards creation.

Indifference or resignation over the destruction of nature is disastrous: the healing community also includes the cosmos. The 'reconciling' community is the church to the degree that it stands for the inseparability of justice and peace, demolishes the dominant hostile clichés, and does not become an echo of power politics but follows the call of the Sermon of the Mount to make peace.

These definitions of the church go far beyond our image of the church, reduced to the official church. We need them if we are to broaden our view and to perceive other possibilities for such living community than those which are all too well known to us. As an example I shall quote from a joint letter which three American bishops, a Methodist, an Anglican and a Catholic from the diocese of Michigan, wrote in the winter of 1988:

Dear Sister Church,

To walk in the footsteps of Jesus is often to be out of step with the people around. In some times and places, that is more evident than in others. For the first three centuries, Christians were 'outlaws', and no one had to remind them that they were out of step. In our own day, the issue of nuclear arms has made us particularly aware of our being out of step... For the past three years we three Bishops have joined our voices with many others seeking peace by jointly calling people to Faith and Resistance Retreats. The retreat experience of coming together to pray, to study and make decisions about actions we might take has been a healing and inspiring experience. The ecumenical prayer vigils and witness (which for some included civil disobedience) at sites in Michigan where nuclear weapons are manufactured or deployed have been a witness to the broader community.[12]

This document shows the change which is taking place in the churches in many parts of the world. The unity of the churches is growing in joint prayer and action. Unity and expectation, the last two criteria of the church in the ecumenical sense, are growing. Leonardo Boff said in an interview:

In the last twenty years many laypeople, proletariat and peasants, have come into the church and have discovered and used the church as a place of freedom where they can work under the protection of the church without being oppressed by the police. And these simple people have converted the bishops, the theologians, the priests. Before the church decided for the poor, the poor decided for the church. This collaboration between church and popular movement is the new form of the church. And it has produced many prophets, for example Helder Camara, the Brazilian forerunner of liberation theology.[13]

The church, interpreted in terms of liberation theology, puts the element of diakonia, of service, at the centre and develops its community and message from being there for one another.

Many women base-theologians in the Third World, also sometimes called 'barefoot theologians', see their task more in looking after the water supply for their community than in writing sermons or articles. They organize the poorest, identify their needs, and visit the city authorities to get material. One of their most important experiences is the way in which koinonia, community, arises out of diakonia and being there for others. The church which comes into being in this way reconciles orthopraxy with the orthodoxy which dominates in the Western churches. It develops the elements of teaching and community from its understanding of service. Base communities gather around concrete tasks and needs, and from the communities, attempts develop to live the new life credibly in another life-style. The main spiritual task of many theologians is then to overcome the basic individualistic understanding of progress – How do I do that? How can I earn enough? How can I bring my family through? – in the direction of community.

In this connection I have heard a wonderful example from El Salvador, told by a pastor in a poor area. He had to marry three couples – and marriage is the exception there, since the majority of the population live together without marrying. These people had eight children in all. The priest asked, 'Why do you want to get married?' Their reply was, 'To serve the community – *al servicio de la communidad.*' They did not marry to be more sure of one another, and the individualistic understanding of marriage as a contract between two people did not play any role. But they believed that they could be there for the community better as married couples.

The connection with liberation theology becomes quite clear here. The life-functions of the church are disclosed through service, diakonia. The building up of the community is an aim completely modelled on the New Testament, if one remembers how in I Corinthians Paul reflects on the building up of a community of equals who are different. People are at different stages on the Christian way (8.7-11; 10.23) and they contribute different gifts and powers (12.1-11)). The goal is the building up of a living community, the 'house of living stones' (I Peter 2.5). Experiences of this kind are had nowadays in base communities. The message is read anew in the service of the poor. In Latin America today there are thousands of pamphlets, leaflets, duplicated catechisms and songs, tiny little texts in popular style which ask questions like: What are we in the world for? Why has Christ come? What follows from this for our life? Simple questions are being raised all over again, as they were during the Reformation in Europe.

And indeed at present a Reformation is taking place in many places among Christians of the Third World. Things are enquired into again, and every woman and every man can understand what is meant. The Bible is also being read anew, as we know from Ernesto Cardenal's conversations in Solentiname.

All that is developing in Latin America from a traditional, extremely ritualized Catholicism, which has hardly any preaching, which only celebrates the mass, which traditionally does not engage in any service, but participates in oligarchic rule, and produces no community because it affirms or tolerates as given by nature its main obstacle, the extreme division of society into classes. The renewal of the church in the direction of the kingdom of God which has grown out of the base communities and which is expressed reflectively in liberation theology is one of the great events of church history in our time. In this process the poor, dispersed, shamed, disorganized people of God is taking part in God's historical liberation.

According to a principle of liberation theology these poor are 'the teachers'. They evangelize us, proclaim the message to us and teach us to read the Bible. Often their theological literacy, their capacity to read in the book of life, seems to be much further developed than among those in our secular world who are subjected to the idols of consumerism. There is a good deal to be learned and discovered from them theologically, but above all they have undertood one feature of the kingdom of God differently from us and more deeply than us, i.e. joy. Perhaps we can learn most from their festivals, their songs, the dedication of their lives, perhaps once again in order to become the church which expresses God's nearness to men and women as joy.

13 The Theology of Peace

The definition of the content of the kingdom of God, its peace and its joy, has seldom become the object of systematic theological questioning. Apart from the historical peace churches, the Quakers, Mennonites and Brethren, the great churches have usually considered the theme of peace relevant only in social and ethical terms. It is completely absent from many outlines of Western theology or merely becomes the application of theological teaching, instead of being understood as the substance of God's action. From a biblical perspective it is difficult to justify this shift of emphasis, the over-theologizing of particular beliefs related to faith and the de-theologizing of others. Peace is a central theme of the biblical writings. The basic significance of *shalom* as faring well, prospering, goes far beyond the so-called negative concept of peace common among us, which means the absence of the open and collective use of violence; in thought under Greek influence, peace is simply the opposite of war. In the philosophy of mutual deterrence the negative concept of peace (*eirene*) is used: the *status quo* of threat, hunger, anxiety, lack of freedom is prescribed, without peace being given a positive content as the fruit of righteousness, which is what happens in biblical thought. The peace of the kingdom of God is the richer concept which combines inner peace with social and external political peace. Eating and health are as much part of *shalom* as community and hope. In *shalom* not only is violence between human beings overcome, but also economic need and exploitation, the lack of political freedom and psychological anxiety. Some Jewish rabbis said that *shalom* is a name of God.

Here I shall first-investigate the biblical tradition and then describe the various attitudes of Christianity to war; thirdly, I shall ask to which of the historical theologies of peace the three theological approaches refer and who are really the peacemakers here.

At many points the Bible speaks of the longing of the peoples for peace, for the end of state violence, and of the hope for the 'prince of peace' who rules in such a way that 'peace will have no end' (Isaiah 9.6f.). The Hebrew Bible indicates that God wants peace, and not the rule of force by arms and war, by saying that God not only converts human hearts but also reforges or destroys the weapons of violence, because these instruments of the rule of force, which we so often see as 'neutral', have in fact long possessed human hearts. Like Gandhi, the Bible, too, knows that in human hands the means – armaments – will become the goals of power and invincible strength: over against that, scripture insists that God is our only 'stronghold', and that love is the only certainty on earth.

> The Lord of hosts is with us,
> the God of Jacob is our refuge.
> Come hither and behold the works of the Lord,
> the wonders that he has done upon earth,
> he makes wars to cease in all the world,
> he breaks the bow and shatters the spear
> and burns the chariots in the fire.
> Be still and know that I am God (Psalm 46.8-11a).

God directs the wars and national catastrophes which are echoed in Psalm 46, on which Luther's hymn 'A Safe Stronghold our God is Still' is based. Despite all preparations for violence and love of violence, God breaks the bows of war, as he broke his own bow in the story of Noah and made it a rainbow of peace (Genesis 9.12-17). God destroys the weapons of murder, God intervenes, the Godhead is with its people to produce peace, and this peace as a basic concept is characterized by the fact that peace and justice belong very closely together. 'If only you had heeded my commandments,' says God to the people. 'Your prosperity (*shalom*) would have become like the river and your salvation (*tsedaqa*, righteousness) like the waves of the sea' (Isaiah 48.18). *Shalom* and *tsedaqa*, peace and justice, belong together, as in this parallelism, which is a characteristic Hebrew way of putting things.

By righteousness the prophets understand a life of community in justice. Those who have built houses will also dwell in them; those who have planted vineyards will also drink their wine. The coming kingdom of peace is conceived of terms of righteousness and justice: God will 'judge between many peoples, and shall decide for strong nations from afar off; and they shall beat their swords into plough-shares, and their spears into pruning hooks; nation shall not lift up sword against nation, neither shall they learn war any more; but they shall sit each under their vine and under their fig tree, and no one shall be afraid' (Micah 4.3f.). These are biblical conceptions of what peace in justice really is. *Shalom* is not an abstract, and in the Hebrew Bible there are no examples of *shalom* denoting the spiritual attitude of inner pece. Moreover the term is usually applied to a community, and rarely to an individual. *Shalom* is a concept of the good life which men and women can live and by which they can die old and full of years, because their days are numbered and they do not perish prematurely through war and injustice.

The foundation of peace is righteousness. 'Grace and truth meet each other, righteousness and peace kiss each other' (Psalm 85.11). The goal is the state in which God has destroyed the chariots and put an end to aggression. Without social justice, without righteousness, there is no peace. According to the prophets the criterion is the right of those without rights – for example women and orphans, who have no male advocate. The lowest class is made the criterion for the prosperity of all: those who have been most deprived of their rights, who have least to say, who not only have no money but also no advocate, no connections, who cannot even go to the authorities because they do not know what they can claim – they are the criterion of what righteousness really is. The excluded, the marginalized, those who are on the lowest rung of the ladder of a society, are lifted up, and the high are 'brought low', so that there is a 'straight highway for God' (Isaiah 40.3f.). Foreign politics and domestic politics are not separated here, as though in foreign politics one can be dominating, imperialistic, intent on arming oneself, while at the same time main-taining law and order at home. Righteousness and peace belong together in the same way as armaments and *law*. Peace in the full sense of the word *shalom* comes about only in conjunction with righteousness. In biblical thinking it is therefore wrong to assert that nuclear weapons have guaranteed us peace for forty years, in so far as over the same period they have guaranteed famine for people in two-thirds of the world. A peace based on deterrence and force, on terror, misery and threat, is anti-biblical, because it makes armaments and not justice the foundation of peace.

That there are two fundamentally different kinds of peace becomes even clearer in the New Testament, as soon as we take into account the political and social structure under which people lived at that time. It is vital to grasp this overall structure in order to understand God's peace in a world without peace and to learn the *Pax Christi* as one's own praxis in contrast to the *Pax Romana*. When I studied theology in Göttingen years ago, no one told me anything about the real world of the New Testament. I regarded the *Pax Romana* as a well-ordered system with good administration. Road building, water supplies, Roman law were regarded as the great cultural achievements of the Romans. As I understood things then, the *Pax Romana*, that guarantee of peace by the empire for the whole of the known earth, followed from *Ius Romanum*, Roman law. I did not connect this world dominated by law and order with the real misery depicted in the New Testament. The many sick people on almost every page of the Gospel reports, the blind, perhaps afflicted with endemic eye diseases, the depressives and schizophrenics, possessed by demons - it did not occur to me to see these as consequences of the blissful *Pax Romana*. I am reporting my own long learning process here to show how one can keep things in one's mind without recognizing the connections, as a result of particular forms of brainwashing which one does not recognize as such. I did not understand the New Testament against its social, economic and political background: Rome's rule of the world defined as the *Pax Romana*.

Luke's Christmas story already speaks of it. 'The time came when a command went out from Caesar Augustus that all the world should be taxed' (Luke 2.1). The emperor Augustus proclaimed his rule, the *Pax Augusta*, as a time of peace. *Pax Romana* was the central theological and political concept, comparable to what we now call the 'free world'. Altars and triumphal arches were erected to peace, harmony and the prosperity of the Roman people. When I stood for the first time in Rome before the altar of peace, the Ara Pacis Augustae (dedicated in AD 11), I was still looking through the eyes of the victors; I still believed in peace as the Romans understood it. In reality this peace meant subjection and misery, plundering and slavery, lack of rights and freedom. Luise Schottroff writes:

Peace and security proclaimed on coins the blessings of the government. After the destruction of the temple in Jerusalem in AD 70,
in AD 75 a temple of peace was built by Vespasian in Rome. The
bloody triumph over the Jewish people was celebrated. To this day
the Jewish people have not forgotten the deadly peace celebrated
by Vespasian.

For the Jews this peace was the final defeat, the destruction
of national identity; the wailing wall in Jerusalem speaks of the
annihilation and must be seen in conjunction with the 'temple of
peace' in Rome: humiliation, suffering and lament for the subjected,
'peace' for the victors. The *Pax Romana* was 'defined quite unsenti-
mentally and without humanistic veiling by the rulers of the Roman
empire: peace and security meant the subjection of other peoples by
victory over them'.[1] The political content of Roman peace consisted
in the central power of Rome as a geopolitical centre subjecting to
itself the peoples on the periphery. Any rebellion, even the first
recognizable stirring of a rebellion, was overthrown. In this context
of necessary peace measures we must also see the crucifixion of Jesus
as a measure which guaranteed the *Pax Romana*. 'Peace' and 'security'
were religio-political terms: Paul saw through them as propaganda
slogans: 'The day of the Lord will come like a thief in the night. When
people say "There is peace and security," then suddenly destruction
will come upon them as travail comes upon a woman with child, and
there will be no escape' (I Thessalonians 5.2ff.). The day of the Lord
is seen as a day of judgment on a world which allegedly has a peaceful
order. Paul recognizes that talk of 'peace and security' is an ideology,
a sham, which is spread over a bloody repression to conceal the reality.
Already in Jeremiah there is a criticism of false peace-propaganda:
'They have healed the wound of my people lightly by saying "Peace,
peace" where there is no peace. Were they ashamed when they
committed abominations? No, they were not at all ashamed; they did
not know how to blush' (Jeremiah 6.14).

We know this 'Peace, peace', or, 'We are all for peace'. Peace
propaganda was also necessary in the Roman empire as part of general
process of tranquillization by the authorities; reality looked different.
The basis of peace was the extensive militarism of the Romans. A
giant professional army was maintained: on present-day calculations
around three per cent of the population was constantly under arms.

People were conscripted or enrolled as mercenaries; among the many people without land or work there were always those who were ready to choose hard but relatively well-paid military service; that meant further misery for the wives and children who were left behind.

Only military power could hold the empire together and guarantee the peace of the *Pax Romana*. For this peace included the systematic plundering of the subject people, of which the Christmas story also tells. The popular census for which Mary and Joseph go to Bethlehem is a consequence of the *Pax Romana* for ordinary people in Palestine. In the Gospel of Luke their journey is connected with the repressive measures of the emperor. The subject peoples are to be taxed. At one point Luke stresses that this taxation was new and unprecedented. With narrative skill he puts representatives of Roman state power at the beginning and the end of his Gospel, so that the references to the Emperor and his representative and to Pontius Pilate supplement each other: the life of Jesus is determined from birth to death by the power structure of the empire. It is not a timeless legend of a hero from the people but the story of liberation from oppression, with the subjection, taxation, compulsory war service and auxiliary service, torture, interrogation, spying, and judicial murder of the innocent which goes with that oppression.

In the story of the birth of Jesus in Luke 2 the peace of God is set over against this kind of peace, the *Pax Romana*. 'Peace on earth and goodwill to the people' (2.14) says the angel; not, however, to the princes and rulers, but to the landless proletariat whom we usually tend romantically to call 'shepherds'. They did not own anything; the herds were simply entrusted to them. They were part of the poor who tremble with fear if one even addresses them. 'They were very afraid' (Luke 2.9). That has often been interpreted in purely religious terms; I would prefer to interpret it as an expression of the anxiety of the subjected in the face of all who are greater, higher or stronger. These wretched people are promised another peace: 'Peace on earth to those with whom God is well pleased.' This is not a peace which comes about in the beyond and exists just for the individual soul, but rather is peace on this earth. The *shalom* of God is a peace which the Jew Jesus conceived of in Jewish terms, i.e. in terms of righteousness. In Luke 2 the *Pax Christi*, as the tradition was later to call this *shalom*, is clearly opposed to the *Pax Romana*. It does not come down from the distant and exalted Rome of the emperor through his governors and imposed rulers, but begins with the poor: they are promised a different life. Peace does not begin in the palace, but in the manger.

One of the basic problems of a Christianity which has been corrupted and become spiritless is that the churches have continually sought to unite the *Pax Christi* and the *Pax Romana* as though they could enjoy both together. Even today, many Christians think that one can live by bearing inwardly in one's heart the peace of Christ which comforts us as individuals and relying outwardly on the *Pax Romana* and the order which it imposes by force. But the *Pax Christi* was never simply space marked out within the peace which the empire had to offer. Christ's peace is not 'of this world', as the Gospel of John puts it. It does not come from the world of domination and subjection. 'My peace I give to you; not as the world gives do I give to you' (John 14.27). This 'other' peace is promised to 'other' people and it attracts other messengers of peace. 'Glory to God in the highest' and 'Peace on earth' belong together: we dishonour God if we prepare war on earth. So we must understand the *Pax Christi* which comes into the world with the birth of Jesus as a history of peacemaking, a history of the interruption of violence. The tradition often expresses the same idea with a concept which we can easily misunderstand: peace as a gift of God. 'He is our peace' (Ephesians 2.14). But this 'gift' is not something that has fallen from heaven, which happens to one like a legacy in the case of the rich or a remission of debt in the case of the poor. The gift of God is the incitement to peace, repeated historically: it draws us into the process of the interruption of violence; it gathers around itself people who follow the other peace and go through the land with the prince of peace. 'God's kingdom is near' was the greeting given by Jesus' messengers; they said, 'Peace be with you!' as a greeting because they too regarded *shalom* as one of the names of God. Jesus and his women disciples and friends proclaimed God's kingdom of peace – and where they were heard, life changed. 'When you enter into a house, first say, "Peace (*shalom*) be to this house." And if a son of peace is there your peace will rest on him; if not, it will return to you' (Luke 10.5f.). For the Jesus movement, a son or a daughter of peace was someone who accepted the message that God's kingdom is near, with all its consequences. Those who rejected this message could be recognized as having drawn God's judgment down upon themselves. 'I have not come to bring peace, but a sword' (Matthew

10.34). This statement by Jesus is not against the *shalom* of God but against those who refuse peace and separate themselves from Christ.

However, historically it has been cruelly misunderstood and misused. The clash between the *Pax Romana* and the *Pax Christi* is clearly noted in the New Testament as being the resistance offered by the Jesus movement,[2] but in the history of the Christian churches, other solutions of the relationship between the two also developed. In essentials there are three different Christian attitudes to war and peace: the earliest Christian pacifism, the theory of the 'just war' and the ideology of the holy war. These are different historical options which Christians have adopted towards peace at different times.

The earliest Christian pacifism arose out of the situation of Christians who were Roman soldiers and had to offer sacrifice to the emperor. They had recognized the divinity of the emperor with two grains of incense put on the sacrificial dish of the Imperator. In Miguel d'Escoto's interpretation of the cross we heard a topical contemporary reference to this practice. Jews and many Christians could not reconcile that with their faith in the one God, and therefore objected to military service. They refused to take the sword. Referring to the fifth commandment, 'You shall not kill', and to the command to love their enemies in the Sermon of the Mount, church teachers until well into the fourth century also thought that war service could not be reconciled with Christian faith. Thus there developed within the early communities a dissociation from political, economic and military power which varied from disinterested loyalty to forced expressions of loyalty and a practice of resistance.

Christians never totally submitted to the power of the state, and practised a pacifism which essentially rests on non-cooperation. 'Do not be conformed to the order of this world' (Romans 12.2) clearly expresses their attitude as resistance against evil and obedience to God, in contrast to the formula in Romans 13.1, 'Let every person be subject to the governing authorities,'[3] which has been overused in Protestantism. This passage, too, can be interpreted in terms of the life of the early Christians. The members of subject peoples had to make declarations of loyalty to Rome like that in Romans 13.1-7. Roman religious policy tolerated alien religions as long as they did not come into conflict with the state authorities – there was a sphere of *religio licita*. In cases of conflict, declarations like this were insufficient, and did not protect Christians from persecution, as we can see from

Paul's own fate. One cannot infer a doctrine of the state in principle from this text, and above all it must not be played off against 'We must obey God rather than human beings' (Acts 5.29). The latter was something which both Jews and Christians took for granted, and it shaped the pacifist practice of the first centuries of Christianity. There were martyrs among the Christians who preferred to die rather than take the sword. The great saint Martin of Tours (316-397) has been remembered and praised in Christian narrative tradition because though he was descended from an officer's family and became a soldier at an early stage, he refused to perform military service.

This earliest Christian tradition was later continued in the peace churches as refusal: refusal to be conscripted, refusal to do military serivce, to pay war taxes, to support war in a variety of forms. Nowadays the questions arise for peace churches in an intensified form, like these. Is it enough to refuse to do military service when the military and industrial complex is swallowing up our taxes and employing half our scientists and engineers? Is not the professional non-cooperation of technologists also a Christian demand today? The 20,000 scientists and engineers worldwide who are refusing to take part in the Strategic Defence Initiative ('Star Wars') are a sign of this kind of refusal to offer the emperor the grains of incense which belong to God. Here are consequences which the Christians among them can base on the earliest Christian pacifism. Two theological motives had an effect here: one is the commandment 'Thou shalt not kill' (Exod.20.13); the other goes back to the first commandment, which Luther calls the principal one. It prohibits the worship of other gods – and in the pacifist tradition the state is the most powerful and the most violent idol. Uncertain justice, conscription, the threat of persecution and its constant renewal characterized the situation of the Christian communities up to the 'Constantinian shift'. Under Constantine, who was well disposed to the Christians, their attitude to state order changed: through the Edict of Milan Constantine gave Christians unqualified public recognition. By transferring the privileges of the old pagan state religion to the Christian church, he relieved Christians of their anxiety and disinterested loyalty and bound them to universal political practice, for which military service and waging war were a matter of course.[4] How was that ethically possible?

The answer to this question is given by the 'doctrine of just war' which Augustine (353-430) formulated in connection with Roman state philosophy and which was later developed by Thomas Aquinas (1225-1274/75). Absurd as it may sound to us that war can ever be said to be 'just', we must understand this church doctrine historically as an attempt to limit and to tame the arbitrariness, brutality and amorality of war. Attempts were made to establish conditions which were essential if a war was to be justified. The most important criteria were:

The authority which declares war must be legitimate.

A prince, a government can declare war, but not a private person.

The ultimate aim must be peace.

The subjective motivation may not be either hatred or vengeance.

The war must be a last resort; there must be negotiations beforehand.

Success must at least appear possible. If the cause is lost from the start, this (extremely pragmatic) criterion comes into force.

These criteria define the *ius ad bellum*, i.e. the legal basis for waging a just war.

It seems to me that the defensive war which Nicaragua has been waging for years against the invading Contras accords with these criteria of a just war.

Further criteria relate to the *ius in bello*; they form the legal basis for conduct within a war.

The means used must be unavoidable for achieving the goal.

These means must be used proportionately, and quantitatively, so that they do not cause more damage than they are supposed to prevent. So they must be proportional to what is wanted.

This criterion plays an important role in the debate about nuclear defence: nuclear war destroys everything, is necessarily 'disproportionate' and therefore cannot in any way include the goal of 'peace'.

The means of a 'just war' must also be applied qualitatively; war against the innocent is to be prevented.

This criterion, too, has found its way into international law, which recognizes a distinction between combatants and non-combatants, for example for the work of the Red Cross. Since the beginning of this century, however, this character has become increasingly meaningless because the number of civilians who are killed in a modern war far exceeds that of the military. As a result of the modern technology of war, war has become total; it has turned into a totalitarian, absolute power which cannot be limited. So theories of just war (or 'defence', which is our name for war) are ethically a thing of the past, even if elements of this theory still crop up even now. The strategies resulting from technologies, for example so-called 'forward defence', destroy all traditional distinctions in the politics of peace; attack is called defence, first strike is in the interest of 'security', most weapon systems bring about disproportionate destruction; psychological preparation for war talks indiscriminately about the 'enemy'. No one has yet devised a defence which would not be structurally capable of attack and to this degree could fall under the theory of the just war.

So even in the strategic plans of the military, concepts keep cropping up which leave the sphere of a 'just defence' far behind and approximate to the worst legacy of Christianity in matters of war and peace: the ideology of the crusade. Here the war becomes 'holy war'; escalation consists in regarding war not just as an evil which if need be can be justified by many clauses, but as an action which is well pleasing to God. In the crusades, the crusaders were granted remission from all sins that they had previously committed if they fell in the Holy War. There are many secular, nationalistic parallels to this kind of homage to soldiers as heroes. The holy war was well pleasing to God because it served to annihilate God's enemies. Therefore anything that offends against the criterion of the 'just war' is permissible in it. In the first years of his presidency Ronald Reagan used many formulas which stand in this tradition, for example when he said that Communism was the 'root of all evil'. Blind anti-Communism which is incapable of making any distinctions is the clearest illustration of the crusade mentality in our world.

What do these three historical positions of Christianity on war and peace mean for the various paradigms of theology? How are they related? And who are the peacemakers of whom Jesus speaks in the Sermon on the Mount? The orthodox position is closest to the doctrine of the just war. Neither the individual Christian nor the church has the authority to decide in matters of war and peace; this is rather the privilege of the authorities. With a reference to Romans 13 and the obedience enjoined there, a theological complex of obedience has developed towards even the most unjust authority which strictly limits the role of the church to proclamation to individuals. All peace action is attributed to 'God alone', and from the theocentric insight that only God brings peace, worldly, human, political peace activity is relativized, said to be unimportant or even condemned. The fundamentalists go furthest in this direction. The following theses come from the broad spectrum of the evangelical camp in Germany:

> Only God brings peace, not Israel and not man... The peace of God has one name: Jesus Christ. We do not need to bring this peace about, far less develop it... There is nothing to be added from our side... Now there is great peace without ceasing... The New Testament nowhere means any other peace than this.

A consequence of this removal of the gospel from our world is the allegation that the beatitude on the peacemakers from the Sermon on the Mount does not refer 'to a changing of the world or to Christian activities in this world', but only to the conduct of the disciples among themselves.[5] Considered objectively, in this orthodox evangelical understanding the removal of faith from the world and the subjectifying of proclamation are in the interests of a theology of military strength, and indeed often of armaments.

In an empirical investigation, the Canadian peace researcher Elbert W.Russell has shown that 'orthodox Christian religious attitudes are connected with militarism and with a whole complex of attitudes consisting in authoritarian, strict, militaristic, nationalistic, ethnocentric, anti-world community, anti-welfare state and anti-humanitarian standpoints'.[6] In extreme cases, as within the apartheid situation in South Africa, but also in the rise of the 'moral majority' in the USA, these attitudes produce a state theology of the kind described in the 1985 South African Kairos Document.[7] There the 'theology of the state' is distinguished from radical 'prophetic theology' and the 'church theology' which stands in the middle. The best example of a state theology outside South Africa is the fundamentalism that has blossomed in the United States since the beginning of the 1980s under the title 'moral majority'. Here 'Armageddon' emerges as a new theological theme, the place which in Revelation (16.16) is designated the scene of the last battle of the nations before the return of Christ. 'God will destroy this earth,' said the popular television evangelist Jerry Falwell, 'the heaven and the earth, millions of people in Armageddon will throng together ... for the final solution (Holocaust) of humankind.'[8] Only the born again Christians will be saved. Military armaments are seen as destined and necessary to fulfil the various stages or 'dispensations' of salvation history. 'There will be no peace until Jesus comes again,' says another preacher. 'Any teaching on peace before his coming again is heresy! That is against God's word.'[9]

These are extreme voices which are popularizing the policy based on armaments and attempt to declare any resistance to it to be un-Christian and anti-biblical. The eschatological theme of Armageddon has taken over the function of the older crusade ideology here.

The most important values of this neo-conservative state religion are 'family, flag and religion', i.e. patriarchal marriage, nationalism taken as an absolute ('America is great because America is good', R.Reagan), and a religion which transfigures the politics of strength.[10] In this state ideology the means of expression in Christian religion are instrumentalized: faith is adapted to an overarching friend-enemy pattern; the content of faith and the relationship to Christ as 'personal saviour' are reduced to militant anti-Communism.

The need for an instrumentalization of religion in the interests of the state and its 'national security' is also postulated from the political side; important documentation for these intentions is to be found in the 1980 paper produced by the 'Committee of Santa Fe' for the Inter-American Security Council, which serves as the basis for present US policy towards Central America.[11] The programmatic introduction to the Santa Fe papers reads, 'The crisis is metaphysical.' This means that the battle between capitalism and Communism is eternal and incessant. War is made a leading political principle and it, not peace, characterizes 'normal international relationships'. Therefore low-intensity warfare against all subversives and those who think otherwise must be eternalized. In this context the role of the church is important for the state: in the metaphysical crisis it is to remain at the service of the empire. In the section on 'internal subversion', liberation theology appears as the enemy which must be 'fought, and not just answered'. So the persecution of Christians which, according to a statement by a Salvadorian priest, is 'raging today as in the times of the Emperor Diocletian', is *de facto* justified. 'Unfortunately Marxist-Leninist forces have used the church as a political weapon against private property and productive capitalism by infiltrating the religious community with ideas which are more Communist than Christian.'[12] The American Foreign Minister Alexander Haig proclaimed one consequence of this kind of theology of the state on 28 January 1981: 'The concept of international terrorism will replace the concept of human rights in our considerations.' At that time Archbishop Oscar Romero had already been murdered – was he too a terrorist?

In the Federal Republic there is hardly a state theology, in the precise sense of the transfiguration of state power by biblical principles, which could justify a system like apartheid or the dirty war in Central America. In its attitude to war and peace the liberal theology which is widespread is best characterized by the concept of a church theology, as the Kairos Document describes it. It is a modern, enlightened church theology, which also contains undigested old traditions from state theology. The church nowadays understands itself as an open forum in which both sides, those in favour of armaments and pacifists, can put forward their positions. As a Volkskirche it wants to seem capable of conversation and mediation. It offers itself as an intermediary, as a neutral position between the fronts. Notes of crusading or of Armageddon are lacking. Reconciliation, peace, non-violence, solidarity with the poor are propagated in a number of places. Are they also practised? Public church statements look, rather, for a peace policy which will not cause offence, will not spoil relations with the powerful. Talk about non-violence mostly serves to exclude the question of the violence practised by the export of weapons and by the economy. This liberal church theology is justified by a theology which is stamped with a deep pessimism.

For example, for Martin Hengel the main motif of the Sermon on the Mount appears to be the 'overwhelming power of our sin'. 'Conceding our impotence' is an imperative which follows from the basic problem which the Sermon on the Mount poses to us. Hengel dismisses real options in peace politics which Christians justify by the Sermon on the Mount as 'political biblicism', and he brackets off the 'better righteousness' of Jesus (Matt.5.20) as 'an ideal of justice which cannot be realized politically by anyone'.[13] The reality of radical love, which is what Ernst Käsemann says that the Sermon on the Mount is all about, is 'disputed or restricted to a small group of those who are particularly holy'.[14] In this theology, the essential content of faith seems to be that we are sinners, not redeemed, not liberated for love. Therefore discipleship of Christ cannot be seriously taken into account within the horizon of the liberal, historical-critical paradigm. The Sermon on the Mount is said to be a private affair: those who attempt to live out its content are dismissed as 'self-appointed' peacemakers who in any case cannot match their own perfectionist claim. The embedding of the Sermon of the Mount in its social and historical context remains rooted in an individualism which is a matter of principle (and in this sense ideological); it therefore remains incomplete and superficial. Käsemann in fact identifies one of the deepest weaknesses of the liberal paradigm when he sums it up by saying: 'The explanation of the Sermon on the Mount as a private matter is the reaction of Enlightenment tolerance and actual rejection of the gospel as God's access to the world.'[15]

At all events, this church theology lacks a social analysis of the reality in which we live today as enemies of God, in the same way as South African church theology, with its limited, restrained and cautious criticism of apartheid. The accusation levelled by the Kairos theologians against their church theology applies equally to the way in which the leading university theologians among us deal with the question of peace:

> Its criticism (supply: of the militarization of West Germany) is, however, superficial and counter-productive because instead of engaging in an in-depth analysis of the signs of our times, it relies on a few stock ideas derived from Christian tradition and then uncritically and repeatedly applies them to our situation.[16]

In taking up these concepts like reconciliation, peace, justice and non-violence, the dominant liberal theology remains remarkably blind to the whole heritage of the peace churches and their traditions, which for example played a significant role during the Vietnam war on the Black civil rights movement.

There is hardly any reflection on who makes a contribution to peace and by what forms of resistance that takes place. The work of the peacemakers is not acknowledged, and they are even defamed. Instead of thanking God for the great movement of women and men for peace, a helpless, anxious, sometimes cynical tone characterizes this vacillating theology.

The position of liberation theology, called 'prophetic theology' in the Kairos paper, is based on the picture of the peacemakers in the Sermon on the Mount. This basic theological motif of the historical subjects who make peace fades into the background in orthodox theology because of its links with the authorities. In the liberal paradigm the tendency to privatize religion and make it a matter of indifference displaces discipleship of Jesus. Who are the peacemakers? On Roman coins the expression 'peacemaker' (Matt.5.9) stands under the image of the emperor. The court men of letters in the world of the time unflaggingly gave the emperor flattering names: bringer of justice, invincible sun, gentle, peacemaker. It is amazing how Jesus applied the word 'peacemakers', which was used by courtiers as a term of flattery for the Most High, to ordinary people, and was referring to them in this beatitude. In a contemporary translation his exclamation would sound like this: 'The upright walk of the peace women who bear no weapons: they are the children of God.'[17]This interpretation of the beatitudes is contextually accurate. The little people who are dependent, and intimidated by power, are to learn to walk upright and become blessed. Jesus, too, could only be referring to those with whom he had dealings every day; he is addressing the women, the fishermen, the people of the Jesus movement, as peacemakers; he means those who bring peace, build it up and produce it, and do not just tolerate passively what is imposed on them. Thus the understanding of peace is quite different from the passivity character-ized by an acceptance of fate and subjection to God which exists down to the present day in church theology. Prophetic theology takes seriously the call of Jesus to his disciples to bring peace and begin another form of life.

The other relationship to violence which was practised in the earliest community is also a characteristic of contemporary Christians: the way of the women followers and friends of Jesus cannot be subjection to the history of violence which is regarded as normal today. The earliest Christian Jesus movement did not join in the militarization of thought, life and action, the assimilation to violence. Christians did not go to the festival games which ran blood, where beasts were urged on against each other and human beings were torn to pieces. Even today the question to Christians of the rich world is: what is your attitude to the main use of force, namely the military? How do Christians behave in the face of power structures? What testimony do they give? Where are they present in the midst of injustice and violence? The question of peace is the call of God to the Christians of the rich world who are not threatened by hunger. Refusal to become accomplices and resistance against the praxis, spirit and logic of deterrence is the answer of Christian minorities to this call which is

directed towards us. What hope bears up these minorities? It is not
that of numerous successes, although the conversions of people in the
last decade from a mild theory of just defence to a position of non-
violent peace are astonishing. Nevertheless people need more hope to
set against the massive propaganda of those who are preparing for
war. This hope is fed by the Hebrew Bible, the Sermon on the Mount,
early Christian pacifism, the example of the peace churches, and many
brave individuals. It is neither for the victory of the free West after
the apocalypse nor for an afterlife for the individual: both these hopes
are unbiblical. The human hope for the justice of God for all people
has a different quality, that of participation in the fight for justice, in
living for God's peace. Where we enter upon this life, we in fact hope
for God. There our hope becomes naked, it removes the false supports
of hope – money and power – and opens itself up to God. Only when
we become capable of peace do we note how much we need God.

14 The End of Theism

It may surprise some people that in the sequence of these lectures God, the foundation of all theological reflection, becomes a theme only at the end. However, during the course of them two reasons for this shift in construction should have become clear. One is the principle of contextuality, to which I am attempting to remain true; this makes it impossible for me to take God for granted without asking questions. Living in a world in which modern science explains and dominates life, it makes no sense to begin from God as a starting point if one wants to make oneself understood in context. What is to be taken for granted is not the supreme being once called 'God', but the impossibility of associating anything at all with this word: our situation is characterized by a pragmatic, unmilitant and painless atheism.

The other reason why God becomes a theme only here, at the end, is connected with the hesitation, the restraint, over possessing a Logos about God which Martin Buber implanted on me. To pose the question of God then means asking how we can speak of God in such a way that God remains a 'You' and not in some sense an object of our 'knowledge', an 'It'.

I shall begin with the end of theism. The conception of a supreme Being at the top of the pyramid of being, which brought all orders into existence and sustains them, is no longer thinkable. God 'is' not as the Himalayas are, a tangible object that can be explored, that can for example be photographed. In other words, theism as the natural assumption of God is incapable of communicating the experiences with God that people have today. And yet it is important to do that. The innermost difficulty of a contemporary God-language, not to mention a God-concept, consists in the fact that Christians today experience an irreconcilable contradiction between the normal atheism of their world on the one hand and the real experiences of God on the other – and in these I include the suffering caused by the absence of God.

However, perhaps this contradiction between 'living atheistically' and 'believing in God' is not so unheard-of and inconceivable as might first appear. For even within theism, i.e. the assumption of a supreme heavenly being who conditions and governs all things, existential belief in God was by no means a matter of course. The letter of James (2.19) and, following it, Luther could already mock it: 'You believe in God? You do well. So does the devil.' In reality atheism and theism are equally remote from an existential faith which shapes the way in which one lives. In the development of my own theology that is expressed in the fact that the question 'Atheism or theism?' has become increasingly unimportant. Neither means much for our living relationship to the ground of life and its goal, to where we come from and where we are going, to creation and redemption. I therefore see the end of theism or the death of the theistic God as an opportunity finally to be able to speak of God in a concrete way, in a way related to praxis. That means bearing witness to God in a world dominated by death and orientated on death.

The intellectual difficulty which I have identified here with the adjectives 'theistic' and 'concrete' is, moreover, as old as Christian theology itself. In it 'God' is both a proper name and also an abstract noun for the deity. This ambiguity introduces a basic problem of theological reflection. The word 'God' first denotes a 'Thou' who can be named by name and addressed in prayer, who has called to life a history with his people and with the individual, and secondly the power of the universe which underlies all things, which explains reality and makes it comprehensible. In the pre-Enlightenment world both spirituality and science had to do with God: the biblical and Greek traditions were fused in a synthesis. Thought and faith had come together in a doctrine of God; the Father of Jesus Christ according to the New Testament and the origin of all that is, that unmoved mover, were understood to be one and the same. In the framework of the Greek philosophical tradition the power of the supreme being was thought of as absolute. God is immutable, infinite, incapable of suffering, all-knowing and all-powerful.

This synthesis of 'Jerusalem' and 'Athens' becomes problematical with the beginning of the modern age. As it develops, natural science emancipates itself from all revelation and speculation about God. But theology too, for its part, gradually detaches itself from the predominance of Aristotelian thought and recognizes that the God of Abraham and Sarah is different from the God of the philosophers. The biblical God is not unchangeable; this God even repents of what he has done (Gen.8.21). The symbols of absoluteness which were developed in classical theology, namely the omniscience, omnipresence and omnipotence of God, cannot really express what the biblical experience of men and women with God means. They give the concept of God an extreme degree of transcendence which goes against religious experience. This super-transcendence, or absolute, unrelated transcendence, leaves the earth godless. Spirit and matter stand dualistically over against each other unreconciled, and silence is kept about that middle level of religious experience which we can call transcendence in immanence, so that it remains unexpressed.

The earliest Christian theology attempted to express faith with the help of the Greek philosophical tradition. It associated biblical piety with the theistic world-view of the hierarchical-patriarchal pyramid with God the Father at its apex, and the association was so close that when this view of the world collapsed, the biblical experience also disappeared. It became incomprehensible and incredible, first to a minority of the enlightened and now to the majority of the population of the industrialized world. The difficulty posed by the natural, as it were naive assumption of God, the end of theism, then led to the present situation, where at the centre of reflection on God a quite different level of reflection has been reached which is no longer interested in proofs for the existence of God: this is the level of linguistic philosophy, of possible, meaningful talk of God.

How can we talk meaningfully and comprehensibly about God when theism is no longer taken for granted? How is the word 'God' to be used at all? What images do we use for God? What language about God is appropriate, i.e. comprehensible? Why do men and women use the language game 'God'?

All conceivable things come under the word God. I recall a theological conference in which the American theologian Harvey Cox suddenly brought out his wallet, held up a dollar bill, and asked, 'Is that what you mean by God? "In God we trust" – on every dollar?' It is important to become clear that the word 'God' as such does not convey anything

definite, any more than does the word 'goddess'. The context determines what content is really to be conveyed here. This is in accord
with the simple obsevation, which one can verify by biblical texts,
that sometimes there is talk of God without the word 'God' ever being
used. One of the best stories in the New Testament does not mention
God at all, and yet we would be blind if we thought that God does not
occur in the story of the Good Samaritan. The story is just about a
man who fell among robbers, and of various passers-by who act in
different ways (Luke 10.25-37). Those involved in the action do not
refer to God. Evidently the narrator has hidden God in this story and
one has to go to look for him: God does not appear here directly.

When we speak of God-language, the actual appearance of the word
God cannot be made the decisive factor. Jesus' procedure is quite
different, as becomes clear in his story of the Samaritan. Anyone who
does not hear God, who does not note that God is acting here and that
precisely for that reason Jesus chose the outsider, the Samaritan, the
Communist, the Turk, in order to point to God beyond the painful
familiarity of the word-fetishists, is hard to help. The same goes for
prayer. Just as not all those who begin with 'O God' and end with
'Amen' are really praying, so conversely it is the case that the lament,
the cry of a person, can be prayer without any religious formulas being
used. The formalisms do not help us here.

I would like to explain how this is so with the help of a fairy tale
which comes from the *Dreams by a French Fireside* which Richard
Volkmann-Leander produced in 1871.[1] The story is about a rich man
who dies and finds himself on the steep road to heaven. When he gets
there, Peter tells him that he should consider what he wants to do up
there: everyone gets precisely what he wants. So the rich man wishes
for a great golden castle, for his favourite food every day and for a
cellar full of gold. And his wish is granted. Peter leads him to this
splendid castle where he can eat and drink to his heart's desire and in
the cellar he finds sacks and chests full of gold and jewels. To begin
with he is happy, but soon he gets bored. He does not enjoy the good
food, and no longer enjoys counting his money. After a thousand years
Peter returns and asks how he is getting on. The rich man complains
bitterly what a miserable place the wretched castle is. 'You hear
nothing, you see nothing, no one bothers. Your much-vaunted heaven
and your eternal bliss are nothing but lies!'

At that Peter is amazed and asks him, 'Don't you know where you

are? Do you think you're in heaven? You're in hell. You wished
yourself into hell! The castle is part of hell.' And with that he leaves
him alone for another thousand years. The rich man weeps, no longer
enjoys anything, becomes depressed and wastes away. When Peter
returns, he begs him at least to show him heaven. Then Peter takes
him to a room in the attics and shows him a knot-hole. The rich man
has to stand on tiptoe and strain to see anything at all, but finally he
sees a golden light and God amidst the clouds and stars. At the same
time he recognizes an old beggar who lived by his house and is now
sitting at God's feet, as he himself had wanted to do. The rich man
cannot have enough of looking at heaven and then he forgets to eat
and count his treasures in the cellar; he just stays by the tiny knot-
hole and watches the beggar laughing. He does not notice that another
thousand years have passed when Peter comes to take him, too, to
heaven.

Why does the rich man not understand that he is in hell? Why does
he imagine that he is in heaven? At the beginning I referred to the
contradiction between life in an atheistic world and its identification
of happiness with riches and success on the one side and the experiences
and deprivations of God on the other. The rich man lives in this
conflict between being rich and being lost, being sated and being
hungry, godlessness and longing. He has all that he wants – or at least
what he thinks he wants. He is unaware that perhaps he needs
something else. He is quite an ordinary person; by God he imagines
precisely what this atheistic world has taught him: riches, things to
consume, success, possessions. Then what is he lacking? Why are the
fulfilments which life offers the individual in a rich world not enough?
I think that the fairy tale is speaking of a longing, a dissatisfaction
over possessions, a quest for the meaning of life, which I now want to
call 'hunger for God'. This is a hunger which can easily be forgotten
if we fill our mouths with other things, but which returns however
much we suppress it, as it does for this rich man in the story, and
makes us believe that we are in heaven. We are dependent on this
hunger for God, even in our splendid castle. The fulfilment that we
experience in our profession, career, relationships, family, cannot still
this hunger; it keeps breaking out, often in quite unexpected places,
for example in the marriage crises which are becoming increasingly
normal when a stage of life comes to an end with education, marriage,
children, building a house. All has gone well and looks good, and

suddenly people find themselves sitting there like the rich man in heaven and asking why it doesn't taste better. Why does it really make no sense, why does it bore us, why did it only look like heaven? Perhaps those who know about the hunger for God among us best are those who have dropped through the usual safety nets: the sick, the depressives, the addicts, many people within our prosperous society who are ill as a result of the specific diseases of prosperity, namely forms of dependence. The addicts see more clearly than the fit.

Someone may perhaps ask what right I have to use the term 'hunger for God' for this hunger, this quest for meaning. Following the lines of a negative theology I would reply that nothing and no one can still this hunger, and that in this nothing there is a statement about what the religions call 'God'. In a variety of images and languages they attempt to speak of the original power of life, of the origin and goal of all things. The religions are concerned with this great X at the heart of the world that has many different names, bears many different faces and is named in a great variety of languages. They all really say nothing but, 'Without this X you are not complete, you are only half there, you lack any connection with the mystery of life. Without this X there is no blessing in what you do, you find no peace, gain no certainty. Without X you are a replaceable cog in the mega-machine.' The experience and feeling of many people is that they are not being used and in this sense are superfluous. The religions respond to this negative experience and say, 'God needs you.'

But is it possible to communicate such a religious certainty to others, to make it capable of being communicated in the conditions of the modern world? How can we speak comprehensibly of God if we are no longer supported by the old ideological certainty of theism? Does that not condemn all talk of God completely and utterly to subjectivity and arbitrariness?

Present-day theological paradigms articulate different answers to this situation. Orthodox theology, often associated with a fundamentalist understanding of the Bible, insists on a God of absolute transcendence who is to be normative not only for piety but also for what is largely a pre-scientific understanding of the world. There is only a very limited adaptation to modernity: that means that God's immanence in human life retreats behind God's transcendence. Biblical concreteness, the history of God with his people, becomes irrelevant. So, as we have seen, the peace of God is interpreted as the transcendent intervention of a power beyond the earth which is no longer understood prophetically as working in, with and through us. The God of orthodoxy is ossified and becomes an objectifiable fetish. The fact that in pietistic communities it is sometimes believed that one can test the faith of a young pastor by counting how often he uses the word 'God' or 'Jesus Christ' is a grotesque expression not only of the primitiveness of this approach but also of its lack of faith: God becomes a calculable object.

From within psychology this God is the deepest symbol of an authoritarian religion. Power is more important to the authoritarian God than justice and love. According to Erich Fromm, authoritarian religion, as opposed to humanitarian religion, is characterized by three structural characteristics:

It calls for the recognition of a higher power which has our fate in its hands and excludes self-determination.

People are subjected to the rule of this power of God without this power having to legitimate itself morally, as love and justice.

A deep anthropological pessimism prevails: people are powerless and insignificant beings, incapable of truth and love, and their denial of their own strength is interpreted as 'obedience'.

Erich Fromm contrasts this authoritarian religion as a paradigm with humanitarian, non-repressive religion.[2] That is not based on a one-sided asymmetrical dependence of powerless people on someone who holds power. Its goal is not subjection and obedience, but union with the will of God as this comes about in exemplary fashion in the living and dying of Jesus. Its sin is not rebellion against the Father, who is understood to be omnipotent, but the failure of human beings created for freedom in which they deny the 'God in us'.

It is claimed that this other non-repressive God appears in liberal theology. This theology has increasingly dispensed with any explanation of the world through the God of the philosophers. It asserts neither that God is to be taken for granted nor that God is needed for our knowledge of the world. Its language is addressed to the individual conscience. It replaces the objectifiable truths of orthodoxy with subjectivity, but this is a subjectivity in dialogue with scripture and tradition. God invites, but he does not compel.

On what basis do we really talk of God? That is one of the questions at issue between orthodoxy and liberalism. Is it at all possible to speak objectively about God, or are there only subjective feelings? The danger of objective statements about God is that they lay claim to an authority outside the world and, often via the concept of 'revelation', truths behind which there can be no questioning are established and used for purposes of domination. But the dangers of a purely subjective language are no less; it so isolates our experience that it really cannot be communicated any more. 'I can't explain it to you, but that's how I feel' can mark the breaking off of communication. Religion then becomes a kind of private neurosis, each person's own system of signs and understanding. But there is a better method in between objective and subjective claims to the truth, in which both are exposed to the test of experience.

'Experience' is a basic concept in feminist theology. Although it is sometimes exaggerated within the religious women's movement so that there is virtually no subsequent reflection on it, it is fundamental to the critical capacity of women and others who are oppressed, who appeal against a dominant theology, opinion or ideology on the basis of their own experience. The most important criterion for this concept is intersubjectivity, in other words the communicability of experience. So, again in connection with the question of God, it is not a matter of my having this God and your having that God, but of the communication of experiences in which we find ourselves together again. One of the most important tasks of feminist theology is to find a common language for God which practises this sharing. The better method for this is dialogue which can be established beyond authoritarian or subjectivistic claims to truth. What is a dialogue, and what do we understand by the dialogical method? Here I want to mention three conditions of dialogue which are indispensable to the liberation thought of feminists and others.

Dialogue must be free of domination. No pressure may be used. If my answer to a question has consequences for my career, if pressure is exercised, for example by an authority, then there is no freedom from domination.

The second condition is intersubjectivity. The different subjects with their experiences become involved in a process of exchange to which all involved contribute with as little restraint as possible.

Here, thirdly, they take a risk which at the same time is the opportunity for dialogue, namely the possibility of change. Readiness to allow oneself to be changed on entering a dialogue with the religious tradition is indispensable. It may be that in the dialogue I have to give up things which were dear and familiar to me. And at the same time the dialogue lives by the hope of all involved that they may make their own experience productive for others.

In its philosophical foundations this method of dialogue related to experience and relevant to praxis represents a factor which goes beyond liberal theology and its God-talk. The intrinsic difficulty of contemporary theological reflection on basic principles seems to me to lie in a certain arbitrariness which has replaced the old necessity of theology. In the process of secularization 'the supernatural and the supra-historical' have become a problem. God is no longer needed to explain world history. For example, Hans Weder writes this in his hermeneutics about the historical-critical method and the secularity of history which it presupposes in principle: 'Methodologically there is a need to exclude God as a historical factor. That means nothing short of the abolition of the necessity of God.'³ This abolition is certainly meant to concern 'God merely in the framework of *worldly* self-understanding', but it is not made clear what other understandings than this there could be.

The questions which an experience-related liberation theology poses to liberal theology are: What God is meant here? On the basis of what experiences is God understood as not necessary? Whose experiences are they which allow us to dispense with God? They are the experiences of the white male European who in the pose of victor stands over against nature and all that appears to him as untamed nature, like wild animals, original inhabitants or women. At all events they are not the experiences of suffering, of being violated, of anxiety about life, of being destroyed. The 'abolition of the necessity of God' can only relate to a God who is thought of in Greek terms. Only the unrelated God is not needed. Weder speaks at another point of the 'Everydayness which in no way calls for a theological interpretation any more than nature calls for the name temple of God.'⁴ That may apply to the objective observer of a timeless nature, but to those who experience the destruction of the temple today in their own bodies, such statements are intolerable. That at least 40,000 people die of hunger every day in fact calls for a theological interpretation; it calls for a God who may not be necessary to explain the world in terms of a scientific understanding, but is necessary for those who fall completely outside this liberal hermeneutics, the victims of everyday brutality.

The basic philosophic assumptions underlying this theology are

still stamped by the Western 'philosophy of the uninvolved onlooker'.
In his book *Marx and the Bible*, José Miranda, the Mexican liberation
theologian, has made a 'criticism of the philosophy of oppression' and
carried on a thorough critical discussion with two most important
traditions of the Western world, the Greek and the Hebrew.[5] He
enriches this old debate and sharpens it up through the perspective of
the mass misery of people in the Third World. However could a
humanism arise, he asks, which was and is blind to social reality in
this urgent and tragic form? A philosophy which regards injustice as
a matter of course is based, as Miranda shows (and in so doing he
resembles the Jewish philosopher Emanuel Levinas),[6] on an ontology
and understanding of being which determines all our thinking and
above all our most important productive force, science. The entity is
seen as a being in itself; it has its essence in itself and can then also
enter into relationship with others on the basis of its being-in-itself.
Over against this, Hebrew thought represents an ontology of being-
in-relationship. Being in relationship to others is the basis of not only
all human life but also all plant and animal life.

To give an example of these different ways of thinking, I want to
recall experiences in hospitals in the Third World. If a patient is
admitted in India, the rest of the family goes too; sometimes there are
twenty people camping on the hospital floor. They are all convinced
that the sick person cannot be healed unless they are there. They
believe that the doctors, for all their resources, only make the sick
sicker if they put individuals in single beds and treat them in isolation.
Their ontology and their understanding of life determines their being-
in-relationship, just as for us the isolation of individual phenomena,
the production of isolated beings, is central. In ecology it is particularly
clear how destructive any thinking in terms of progress is which does
not take account of chains, involvement, interweaving, and is then
fond of declaring the damaging consequences of a measure to be 'side-
effects'. That is the consequence of the ontology of being-in-oneself
or objectification. Objectification is always also domination, the control
of isolated individual parts. The understanding of science which
follows from this ontology is related to neutrality and objectivity. As
far as it is concerned, living human praxis fades into the background.

Now this Greek way of thinking has also moulded Western theology
down to its liberal offshoots and above all has damaged its understanding of God. God is God in himself, unrelated to his creatures. He does

not need them and is all-sufficient in himself. In the words of the Westminster Confession, he has 'sovereign rule over them, through them, for them, or upon them, to do whatever pleases him'.[7] The theological technical term for this complete independence of God is his 'aseity'. In the understanding of scholastic theology God exists *a se*; he derives himself from himself and not from another. Only God has this privilege of being *a se*: it ensures his infinite superiority. God could create the world, but he could also have left it alone. God is not concerned with those who love him. Theologians of relationship have always objected to this being of God *a se*. In the saying 'God does not live without me', the mystic Angelus Silesius (1624-1677) remarks:

> I know that without me
> God cannot live a moment.
> If I become nothing,
> He must of necessity give up the ghost.[8]

As we saw, Karl Barth, who regarded the assumption of the aseity of God as indispensable to the freedom of God, speaks of the mystical 'impertinence' of Angelus Silesius.

Today, the dispute over whether God can be thought of beyond us as resting in himself and unrelated, or whether God is the relationship itself and can be thought of only as relationship, seems to me to be one of the most important arguments between male-patriarchal and feminist theology. Is sovereignty the essential characteristic of God – or is it his capacity for relationship? This question seems to me to lie behind the much-discussed question of images of God. It is easy for theologians within the iconoclastic tradition of Judaism and Protestantism to assert that of course God is neither male nor female for them, but 'wholly other'. This statement evades the real problem, which lies in the substance of what we mean by 'male' of 'female'. If God is the absolute Lord, superior to the world, who allows or takes responsibility for Auschwitz, is his unassailable power the most important thing for him and is 'He' in this sense anything other than the projection of the masculine will to power? A series of theological trends, including North American process theology, but also Jewish thinkers like Abraham Joshua Heschel, Hans Jonas and Harold Kushner, reject the conception that God can be unrelated sovereignty, superior to the world and dependent on no one.

This brings me to the paradigm of liberation theology. The concept of need, of dependence, is essential to its ideas of God, whether they have a feminist, Latin American or African stamp. Just as we need God, so God needs us. Just as we wait on God, so God waits on our appearing; that, too, is an old mystical insight. Only if we understand this being needed by God do we really learn to think in a liberating way. In that case patriarchal thinking is overcome, not only by saying 'Goddess' instead of 'God', but by demonstrating the mutual dependence of us human beings on the power of life, and the power of life on us.

In this context, feminist thought provides that comprehensive criticism of domination and power without which a liberating theology cannot work. One of the main difficulties of thinking of God consists in the fact that while God embodies power in a sense which has still to be determined, this power cannot be that proclaimed by the authoritarian religion which we find at the top of a hierarchy. By hierarchy I understand a 'hallowed' order behind which questions cannot be asked, in which the higher level in each case has power over the lower. The appearance of the pyramid of being in patriarchal religions is: God, imagined as masculine, is at the top, and has male people in charge below him; then come women, animals, plants, and finally the earth. The higher level in each case has the right to use what is below it. The subject-object relationship is presupposed. This can be a caring relationship, just as there are also gentle forms of patriarchal culture, but that does not alter the basic structure in which God remains as the unrelated major subject, whose most important function is rule. This God is worshipped because he has power. The criticism of this patriarchal understanding of God in the various liberation theologies has roots in the indigenous cultures of the peoples who experienced the God of the white invaders and his imperialistic claims; another root is the biblical tradition itself with its philosophical developments.

15 Who is Our God?

I have mentioned Martin Buber (1878-1965) several times in this book and want to go into his significance for a feminist theology, i.e. for a non-imperialist understanding of God. Buber's book *I and Thou*, which appeared in 1923, is about the basic distinction between the I-Thou relationship and the I-It relationship. We always live in a twofold bond, on the one hand related to the It, as for example in work and productivity, and on the other related to a Thou, as in the relationships of taking and giving, of dependence on one another and being directed towards one another. The greatest danger for our humanity consists in our dropping out of I-Thou relationships and reifying them so that they become I-It relationships. In any personal relationship to the other it may happen that we make the other person a manipulable object, and use him or her in some sense of the word. The irreplaceable Thou then becomes a replaceable object, a giver of comfort, a money machine, a slave. The other person, who should always be an end, as Kant said, is then made into a means. I humiliate him or her by reducing them to the I-it relationship. The true I-It relationship can only be thought of in mutuality.

Buber says: 'You know always in your heart that you need God more than everything; but do you not know too that God needs you – in the fullness of his eternity needs you? How would human beings be, how would you be, if God did not need them, did not need you? You need God in order to be – and God needs you, for the very meaning of your life.'[1] Buber attempts to decipher the 'supreme meeting' with God from which we do not emerge the same being, and identifies three elements in this encounter. The first is 'whole fullness of real mutual action, of being raised and bound up in relation: human beings can give no account at all of how the binding in relation is brought about, nor does it in any way lighten their lives – it makes life heavier, but heavy with meaning.' Real encounter in love can only take place in mutuality, not in an asymmetrical relationship of dependence. Giving and taking are two-sided: we know God only if we also know how much God needs us. There is a false Christian way of reducing love to a sheer giving, which is often thought through in terms of the parent-child model, and above all glorified in the image of the mother who gives without limit and gets nothing herself. But these illusions, which are alien to reality, lead to neuroses, and do so on both sides of such a relationship. Love itself wants mutuality; God wants our joy, our power, our creative participation, and not us as mere vessels of divine inpouring. We are to earn interest with our pounds (Luke 19.11-27). All our relationships, including those with weaker, sick partners, at least tend towards mutuality. For it is precisely out of the mutuality of encounter that meaning arises.

The second element in Buber's deciphering of the experience of God is 'the inexpressible confirmation of meaning. Meaning is assured. Nothing can any longer be meaningless. The question about the meaning of life is no longer there.' I can only confirm these last thoughts of Buber from my own experiences. In the years after the German catastrophe I experienced an intensive phase of meaninglessness, of the despair of youth, of European nihilism. Existentialism, represented above all by Sartre and Camus, shaped this phase of my development. In traditional terms, I was looking for God, but what I found was Heidegger's 'nihilizing nothing' or Sartre's statements from *Les jeux sont faits* that hell is the other person. The experience of meaninglessness had become virtually a condition of my spiritual existence. At that time I kept thinking that there must be an answer to the question of being, and imagined it as a key statement occuring to one in a dream. The adults who had given up the question of meaning and regarded the dismissal of such questions as wisdom and higher maturity disgusted me. I hoped for greater clarity about meaning, probably connecting an aim in life with support in the present. But while I was still looking for an answer in the form of a statement – 'Such and such is the meaning of life' – I experienced, as Martin Buber puts it, that: 'The question about the meaning of life is no longer there. But were it there, it would not have to be answered. You do not know how to exhibit and define the meaning of life, you have no formula or picture for it, and yet it has more certitude for you than the perceptions of your senses.' And it is certainly surer than the reflections in your mind. We do not find meaning as a something, as a formula, which would then be valid for ever. And yet there is a receiving of meaning in which the questioning falls silent, because we live by the meaning itself. That is the basic experience of love. It also occurs in the basic experience of becoming a mother. A certainty appears in which nothing can become meaningless any longer.

The third thing that Buber mentions here alongside mutuality and the experience of meaning is that meaning must be done, must be lived out by us. 'It does not wish to be explained (nor are we able to do that) but only to be done by us. Thirdly, this meaning is not that of "another life" but that of this life of ours, not that of a world "yonder" but that of this our world of ours, and it desires its confirmation in this life and in relation with this world.' Doing, proving, living – this thought comes from the depths of Judaism. Also Jewish is the statement: 'The assurance I have of it does not wish to be sealed within me, but it wishes to be born of me into the world.' Here God is understood as will, not as being resting in itself. Of course God remains an infinite mystery that we cannot interpret, but in ethical terms that is a foolish statement, because what God wants of us is quite clear and recognizable: 'You have been told what is good and what the Lord requires of you' (Micah 6.8). It is quite clear how meaning is to be received and to be brought into the world.

Perhaps Buber's approach can be summed up in his saying, modelled on the first sentence in the Bible, 'In the beginning was the relation-ship.' Here God is not spoken of as the supreme object, but as the mutual, significant, actively experienced relationship to life. God is not found as a precious stone or as blue flowers, as Novalis pictured, but God happens. God spent this Tuesday afternoon with me – that is a meaningful statement, an attempt to identify the experience, the encounter, which puts us in relationship. The search is then subsequently often understood as a wrong road. Our everyday life, our real, inconspicuous relationships, were all too hazy to us. What takes place in the encounter with God is that the searching ends not with finding, but with being found. God was always already standing behind me, even when I was rushing in the other direction.

A theological consequence of this approach by the God who encounters us is the linguistic form in which we can communicate

God. Only secondarily can it be the principle, the awareness, the dogma. Religious language destroys itself if it talks about God in the I-It relationship. Prayer or narrative is possible talk of God. In the narratives of the New Testament God appears, God happens. If we tell stories of God and are concerned about the narrative method, we are telling what God does or how God conceals himself, how God acts. And in prayer we ask God to do something worth telling of, to appear, to show power for good, to change us. In these two linguistic forms we talk of God more as an event than as a substance. We speak from and to God, instead of 'about' him.

The question which is often put to me, 'Do you believe in God?', usually seems a superficial one. If it only means that there is an extra place in your head where God sits, then God is in no way an event which changes your whole life, an event from which, as Buber says of real revelation, I do not emerge unchanged. We should really ask, 'Do you live out God?' That would be in keeping with the reality of the experience.

Criticism of the false ontology of being-in-oneself and the theology of the God who is in himself is nowadays made from various directions. Biblical thought in its otherness, the personalism of Martin Buber, the basic Marxist idea of the priority of those who work and suffer over the needs of capital and its 'material pressures', existentialist philosophy with its attempt to deobjectify people, process theology with its conception of the God who develops further, who cannot remain behind the ethical level of the democratic consciousness, but above all feminist theology with its insistence on a relational, non-patriarchal language, which is in a position to communicate experiences with God existentially – these are attempts to overcome the ontological lack of relationship and to think of God beyond theism and atheism.

One of the most difficult problems in this connection is the question of the power of this God of relationship, this God of the life which calls and answers. Is not the God of the powerless also powerless, the God of women also pushed to the periphery and trivialized, the God of the peacemakers also unprotected and an object of mockery? So why do Christians refer to a higher being if this God is not omnipotent? What does it mean to think in theological terms of God's renunciation of power, which shapes the story of Jesus of Nazareth?

The Christian assumption that we recognize God most clearly in this figure of someone tortured to death goes completely against our fixation on power and domination. Christ appears in the Gospels as the man for others, has nothing but his love: no weapons, no magical tricks, no privileges. It is false christology to imagine Christ as a Greek god, a figure who can do anything, and who has a return ticket to heaven. That is really a denial of the incarnation. Christ refused to do miracles if they were asked of him as a proof. He refused to come down from the cross, and the original witnesses undestood that quite clearly, when they mocked him and said, 'If you are the Son of God, come down from the cross and then we will believe in you' (Matt.27.42). For those who mocked him, God was identical with power and rule. But the only capital with which he came into the world was his love, and it was as powerless and as powerful as love is. He had nothing but his love with which to win our heart. Perhaps the abstractness of the search for the meaning of life can be overcome where we do not find the back-up of a father but the face of a human being at the centre of power. In fact we are not saved by any 'higher being, god, emperor or tribune', as the Internationale puts it. No higher being can save us, because the only salvation is to become love. More than that is not promised to us. All other deliverance is based on a mere shift from a bad state to a good state, to another place, to another time, which does not change us in the process. Such hope for power, for the intervention of an omnipotent superiority and unassailability, has always deceived people. God is not the extension of our false wishes, nor the projection of our imperialisms.

And yet that is still not the whole story. It is possible to understand the cross of Christ in this language of powerless love, but it is impossible to articulate the resurrection as long as we regard all power as 'evil', as tyrannical, as split off and masculine. I note that tendency in a critical attitude to my own theology, which can be understood in three different stages. I had left behind belief in an omnipotent father 'who rules all things so gloriously', derived from theism. For me, the metaphor of the 'death of God' meant deliberately giving up the notion of the omnipotence of God as theologically and ethically impossible. In the light of Auschwitz the assumption of the omnipotence of God seemed – and still seems! – to me to be a heresy, a misunderstanding of what God means. From this criticism of the theistic-patriarchal God I developed a position in which the cross of Christ stands in the centre, as an affirmation of the non-violent impotence of love in which

God himself is no longer one who imposes suffering, but a fellow sufferer.

The difficulty of this position is connected with the question of the power of this non-violent God. Is power really evil, or can we say something about the good power, the power of God, the victory of life over death wishes? The third position attempts to think of the resurrection of Christ and our escape from death as participation in God's power.

The transition from the second to the third position is connected with my growth into the theologies of liberation. I slowly came to understand that outside the power to shout and shoot, outside the power of the imperium, there are yet other forms of power which arise out of our being bound up with the ground of life. The grass that grows into the light through the asphalt also has power: not power to command, to rule, to manipulate, but a power which comes to life from a relationship. How can we distinguish good power, the power of life, from evil power, the power to dominate? This question is central for a feminist and thus humane way of thinking. The most important criterion for answering it is that good power is shared power, power which distributes itself, which involves others, which grows through dispersion and does not become less. In this sense the resurrection of Christ is a tremendous distribution of power. The women who were the first to experience it were given a share in the power of life. It was the tremendous certainty of God which now entered their life.

In the thought of a feminist liberation theology within the First World the concept of God has taken on a new significance, in that the relationship of the omnipotent God to helpless men and women is now understood in a different way. Real relationship means that an exchange takes place and that people gain a share in the creative, good, non-compelling power of God. Above all Jewish thought has helped me to clarify this participation in God. In the Talmud the image of God in human beings is not understood as a spiritual image; rather, we are the image of God, which means that we can act like God. Just as God made clothes for Adam and Eve, so too we can clothe the naked. Just as God fed Elijah through a raven, so we too are to feed the hungry.[2] For Christians, nothing is more false than so to stabilize the idea of God's omnipotence and human helplessness that there is no longer any exchange between the two. In that case a reified transcendence comes about instead of the *imitatio dei* which is offered us in Jewish thought.

The task of a liberating theology is to overcome just this kind of reified transcendence. Reified transcendence portrays the God who can only act as a superman, who thus acts independently, untouchably and powerfully. I think that all three statements about the absoluteness of God – his omnipotence, omniscience, omnipresence – all three 'omnis' express a fatal imperialistic tendency in theology: the power of the independent ruler. This God is in fact no more than the dream of a culture dominated by males. For me that has become clear from one of the male myths of North American popular culture. It is the dream which is entitled 'Go west'. The action in these films and stories usually follows the same pattern. A village is dominated by a brutal band of criminals. More and more people get murdered. The sheriff is powerless, and people no longer dare go out on the streets. One day a young man rides in; in a short time he gets the better of the villains and creates law and order. The sheriff promises him his daughter, who has fallen hopelessly in love with the handsome stranger. But the night before the wedding the cowboy saddles his horse and rides off. New adventures are waiting: greatness is not to be tied to anyone, independence is a central value. This myth is about independent male heroes who owe no one anything, who need no one, for whom mutual help, exchange and community are secondary matters. His strengths lie in himself alone, and to this degree this primal story reflects a God who equally needs no one, a male God.

One cannot understand feminist theology as long as one believes that it is simply a change of position or an exchange of pronouns. It is in fact about another way of thinking of transcendence, of no longer understanding it independently of everything else and in terms of domination over all others, but as bound into the web of life. In one of his aphorisms about love Goethe says, 'Voluntary dependence, the finest state, and how would it be possible without love?' God is no less voluntarily dependent than we all can be in love. That means that we move from God above us to God in us, that we overcome the false conception of transcendence in hierarchical terms. We cease to project God as the omnipotent one over against whom we then stand in total helplessness, and thus also change the relationship of this world to the other world or, to use another geometrical picture, of the horizontal and vertical.

In his book *The Socialist Decision*, Paul Tillich says something about the hope that has helped me on the way from the second position, determined by helplessness, to the third position, determined by liberation:

Human expectation is always both other-worldly and this-worldly at the same time. More precisely, the opposition does not exist for expectation. Any analysis of prophetic expectation shows that clearly. The coming order of things is seen in historical continuity with the present. It is this-wordly. But the concepts used to describe what is to come presuppose a complete transformation of the present, the abolition of the laws of the nature. The this-worldly is in truth other-worldly. And so miracles are expected. Miracle stories are told. This world and the beyond, transcendence and immanence, enter into another relationship.[3]

I have had similar experiences with hope in which transcendence and immanence emerge at the same time, in many services and gatherings which were related to the Christian expectation of another peace and another social order. Here, too, the immanence of the historical content of hope, like the renunciation of the means of mass destruction, the remission of debts for the poorest, the protection of water, etc., is quite clear. Many non-religious groups have made similar demands. To this degree the historical continuity of the expectation is obvious to all. Nevertheless, something of 'other-wordliness', underivability, the expectation of miracles, is also involved. Prayer brings assurance, comfort and strength. The real hopes for an earth without violence and exploitation are still always obligations on the self. Without commitment they remain mere illusion. They bind people together; they collect and concentrate our wishes. They realize something of the other relationship between transcendence and immanence, which I want to identify with the statement: 'Transcendence is radical immanence.'[4] This notion seems to me to be fundamental to a theology of liberation.

First of all it contains a liberation of theology from the thousand-year old burden of doctrines about divine transcendence which start from the notion that human society is basically incapable of ordering itself rightly. It is thought to be too sinful and too finite; the notion prevails that for its own prosperity society needs a higher, more comprehensive, authority to which human beings must be subject.

How immanence is related to transcendence has been understood in very different ways in the course of the history of Christianity. Earliest Christianity in its apocalyptic imagined a divine destruction of this terror-filled world, which was to be followed by a new age under the rule of Christ. The Fourth Gospel saw the relationship between transcendence and immanence in the image of a peaceful flock under the good shepherd. The Constantinian establishment thought in theocratic terms: God is the true ruler over this world, and all earthly order must be modelled on him. Pietism, to chose a modern model, imagines the human heart as the place where men and women are subjected by God; some people also believed that the Christian community is the leaven for the whole of society.

But all these variations on the theme of dependence on the more original and higher authority of God have one idea in common: that the divine transcendence rests on power and wisdom outside society. Transcendence is regarded as wholly other. The words that we use to express other-wordliness are 'over', 'above', 'beyond', 'more than', 'other than', 'free from', 'over against', 'outside', 'totally different'. And the theo-political terms which go with them are government, lordship, kingship, order, obedience. Here the relationship between transcendence and immanence was thought of in hierarchical terms, although we have to note that Christianity has never denied the immanence of God. God was in Christ always also within, not just above; always also present, not just beyond; always also 'part of' and not just 'free from' earthly limitation. In the history of modern theology the relationship between immanence and transcendence has been interpreted as being dialectical or paradoxical, but these beginnings of a break-up of hierarchical thought have never gone far enough. God's transcendence, often complained about as being his male side, was always still higher, more true, more authentic than his immanence, which nowadays is being reclaimed by feminist theology.

Feminist liberation theology, to the degree that it is done by white women in the rich countries, participates in one of the most important tasks of ethics, posed by the Enlightenment and the democratic understanding of society which followed it, namely the demystification of power. This critical contribution has consequences for the pattern of transcendence and immanence. Now it can no longer exist as one of 'above' and 'below'. God as absolute power, i.e. detached power free from ties, only legitimates a hierarchical, oppressive society with its racism, sexism, class injustice and imperialism over nature. The conception that the divine transcendence is the opposite of immanence and that 'God does what he wills' has not made it any clearer how transcendence and immanence are really to be reconciled. That is the real task of theology today, but it would then have to abandon the old scheme. Just as we criticize the omnipotence of God and democratize monarchistic absolutism, so too we work with another concept of transcendence.

Both transcendence and immanence are related to the same matter, the same one creation. The difference lies in the fact that transcendence concentrates and hallows any phenomenon of immanence to which it is applied. Transcendence is radical; in other words, it is immanence loved and affirmed from the roots. If in our immanence, in what we experience and do, we really enter into the radicality of love, then our immanence contains transcendence. In that case what we call 'God' appears in our everyday affairs. The compassionate man from Samaria finds God and is found by God on the road. So, too, the truth, love, beauty of God can shine forth in our everyday life. The mystics have always said that God is as it were lying on the streets, if only we could learn to see. They have said that there are more possibilities than experiences mediated in cultic religious terms in which we become sure of God. God condenses and hallows what is around us, so that we catch sight of it in God's radical immanence of God. Do we thus give up the vertical? Have we sacrificed the vertical for the horizontal, a charge constantly levelled against political theology? I believe that this criticism is no more than a superficial one, because an approach in terms of two levels, one on which we reflect on the links between our banks and South Africa, and a higher one, in which God dwells, does not really get us any further. Rather, we must find the point at which the horizontal and the vertical touch. Just how serious Christianity is first emerges when Christians collaborate and suffer together on the lower level and know that God is 'within it', within this radical immanence. 'He who says that he is in the light but hates his brother is still in the darkness' (I John 2.9). According to I John, being in love means abiding in God and knowing God in us (4.16). Radical immanence means that God hallows our everyday life, that God is 'in' our this-wordliness if we have not destroyed our commitment through 'hatred' – disguised as normality and indifference.

My experience in many committed groups tells me that those who lack transcendence also fall short on immanence. Moreover they lack clarity and compassion; they are not as 'with it' as human beings can be in God, have not gone as far in love as love expects. For the self-centred, cold immanence which Bonhoeffer called 'flat this-worldliness' leaves a dangerous wake behind it. It prevents us from thinking beyond what is given; it compels us to become the slaves of pressure of circumstances, destroys our concept of what life really is, so that we no longer dare to think of freedom at all. Caught up in this wake, we become adapted to impoverished, destroyed reality, so that we utterly fail to perceive its depth, which in fact cries out for transcendence. In that case we do not perceive the reality in which people are continually perishing, are continually being mutilated even in our own countries, are perishing spiritually and mentally for lack of transcendence in a fat and stupid immanence. In the depth of this-worldliness, life, fettered and tormented by us, cries out for liberation. We cannot afford to do without even a ray of transcendence.

And that brings me back to the beginning of this book, where I spoke of the experiences of God which, even today, without theistic preliminaries, people have in the midst of this-worldliness. Theology is the often desperate attempt to make these experiences communicable, to hand on to others the bread of life which I eat with others, including the spiritually hungry by whom I am surrounded. Is it possible to communicate the certainty of God? I have great doubts about reflective theological language. I can relate my experiences of the presence of God in the same way as the friends of Jesus, women and men, told miracle stories. Reflection, analysis of reality, criticism of the world of death with which we are surrounded – in theory I can mention all that in the language of science. But theology requires more; it really calls for the impossible. As a handmaid of faith it should be helping to articulate the certainty of God.

Some time ago I met a young black woman from South Africa in New York. In my seminar she spoke about her work for the liberation of her people, of how she worked in the YMCA, brought young people together, studied the Bible with groups, visited friends in prison, organized the neighbourhood by going from house to house, and how they prayed together. While this young woman was talking, it became increasingly clear that she was borne up by a power that those of us who were listening did not know in this form. I suddenly understood what the innermost certainty of God can bring about in a person.

Someone asked her how long she thought apartheid would last. She answered quite calmly, 'Perhaps we shall be free in 1990, perhaps it wil take even longer.' She sat down and listened to us, and I had the feeling that this X that we are seeking was in her, involvement in the meaning of life. The Quakers call it 'that of God' in each person. This young woman simply knew what she was living for. She lived from meaning, and was no longer in search of it. The meaning was there and was visible in her. I thought of what she expected on her return to South Africa: possibly imprisonment, torture or death. That was also quite clear to her. At the same time I had a strong feeling, as if I heard another voice saying, 'They will not destroy this young woman. She is indestructible. Of course they can murder her; every human being can be killed. But they cannot destroy her. God is strong in her, God is beautiful in her.' She said that her only theological principle was 'I am made in the image of God'. She took up the Christian doctrine of creation in this way and applied it to herself. And with quiet pride she added: 'And my human dignity remains, even if it is repudiated throughout the society in which I live.' This theme of the image of God in every person is an important theme for South African theology in particular, because the apartheid theologians deny that it applies to black people. At this moment that bond with God without which we cannot emanate either freedom or beauty was quite visible.

Later, I reflected on this encounter, and it became clear to me that this young woman in sweatshirt and trainers is what the religious tradition teaches me to call an angel. An angel is a messenger who makes God visible. For our self-education as Christians it is important for us to pay attention and draw the attention of others to the messengers, so that we see them and do not trivialize them away.

An angel who makes God visible binds me to power, the good power of light. Such a messenger does not of course come to tell us the meaning of life: to assume that would be rationalistic folly. But she comes to protect the meaning of life, so that it is not destroyed by the trivial way in which we so readily treat life. It is not the case that we have to give meaning to life or produce the fulfilment. Rather, life gives us meaning, if we do not constantly get in its way and overpaint it with all too many things, as the rich man in hell did. Meaning is like the sun, to use a biblical image; it is already there before us. We can prevent it coming to us, but we cannot prevent it shining. We can so shut ourselves away that the voices of the messengers do not get to us, that they shrivel up in our cold, like so many Third World Christians who come to Europe. We are very strong in our emptiness, our capacity to protect ourselves. But if we open our hearts, the knowledge breaks through that we too are part of the totality of good, we too are being used. The certainty of God in us does not then grow as a certainty of authoritarian might that it will be right in the end, but as the certainty of the subversive power of justice.

I am often asked from where people in the liberation and peace movements get the courage and the power to fight and hope in the face of the gigantic superiority of weapons and technologies, capitalism and corrupted science. In fact there is no explanation in terms of 'this world'. Paul, who believed in the other God of Jesus under the conditions of the Roman empire, expressed this certainty in Romans with the words: 'For I am sure that neither death, nor life, nor angels, nor principalities, nor things present, nor things to come, nor powers, nor height, nor depth, nor anything else in all creation, will be able to separate us from the love of God which is in Christ Jesus our Lord' (Romans 8.38f.). In these words we find the link with the whole, and in them God is present.

I think that one danger in our lives is that we often confuse the meaning of life with success. In this way we remain at the spiritual level of capitalism, which regards success as the supreme value. It is also conceivable to the believer that the enemies of God will succeed in destroying this creation. In that case the truth of Jesus would end in tragedy. But would it be destroyed as truth? In that case God would sit over the ruins of this radioactive planet, weeping. Faith does not mean living without anxiety. If we are serious about understanding God's being in social terms, thinking of God as the power at the beginning, the power of relationship, then the continuation of creation depends on the strength of love among human beings. Whether or not the nuclear winter comes depends on how many people rise from the death of unrelatedness and are converted. God lures anew each day, to repent.

Notes

1. What is Systematic Theology?

1. 'Theology', in K.Rahner and H.Vorgrimler, *Concise Theological Dictionary*, Burns and Oates (1965) ²1983, 497.
2. Van A.Harvey, 'Theology', in *A Handbook of Theological Terms*, Macmillan, New York 1964.
3. D.Eich and C.Rincon, *La contra. Der Krieg gegen Nicaragua*, Hamburg nd.
4. H.Peukert, 'Fundamentaltheologie', in P.Eicher (ed.), *Neues Handbuch theologischer Grundbegriffe*, Munich 1984.

2. Orthodox, Liberal, Radical – Three Basic Theological Frameworks

1. T.S.Kuhn, *The Structure of Scientific Revolutions*, University of Chicago Press ²1970.
2. Hans Küng, 'Paradigm Change in Theology: A Proposal for Discussion', in Hans Küng and David Tracy (eds.), *Paradigm Change in Theology*, T.& T.Clark 1989, 3-33.
3. H.Richard Niebuhr, *Christ and Culture*, Faber and Faber 1952.
4. Paul Tillich, *The Protestant Era*, University of Chicago Press 1948.
5. Cf. R.McAfee Brown, *Saying Yes and Saying No: On Rendering to God and Caesar*, Westminster Press 1986, 29-40.

3. The Use of the Bible: From the Orthodox to the Liberal Paradigm

1. M.Veit, 'Wovon leben wir Linken?', *Junge Kirche. Zeitschrift europäischer Christen*, January 1988.
2. E.Schüssler Fiorenza, ' "For the Sake of Our Salvation": Biblical Interpretation and the Community of Faith', in *Bread Not Stone: The Challenge of Feminist Biblical Interpretation*, Beacon Press 1984, 24.

4. The Use of the Bible: From the Liberal Paradigm to the Paradigm of Liberation Theology

1. For its place in the history of theology see my article 'Eine Erinnerung um der Zukunft willen', in E.Schillebeeckx (ed.), *Mystik und Politik. Theologie im Ringen um Geschichte und Gesellschaft. Johann Baptist Metz zu Ehren*, Mainz 1988, 13ff.
2. A.von Harnack, *What is Christianity?*, reissued Harper Torchbooks 1957, 63, 67, 70.
3. R.Bultmann, *This World and the Beyond*, Lutterworth Press 1960.
4. See for example P.Tillich, *Systematic Theology*, Vol.1, University of

Chicago Press 1951; reissued SCM Press 1978, 122f., etc. This theme appears in many of his books.

5. G.Gutiérrez, *We Drink from our Own Wells*, Orbis Books and SCM Press 1985.

6. Cf. L.and W.Schottroff, 'Vom Umgang mit der biblischen Tradition', in *Die Parteilichkeit Gottes*, Munich 1984, 7-13.

7. L.and C.Boff, *Introducing Liberation Theology*, Burns and Oates and Orbis Books 1989.

8. These five fundamentals were – and are – the following: the inspiration and infallibility of the Bible; the doctrine of the Trinity; the Virgin Birth and the divinity of Christ; the theory of vicarious atonement through Christ; and finally the physical ascension, resurrection and second coming of Christ.

9. E.Cardenal, *The Gospel in Solentiname*, Orbis Books 1982.

5. The Understanding of Creation

1. P.Teilhard de Chardin, *Letters from a Traveller*, Collins and Harper and Row 1962.

2. D.Sölle with Shirley Cloyes, *To Work and to Love*, Fortress Press 1984, 13-21.

3. Ibid., 69ff.

4. W.Schottroff, 'Gleichgeschlechtliche Liebe', in L.and W.Schottroff, *Die Macht der Auferstehung. Sozialgeschichtliche Bibelauslegungen*, Munich 1988, 126-32.

5. E.Fromm, *You Shall be as Gods*, Jonathan Cape 1967.

6. F.Gogarten, *Der Mensch zwischen Gott und Welt*, Heidelberg 1952, esp.350-81.

7. A.Boesak, *Black and Reformed. Apartheid, Liberation and the Calvinist Tradition*, Orbis Books 1984; *If This is Treason, I am Guilty*, Eerdmans 1987 and Collins, Fount Books 1988.

8. G.Gutiérrez, *A Theology of Liberation*, Orbis Books 1973 and SCM Press 1974, 154, 161.

9. Quoted from ibid., 186 n.89.

10. Cf.C.Heyward, *The Redemption of God. A Theology of Mutual Relation*, University Press of America 1982.

11. H.-Eckehard Bahr/H. and G.Mahlke, D.Sölle/F.Steffensky, *Franziskus in Gorleben. Protest für die Schöpfung*, Frankfurt am Main 1981.

6. The Understanding of Sin

1. D.Sölle and H.E.Bahr, *Wie den Menschen Flügel wachsen. Über Umkehr aus dem Gewalt-System*, Munich 1984, 49-60.

2. L.Schottroff, 'Die Schreckensherrschaft der Sünde und die Befreiung durch Christus nach der Römerbrief des Paulus', *Evangelische Theologie*, November/December 1979.

3. R. Niebuhr, *The Nature and Destiny of Man*, Nisbet 1941, 1943 (two vols.).

4. F.D.E.Schleiermacher, *Speeches on Religion to Its Cultured Despisers*, reissued Harper Torchbooks 1958, 71.

5. Cf. Paul Tillich, *Systematic Theology* 2, University of Chicago Press 1957, reissued SCM Press 1978, 44-78.

6. Cf. D.Sölle, *Choosing Life*, Fortress Press and SCM Press 1981, 'Sin and Estrangement', 20-40.

7. See Tillich, *Systematic Theology*, Vol.2 (n.5), 57ff.

8. V.Saiving, 'The Human Situation: A Feminine View', in *Womanspirit Rising: A Feminist Reader in Religion*, ed. Judith Plaskow and Carol Christ, Harper and Row 1979.

9. Ibid.

10. *Schleiermacher-Auswahl* (with a postscript by Karl Barth), Gütersloh 1983, 274.

7. Feminist Liberation Theology

1. The translation in the text, and that of Micah 6.6f. which follows, is based on the German of *Die neue Basisbibel*, Neuwied 1982.

2. Cf. M.Bührig, *Die unsichtbare Frau und der Gott der Väter. Eine Einführung in die feministische Theologie*, Stuttgart 1987, 9-37.

3. D.Sölle, *Und ist noch nicht erschienen, was wir sein werden. Stationen feministischer Theologie*, Munich 1987, 170-4.

4. P.Trible, *Texts of Terror*, Fortress Press 1984.

5. E.Schüssler-Fiorenza, ' "For the Sake of Our Salvation", Biblical Interpretation and the Community of Faith', in *Bread Not Stone: The Challenge of Feminist Biblical Interpretation*, Beacon Press 1984, 40f.

6. L.Schottroff, 'How my mind has changed, or: Neutestamentliche Wissenschaft im Dienste der Befreiung', *Evangelische Theologie* 48.3, 1988, 247-61.

7. V.Mollenkott, *The Divine Feminine. The Biblical Imagery of God as Female*, Crossroad Publishing Company 1984.

8. Cf. E.Schüssler-Fiorenza, ' "For the Sake of Our Salvation" ' (n.5).

8. The Understanding of Grace

1. 'Theology', in K.Rahner and H.Vorgrimler, *Concise Theological Dictionary*, Burns and Oates (1965) [2]1983, 196.

2. Paul Tillich, *Systematic Theology*, Vol.3, University of Chicago Press 1963, reissued SCM Press 1978.

3. Cf. L.Siegele-Wenschkewitz (ed.), *Verdrängte Vergangenheit, die uns bedrängt. Feministische Theologie in der Verantwortung für die Geschichte*, Munich 1988.

4. Cf.C.Heyward, *The Redemption of God. A Theology of Mutual Relations*, University Press of America 1982.

5. Cf. D.Sölle, 'Die vermauerte Gnade', in *Sympathie. Theologisch-politische Traktate*, Stuttgart 1978.

6. Cf. D.Sölle, 'Der Mensch zwischen Gott und Materie. Warum und in

welchem Sinn muss die Theologie materialistisch sein?', in W.Schottroff and W.Stegemann (eds.), *Der Gott der kleinen Leute. Sozialgeschichtliche Bibelauslegungen 2, Neues Testament*, Munich 1979, 30ff.

7. E.Käsemann, *Commentary on Romans*, Eerdmans and SCM Press 1980, 176.

8. E.Käsemann, 'On Paul's Anthropology', in *Perspectives on Paul*, SCM Press and Fortress Press 1971, 21.

9. C.Blumhardt, *Worte*, ed. J.Harder, Wuppertal 1972, 111.

9. Introduction to Black Theology

1. J.Cone, *A Black Theology of Liberation*, Lippincott 1970.

2. F.Crüsemann, 'Die unveränderbare Welt. Überlegungen zur "Krisis der Weisheit" beim Prediger (Kohelet)', in W.Schottroff/ W.Stegemann (eds.), *Der Gott der kleinen Leute. Sozialgeschichtliche Auslegungen*, Vol.1, Munich 1979.

3. J.Cone, 'Schwarze Theologie in der amerikanischen Religion', *Weltmission heute*, no.3, EMW Hamburg 1988, 62.

4. Ibid., 60.

5. Ibid., 63.

10. Who is Jesus Christ for us Today?

1. B.Brecht, *Gesammelte Werke* 12, Frankfurt 1967, 380.

2. In H.Spaemann (ed.), *Wer ist Jesus von Nazareth – für mich? 100 zeitgenössische Zeugnisse*, Munich 1973, 21ff.

3. See Eberhard Busch, *Karl Barth. His Life from Letters and Autobiographical Texts*, SCM Press and Fortress Press 1976, 81f.

4. K.Barth, *The Epistle to the Romans*, Oxford University Press 1933, 98.

5. A.von Harnack, *What is Christianity?*, reissued Harper Torchbooks 1957, 68.

6. Karl Barth, *Romans* (n.4), 29f.

7. Recording of the *Misa Nicaraguense* by Meija Godoy.

8. Ibid.

9. J.D.Salinger, *Franny and Zooey*, Penguin Books 1964, 155f.

10. Ibid.

11. Cross and Resurrection

1. F.D.E.Schleiermacher, *The Christian Faith*, T. and T.Clark 1928, 'The Person of Christ', 377-424.

2. E.Troeltsch, *Glaubenslehre*, 1925, 104f.

3. L.Schottroff/B.von Wartenberg-Potter/D.Sölle, *Das Kreuz – Baum des Lebens*, Stuttgart 1987, 10f.

4. Ibid., 11.

12. The Kingdom of God and the Church

1. P.Potter, 'Report of the General Secretary', in the Official Report of the Sixth General Assembly of the World Council of Churches, WCC, Geneva.

2. Germany still has the highest density of atomic weapons inthe world: Mutlangen has Pershing 2s, the Hunsrück cruise missiles. Brokdorf is a nuclear power plant, highly controversial.

3. Potter (n.1).

4. D.Bonhoeffer, *Gesammelte Schriften* I, Munich 1958, 144f. There is an English translation in Edwin H.Robertson (ed.), *No Rusty Swords*, Fontana Books 1970, 157.

5. Synod of the Evangelical Church in Germany, *Glauben heute, Christ werden – Christ bleiben*, Gütersloh 1988, 28.

6. Ibid., 29.

7. D.Bonhoeffer, *Gesammelte Schriften* I (n.3), 147 = *No Rusty Swords*, 159f.; cf. the application of Bonhoeffer to contemporary economy in U.Duchrow, *Weltwirtschaft heute – Ein Feld für die Bekennende Kirche?*, Munich 1986.

8. D.Bonhoeffer, *The Cost of Discipleship*, SCM Press and Macmillan, New York 1959, 23.

9. Ibid., 28.

10. Dietrich Bonhoeffer, *Letters and Papers from Prison. The Enlarged Edition*, SCM Press and Macmillan, New York 1971, 382f.

11. *Life and Peace Review*, 1988. Cf. P.E.Arns, *Von Hoffnung zu Hoffnung: Vorträge, Gespräche, Dokumente*, Düsseldorf 1988.

12. Letter of the Robert H.Whitaker School of Theology, 1 January 1989, Diocese of Michigan.

13. L.Boff, interview in *Publik-Forum*, 24 June 1988.

13. Theology of Peace

1. L.Schottroff, 'Der doppelte Begriff von Frieden', in Aktion Sühnezeichen/Friedendienst (ed.), *Christen im Streit um den Frieden, Positionen und Dokumente*, Freiburg 1982, 135.

2. Cf. L.Schottroff, *Der Sieg des Lebens, Biblische Tradition einer Friedenspraxis*, Munich 1982, esp.23-47.

3. On Romans 13 cf. L.Schottroff, ' "Gebt dem Kaiser, was dem Kaiser gehört, und Gott, was Gott gehört." Die theologische Antowrt der urchristlichen Gemeinden auf ihre gesellschaftliche und politische Situation', in J.Moltmann (ed.), *Annahme und Widerstand*, Munich 1984, 15-48.

4. Cf. M.Mettner/J.Thiele, *Entwaffnender Glaube. Frieden als Themas in Religionsunterricht, Jugendarbeit und Erwachsenenbildung*, Munich 1983, 86ff.

5. K.Henning, 'Der Friede Gottes und der Friede der Welt – 18 biblische Thesen zum Frieden', in *Christen im Streit für den Frieden* (n.1), 48-51.

6. E.W.Russell, 'Christentum und Militarismus', in *Studien zur Friedensforschung*, ed. W.Huber/G.Liedke, Stuttgart and Munich 1974, 101f.

7. *Challenge to the Church. The Kairos Document. A Theological Comment*

on the Political Crisis in South Africa, ed. the Kairos Theologians, Braamfontein 1985 and Eerdmans 1946. See also the titles for further reading.

8. Jerry Falwell, Television address from Lynchburg, Virginia, 2 December 1984.

9. Jim Robinson, Broadcast address 1984. Cf. G.Halsell, *Prophecy and Politics. Militant Evangelists on the Road to Nuclear War*, New York 1986.

10. Cf. D.Sölle, 'Christofaschism', in *The Window of Vulnerability*, Fortress Press 1991.

11. U.Duchrow et al. (eds.), *Totaler Krieg gegen die Armen. Geheime Strategiepapiere der amerikanischen Militärs*, Munich 1989.

12. Ibid., 63. Cf. B.Päschke, *Befreiung von unten lernen. Zentralamerikanische Herausforderung theologischer Praxis*, Münster 1986, 68f.

13. M.Hengel, 'Die Bergpredigt in der aktuellen Diskussion', in *Christen im Streit für den Frieden* (n.1), 61.

14. E.Käsemann, 'Bergpredigt – eine Privatsache?', in ibid., 79.

15. Ibid., 82.

16. Kairos Document (n.7), Chapter 3, Introduction.

17. 'Leute, Gott will den aufrechten Gang!', translated by H.R.Hilty into German, from *Neue Wege, Beiträge zu Christentum und Sozialismus*, Zurich, March 1989.

14. The End of Theism

1. R.von Volkmann-Leander, *Träumereien an französichen Kaminen. Märchen*, Stuttgart 1973, 106ff.

2. E.Fromm, *Psychoanalysis and Religion*, Yale University Press 1950, reissued Bantam Books 1970.

3. H.Weder, *Neutestamentliche Hermeneutik*, Zurich 1986, 74.

4. Ibid., 229.

5. J.Miranda, *Marx and the Bible. A Critique of the Philosophy of Oppression*, Orbis Books and SCM Press 1974. Cf. also D.Sölle, 'Gott ist Gerechtigkeit', in *Sympathie*, Theologisch-politische Traktate, Stuttgart 1981, 114-24.

6. E.Levinas, *Wenn Gott ins Denken einfällt. Diskurs über die Betroffenheit von Transzendenz*, Freiburg and Munich 1985.

7. D.W.D.Shaw, 'God', in Alan Richardson and John Bowden (ed.), *A New Dictionary of Christian Theology*, SCM Press 1983 (US title: *The Westminster Dictionary of Christian Theology*, Westminster Press), 237.

8. Angelus Silesius, *Cherubinischer Wandersmann*, Stuttgart 1984, I, 8.

15. Who is Our God?

1. Martin Buber, *I and Thou* (1923), translated by R.Gregor Smith, T. and T.Clark ²1958, 107, 139ff.

2. Cf. D.Sölle with Shirley Cloyes, *To Work and to Love*, Fortress Press 1984, 75f.

3. P.Tillich, *The Socialist Decision* (1933), 1980.

4. Cf. T.Driver, *Patterns of Grace: Human Experience as the Word of God*, Harper and Row 1977.

For Further Reading

1. What is Systematic Theology?

Dorothee Söelle and Fulbert Steffensky, *Not Just Yes and Amen: Christians with a Cause*, Fortress Press 1985, 1–50

2. Orthodox, Liberal, Radical – Three Basic Theological Frameworks

Gustavo Gutierrez, *A Theology of Liberation*, second, revised, edition, Orbis Books and SCM Press 1988

Beverly Wildung Harrison, 'Theological Reflection in the Struggle for Human Liberation', in *Making the Connections: Essays in Feminist Social Ethics*, Beacon Press 1985, 235–65

Alisdair Heron, *A Century of Protestant Theology*, Lutterworth Press and Westminster Press 1980, 1–67

William Hordern, *A Layman's Guide to Protestant Theology*, revised edition, Collier Macmillan 1968, xiii–110

Theo Witvliet, *A Place in the Sun: An Introduction to Liberation Theology in the Third World*, SCM Press and Orbis Books 1985

3. The Use of the Bible: From the Orthodox to the Liberal Paradigm

Rudolf Bultmann, *Jesus Christ and Mythology*, Scribners and SCM Press 1958

Rudolf Bultmann, 'New Testament and Mythology', in H.W. Bartsch (ed.), *Kerygma and Myth*, SPCK 1972, 1–41

Helmut Gollwitzer, 'The Bible', in *An Introduction to Protestant Theology*, Westminster Press 1982, 46–62

Dorothee Sölle and Fulbert Steffensky, *Not Just Yes and Amen: Christians with a Cause*, Fortress Press 1985, 51–96

4. The Use of the Bibles: From the Liberal Paradigm to the Paradigm of Liberation Theology

Karl Barth, 'The Word of God as The Task of Theology', in *The Word of God and the Word of Man*, Harper Torchbooks 1957

Cain Hope Felder, *Troubling Biblical Waters: Race, Class, Family*, Orbis Books 1989

'The Kairos Document: A Moment of Truth', in *The Kairos Covenant: Standing with South African Christians*, ed. Willis Logan, Meyer-Stone Books and Friendship Press 1988, 1–43

Kwok Pui-Lan, 'Discovering the Bible in the Non-Biblical World', in *Lift Every Voice: Constructing Theologies from the Underside*, ed. Susan Brooks Thistlethwaite and Mary Potter Engel, Harper and Row 1990, 270–82

Letty Russell (ed.), *Feminist Interpretation of the Bible*, Westminster Press 1985

Elizabeth Schussler Fiorenza, *Bread Not Stone: The Challenge of Feminist Biblical Interpretation*, Beacon Press 1984

Willy Schottroff and Wolfgang Stegeman (eds.), *God of the Lowly: Socio-Historical Interpretations of the Bible*, Orbis Books 1984

Renita J. Weems, *Just a Sister Away: A Womanist Vision of Women's Relationships in the Bible*, LuraMedia, San Diego, Ca. 1988

5. The Understanding of Creation

Pierre Teilhard de Chardin, *The Phenomenon of Man*, Collins and Harper and Row 1959

Carter Heyward, *Touching Our Strength: The Erotic as Power and the Love of God*, Harper and Row 1989

Jürgen Moltmann, *Theology Today*, SCM Press 1988 and Trinity Press International 1989

Rosemary Radford Ruether, 'Women, Body, and Nature: Sexism and the Theology of Creation', in *Sexism and God-Talk*, Crossroad Publishing Company and SCM Press 1983, 72–92

George Tinker, 'The Integrity of Creation: Restoring Trinitarian Balance', *The Ecumenical Review* 41.4, 1989, 527–36

Susan Brooks Thistlethwaite, 'Class and Creation' and 'Creating and Destroying Grace: Nature and the Fall', in *Sex, Race and God: Christian Feminism in Black and White*, Crossroad Publishing Company 1989, 44–76

Vitor Westhelle, 'Creation Motifs in the Search for a Vital Space:

A Latin American Perspective', in *Lift Every Voice*, ed. Susan Brooks Thistlethwaite and Mary Potter Engel, Harper and Row 1990, 128–40

6. *The Understanding of Sin*

Sheila Collins, 'Class, Family, Forgiveness', in *Christianity and Crisis*, 17 April 1978, 82–8

Rosemary Radford Ruether, 'Christology: Can a Male Saviour Save Women?' and 'The Consciousness of Evil: The Journeys of Conversion', in *Sexism and God Talk*, Crossroad Publishing Company and SCM Press 1983

7. *Feminist Liberation Theology*

Sheila Collins, *A Different Heaven and Earth*, Judson Press 1974

Virginia Fabella and Mercy Amba Oduyoye, *With Passion and Compassion: Third World Women Doing Theology*, Orbis Books 1988

Elisabeth Schüssler Fiorenza, *In Memory of Her: A Feminist Theological Reconstruction of Christian Origins*, Crossroad Publishing Company and SCM Press 1983

Beverly Wildung Harrison, *Making the Connections: Essays in Feminist Social Ethics*, Beacon Press 1985

Judith Plaskow, *Standing Again at Sinai: Judaism From a Feminist Persepctive*, Harper and Row 1990

Letty Russell et al. (eds.), *Inheriting Our Mothers' Gardens: Feminist Theology in Third World Perspective*, Westminster Press 1988

Susan Brooks Thistlethwaite, *Sex, Race and God: Christian Feminism in Black and White*, Crossroad Publishing Company 1989

8. *The Understanding of Grace*

Mary Pellauer with Susan Brooks Thistlethwaite, 'Conversation on Grace and Healing: Perceptives from the Movement to End Violence Against Women', in *Lift Every Voice*, ed., Susan Brooks Thistlethwaite and Mary Potter Engel, Harper and Row 1990 pp. 169–285

9. *Introduction to Black Theology*

James Cone, *For My People: Black Theology and the Black Church*, Orbis Books 1984

Cornel West, *Prophesy Deliverance! An Afro-American Revolutionary Christianity*, Westminster Press 1982

Delores S. Williams, 'Black Theology's Contribution to Theological Methodology', *Reflection* (Yale Divinity School), Vol. 80, no. 3, January 1983

Gayraud Wilmore and James Cone (eds.), *Black Theology: A Documentary History, 1966–1979*, Orbis Books 1979

10. Who is Jesus Christ for Us Today?

Ernest Bloch, *The Principle of Hope*, Blackwell 1988

Jacquelyn Grant, *White Women's Christ and Black Women's Jesus: Feminist Christology and Womanist Response*, Scholars Press 1989

Carter Heyward, *Speaking of Christ: A Lesbian Feminist Voice*, Pilgrim Press 1989

Walter Lowe, 'Christ and Salvation', in *Christian Theology: An Introduction to its Traditions and Tasks*, ed., Peter Hodgson and Robert King, Revised edition, Fortress Press 1985, 222–48

Raymond L. Whitehead, 'Christ and Cultural Imperialism', in *Justice as Mission*, ed., Terry Brown and Christopher Lind, Trinity Press: Burlington, Ontario 1985, 24–34

11. Cross and Resurrection

Rita Nakashima Brock, *Journeys By Heart: A Christology of Erotic Power*, Crossroad Publishing Company 1988

Joanne C. Brown and Carol R. Bohn (eds.), *Christianity, Patriarchy and Abuse: A Feminist Critique*, Pilgrim Press 1989

Albert Nolan, *Jesus Before Christianity*, Orbis Books 1978

Jon Sobrino, *Christology at the Crossroads: A Latin American Approach*, Orbis Books and SCM Press 1978

Dorothee Sölle, 'Resistance: Toward a First World Theology', *Christianity and Crisis*, 23 July 1979, 178–82

12. The Kingdom of God and the Church

Gregory Baum, *Compassion and Solidarity: The Church for Others*, Canadian Broadcasting Corporation Enterprises, 1987

Bruce Birch and Larry Rasmussen, *The Predicament of the Prosperous*, Westminster Press 1978

Leonardo Boff, *Church: Charism and Power. Liberation Theology and the Institutional Church*, Crossroad Publishing Company and SCM Press 1985

Beverly Wildung Harrison, 'Keeping Faith in a Sexist Church: Not For Women Only? in *Making the Connections*, 206–34

Carter Heyward, *Our Passion for Justice: Images of Power, Sexuality and Liberation*, Pilgrim Press 1984

Willis Logan (ed.), *The Kairos Covenant: Standing with South African Christians*, Meyer-Stone Books and Friendship Press 1988

Pastoral Team of Bambamarca, *Vamos Caminado: A Peruvian Catechism*, SCM Press and Orbis Books 1984

Susan Brooks Thistlethwaite, *Metaphors for the Contemporary Church*, Pilgrim Press 1983

13. Theology of Peace

Robert McAfee Brown, *Religion and Violence*, Second edition, Westminster Press 1987

'The Kairos Document: A Moment of Truth', in *The Kairos Covenant: Standing with South African Christians*, (ed.), Willis Logan, Meyer-Stone Books and Friendship Press 1988, 1–43

John Macquarrie, *The Concept of Peace*, SCM Press and Trinity Press International 1989

Theodore Runyon (ed.), *Theology, Politics and Peace*, Orbis Books 1984

Susan Thistlethwaite, *A Just Peace Church*, Pilgrim Press 1986

Jim Wallis (ed.), *Waging Peace: A Handbook for the Struggle to Abolish Nuclear Weapons*, Harper and Row 1982

James E. Will, *A Christology of Peace*, Westminster/John Knox Press, 1989

14. The End of Theism

José Miguez Bonino, *Room to Be People*, Fortress Press 1980

15. Who is Our God?

Beverly Wildung Harrison, 'Sexism and the Language of Christian Ethics,' in *Making the Connections, Essays in Feminist Social Ethics*, Beacon Press 1985, 22–41

Carter Heyward, *The Redemption of God: A Theology of Mutual Relation*, University Press of America 1982

Dorothee Sölle, 'God's Pain and Our Pain', in *The Future of Liberation Theology*, ed., Marc Ellis and Otto Maduro, Orbis Books 1989, 326–33

Susan Brooks Thistlethwaite, ' "I Am Become Death": God in the Nuclear Age', in *Lift Every Voice: Constructing Theologies for the Underside*, ed., Susan Brooks Thistlethwaite and Mary Potter Engel, Harper and Row 1990

Index of Biblical References